AKIBA

AKIBA

Scholar, Saint and Martyr

BY

LOUIS FINKELSTEIN

Mind and spirit remain invincible.

—MILTON.

A TEMPLE BOOK

ATHENEUM 1985 NEW YORK

TO

DOCTOR CYRUS ADLER

*My friend and guide through two decades, a true disciple of
Hillel, who loves peace, and pursues peace, loves people
and, through precept and example, brings
them nearer to the Law.*

*Published by Atheneum
Reprinted by arrangement with
The Jewish Publication Society of America
Copyright © 1936 by Louis Finkelstein
Copyright renewed 1964 by Louis Finkelstein
All rights reserved
Library of Congress catalog card number 62-12354
ISBN 0-689-70230-2
Manufactured in the United States of America by
Fairfield Graphics
Fairfield, Pennsylvania
Published in Canada by McClelland and Stewart Ltd.
First Atheneum Printing January 1970
Second Printing March 1975
Third Printing April 1978
Fourth Printing October 1981
Fifth Printing May 1985*

CONTENTS

iii

FOREWORD

Akiba ben Joseph, the hero of this narrative, ranks in depth of intellect, breadth of sympathy and clarity of vision with the foremost personalities in the Hebrew tradition: Moses and Isaiah among the prophets, Maimonides, Crescas and Spinoza among the philosophers. He dominates the whole scene of Jewish history for eighteen centuries, from the period of the Second Isaiah, about 540 B.C.E. until the rise of the Spanish school of Jewish philosophers about 1100 C.E. Certain aspects of his genius appear also in other distinguished leaders of his people. The authors of Ruth and Jonah were his equals in universality of outlook and human tenderness; the Maccabees and the Zealot leaders, in courage and devotion to principle. Hillel, the founder of the plebeian School of Pharisaic learning, and Saadia Gaon, the pioneer in the study of medieval Jewish philosophy, shared his originality of thought; Gamaliel I, who reformed the judicial system of Palestine, and Gershom ben Judah, who in the chaos of tenth century Europe created a federation of German-Jewish communities, were as great in legislative insight. But Akiba alone combined all these qualities; and above all, he possessed that colorful personality which made him the most revered, as well as the most beloved, of talmudic sages.

In our own generation special interest attaches to Akiba as one of the builders of civilization. His specific teachings have, naturally, exerted their profoundest influence on the development of Judaism. Wherever Jewish traditions are studied and observed, Akiba's decisions and doctrines are recognized and authoritative. But in a wider sense, the contour of western thought generally has been affected by his philosophy. His ideas molded those of Maimonides, Gersonides and Crescas. These men influenced a whole series of Latin writers from Thomas Aquinas to Spinoza, who in turn laid the foundations of modern thought. If, as has been said, "Spinozism is not a system, but a habit of mind," it is a habit of mind which derives, in large part, from Maimonides among the medievalists, and Akiba among the talmudic sages. The careful student will soon recognize the close relationship between Spinoza's *Amor Dei Intellectualis* and Akiba's teachings that worship is an expression of love, and that study is the highest form of worship. The amalgam of rationalism and mysticism, which was basic to the advanced Jewish philosophy of the Middle Ages, the conception of a God who was real but not anthropomorphic, could hardly have taken the form it did without the authoritative support of Akiba. Certainly the unequaled freedom and tolerance of later Jewish thought was in large part a result of Akiba's victorious assertion of his right to be original. Even the absorbing concern with the ethical, which was characteristic of all Jewish thought, and has been perhaps its main contribution to the modern mind, gained in impressiveness from Akiba's teaching.

Perhaps, however, it is the reconstruction of the social conflicts of his time which makes Akiba's life and teaching particularly relevant to us. Despite the vast changes which civilization has undergone since then, the issues which confronted him are once more with us, though in somewhat new form. The problems of international peace, universal education, the status of woman, the rights of laborers, the prerogatives of hierarchy, the removal of superstition from religion, and the advancement of pure scholarship are still unsolved. Artisans have been succeeded by factory hands; Samaritans and Ammonites by powerful nations; scriptural studies by modern science. Yet the questions he poses, and the solutions he offers, still remain strangely applicable to our own time.

The correspondence between the two ages becomes particularly marked when we consider the last twenty years of his life. The collapse of Palestinian civilization through the rise of extremists closely parallels the eclipse of reason in our own day. His determined effort to avert cultural disaster in the midst of political and economic chaos, and his ultimate victory, in spite of apparent, temporary defeat, is of permanent significance to the statesman and the sociologist, as well as to the historian and the general reader.

Yet, in spite of his heroic proportions and world significance, Akiba has remained unknown outside the limited circles of Talmud students. Whereas whole libraries have been written about Paul the Apostle and Augustine the Philosopher, the Christian teachers who most nearly approximate his genius, the literature about Akiba covers no more than seven or eight hundred printed pages. His best biography in any language is a brief article by Professor Louis Ginzberg in the Jewish Encyclopedia.

The contrast between Akiba's importance and the meager studies devoted to him is particularly surprising in view of the wealth of relevant source material. His opinions and adventures, carefully recorded by faithful disciples, are to be found on almost every page of the Babylonian Talmud, with its eighteen massive tomes, as well as in the smaller, more compact Talmud of Jerusalem, and its kindred Palestinian works.

The difficulty has been that these books were practically

sealed to all but rabbinic students. The gifted translators who popularized the Hebrew Scriptures, and made them man's foremost literary treasure, had no interest in the Talmud, and, in any event, were helpless in their approach to it. The enormous compass of the work, its curious dialectic, its peculiar idiom, its constant use of ellipsis and obscure academic terms, combined to discourage even the boldest investigators.

The Jewish scholars who knew Akiba never thought of writing his biography. For them he was not a figure out of a remote past, but a contemporary. He was their companion, and their intimate friend. The talmudic world in which he moved was as much part of their lives as the paths and by-paths of their own villages. The best hours of each day were devoted to reconnoitering its hidden glades. Its study was not merely a religious duty, but a cultural pleasure. It was their hobby, their pastime, their sport, their theater, their concert house, their cinema, their newspaper, their radio, their life. The poetic outburst of the ancient psalmist, "Had not Thy law been my delight, I should have perished in my affliction," became literal truth for the Jew of the Middle Ages. Facing continual danger and persecution, he escaped from the apparent reality of his dismal and sordid existence into the true reality of biblical and talmudic learning. He could think of no higher pleasure than that which rose from the folios of his text. The study of the Talmud did not lead to Paradise; it was Paradise. God, Himself, the Jew imagined, must enjoy the study of the Torah!

Such scholars could not write a "life" of Akiba. Their regard for the master resembled that of children for distinguished parents, or disciples for a renowned master. They loved and admired him; and intuitively felt the greatness of his genius. But their feelings remained unanalyzed and inarticulate. Being continually with him, they accepted his contribution to their life and thought as a matter of course, and could not appreciate the rarity of his gifts or his place in world history. His brilliance as rabbi and teacher obscured for them his equal distinction as a man.

There was, however, another, more inclusive, reason for the failure of Jewish scholars to describe Akiba: their aversion to biography. It was almost as if the commandment against human images were extended from sculpture to literature. Not that these scholars were deficient in the art of narrative or character delineation. The Hebrews were the fathers of history, and, indeed, of all non-poetical composition. Their histories of the patriarchs, the judges and the early kings, are to prose what Homer is to poetry. Unaffected power, smooth-flowing rhythms, simple yet passionate diction, the attainment of that highest art which is the absence of all studied effect, have made these works the literary as well as the spiritual guides of half the human race. The Book of Samuel has been built up about a contemporary chronicle which remains to this day a classic. Nothing written in the three thousand years since its time surpasses it in objectivity, precision, or vividness of portrayal. The writer's clear analysis of opposing issues and hidden motives, his masterful selection of the relevant material, and rejection of the incidental, establish him as the world's first true historian. The panegyrics which the Egyptians, Babylonians and Assyrians wrote in honor of their imperial masters, the folk tales which Herodotus so assiduously gathered into his chronicle, the mythological reconstruction of early Roman history by the writers of the Republic, important as they are, fall short of the method and style of this unnamed literary master, the Thucydides of the tenth century B.C.E.

But these biblical works, excellent as history, are not biography. The depiction of personality is regularly subordinated to the story of the nation. The histories of the Patriarchs are, as the talmudic sages with their uncanny insight remark, "symbolic for their descendants." The early Israelite kings and judges figure in the accounts concerning them only as organs of the body-politic. The religious historian deals with them as instruments in the spiritual development of his people; those decades of their lives which were not pertinent to his interpretation of events are left unchronicled. That the characters nevertheless are so vivid and distinct is simply proof of the author's superlative genius; the sparks from his anvil are brighter than the full flame of many another craftsman.

The so-called "biographies" of Elijah, Elisha and Isaiah, from which certain chapters in the Book of Kings are supposed to be excerpts, were not life-histories in the ordinary sense of the word. They were collections of tales, intended to increase respect for the prophets as religious teachers. The biographical notes which Baruch ben Neriah apparently added to the Book of Jeremiah simply provide the necessary background for the prophet's addresses.

This literary subordination of the individual doubtless was a result of the strong group-consciousness in primitive Hebrew thought. Like other ancient peoples, the Hebrews did not at first recognize the significance of the individual. The unit of moral responsibility as well as of human interest was the clan, the tribe or the nation. It was not long, however, before the prophets realized how important the individual is in the moral sphere. The principle of individual responsibility begins to emerge in the eighteenth chapter of Genesis, and reaches its highest expression in the Book of Ezekiel. But the development of ethical thought left literary fashion unchanged. The individual, who had at last become recognized as the unit of ethical teaching, still remained without significance to the chronicler. This doubtless explains the amazing preponderance of anonymous and pseudonymous books in ancient Hebrew literature. The authors of only a small fraction of biblical books, and of but one of the apocryphal works, are known by name. And, indeed, to this day, Hebrew writing contains a curious disproportion of noms de plume. Even when the names of the authors are known, the rabbinic scholar usually refers to them by the titles of their books. He will say that "The Duty of the Heart" (*Hobat Halebabot*) was a Spanish Rabbi of the eleventh century, when he really has in mind the famous Bahya ibn Pakuda, the writer of that saintly volume; he will say that the "Path of the Righteous" (*Mesilat Yesharim*) wrote dramas in the Italian style, when he means this was done by its compiler, Moses Hayyim Luzzatto. This seems peculiar to those unaccustomed to the habit, but is in reality no more strange than the opposite practice, common in other groups, of referring to books by the names of their authors. We speak of reading "Shakespeare," when we mean "Hamlet" or "Julius Caesar"; "Milton," when we mean "Paradise Lost"; "John Bunyan," when we mean "Pilgrim's Progress." The difference in fashion reflects a difference in point of view. The ancient Hebrew was interested in the work, the introspective modern is primarily concerned with the writer behind it.

The lack of suitable life-sketches of the rabbinic sages is especially deplorable because only biography can serve as an introduction to the spirit of the Talmud. Neither translations nor *"einleitungen,"* no matter how excellent, adequately meet this need. The most accurate and literary translation can remove only one impediment to the study of the Talmud— that of language. The difficulties which arise from its recondite allusions, its concise style, and its special forms of argument, remain, and make a lifetime of devotion necessary for the mastery of the text. The formal "Introductions" to the Talmud, on the other hand, deal only with its externalities; they give the reader no opportunity to see it from within. They list its treatises and chapters, briefly summarize the themes discussed, arrange the authorities mentioned in chronological order, and attempt to explain the strange terminology and dialectic. But they cannot undertake to discuss motives and characters, parties and issues, the changing scenes and the human actors. Above all, they cannot recreate the spirit which animates the work.

The lack of such intimate descriptions of the rabbinic world, especially in its earliest phases, has been disastrous to the study of western religious history. Much in Christianity which only an appreciation of the talmudic sages could make explicable has remained a mystery; as, likewise, that in Judaism which a study of the Christian revolt might have illumined has remained in darkness. The conception of Pharisaism as narrow bigotry, and of the apostles as opponents to the rabbinic ethics is only part of this tragic misinterpretation. Forgetting that Paul described himself, *after his conversion,* as a "Pharisee the son of a Pharisee"; that his double standard of religious observance for Jews and Gentiles had its roots in the older tradition; that he and the other apostles were frequently saved from punishment by the descendants of Hillel; and that the Roman proselytes to Palestinian religion, like many Jews in the Diaspora, for decades drew no distinction between Judaism and Christianity; forgetting all these things, scholars created false antitheses, and made a crude and impossible reconstruction of the annals of Palestine during the first century of the Christian era. The effect of this misinterpretation has been especially tragic for a large proportion of the modern Jews. Unable to read the literature of their people in its original tongue or in adequate translation, they cease to appreciate the true greatness of the rabbinic authorities, and accept the judgment of the world regarding them. Only in recent years have Schechter's researches in Jewish theology, Herford's authoritatives studies of the Pharisees and Pharisaism, Dalman's analysis of the correspondence between rabbinic Judaism and Christianity, Moore's monumental work on rabbinic Judaism, and Torrey's masterful reconstruction of the spirit of the later prophetic writers, begun to clear the mists surrounding the origins of rabbinic Judaism and Christianity and enabled us to see the development of both religions in true perspective.

The portrayals of the late prophetic and early rabbinic scenes which these unforgettable masters have painted on their vast canvases, excellent and lifelike as they are, necessarily suffer from two deficiencies. Being group representations, they cannot indicate the full significance of the component individuals; and being "still" pictures, they cannot reproduce the dynamic quality of talmudic civilization. To supply these needs, we must turn to biography where we can see at least one individual in every facet of his life, and follow each development of his thought and career. No better choice for this purpose can be made than Akiba ben Joseph, the foremost teacher of the rabbinic world. Making him our guide, participating in his struggles, sharing his adventures, listening to his arguments, we may hope to emerge with a clear understanding of the talmudists' lives, their aspirations and their significance.

The desire to depict the great sage came to me, however, long before I realized his significance in the history of human letters. Indeed, the present volume may be described as the fulfillment of a life aspiration which I probably owe to the influence of my father, whose enthusiasm for Akiba has remained with me since childhood days.

Still, the early impulse might not have been translated into action at this time without the stimulus of two eminent scholars, Professor F. C. Porter of Yale and Professor A. D. Nock of Harvard. At a symposium held in conjunction with the meeting of the Society of Biblical Literature, in December, 1929, the former remarked on the importance of a biography of Akiba, and told how he himself had been moved when he read the story of the martyrdom. During a visit to Cambridge in March, 1935, I recalled this incident to Professor Nock, who immediately suggested that he would be pleased to devote a full number of the *Harvard Theological Review* to a monograph on the subject.

Returning home, I set aside all other tasks, and began to write the work. It soon became evident to me that it could not be compressed into the limits of a periodical, no matter how generous the editor was willing to be in the matter of space. Nevertheless, I did not desist from the task. The work grew until it emerged as the present book.

I have attempted no panegyric of the master; he would, like Cromwell, have tolerated no painter who omitted his wrinkles and his scars and tried to flatter him by being false to him. His humble beginnings, his first awkward attempts to free himself of their effects, his hypersensitivity to bad manners, his temporary lapse from his own teachings when he approached his ninetieth year, are as much part of him as his indomitable will, his unfailing courtesy, his copious mind, his resilient spirit, his fine humor, and his ability to recapture his youthful idealism, purpose and intellectual courage in the crisis of his life's last years. I have tried to say as little about Akiba as I could. Wherever possible his words are transmitted as he uttered them. It was my purpose to let the reader see him not through my eyes, but as he appears in the pages of the Talmud. Whenever the evidence was too technical to be included in the text itself, it has been added in the Appendix, in the supplementary discussions, and in the notes at the end of the volume.

I approached the final chapter of the book with a peculiar gripping of the heart. It was as though I had voluntarily joined Judah Ha-Garsi in watching our Master being taken from us. When I had finished the task, I thought of Tineius Rufus and the part he played in that tragedy, in the execution court of Caesarea. He doubtless considered the event a trifling, if rather unpleasant, incident in his career. He had liked Akiba, and would have preferred to spare the old man; but naturally the interests of the Empire came first. How the Roman general would have been surprised had he been told that before many centuries had passed he would be recalled in history only through his association with the Jewish sage. Yet the impossible has happened. Nothing is recorded of Rufus's conversation save what he said to Akiba; nothing is known of his battles, save those he fought against the Jews. The empire he defended perished centuries ago; it is only where students gather to pore over the Talmud that the brilliance of Akiba's glory lends a slight luster of immortality also to his executioner.

Could anything have demonstrated more completely the truth of Akiba's teaching, that intellect alone is powerful, and that violence is self-defeating? Had the Romans but been able to grasp this idea, had they realized that in using force to crush opposition they were training barbarian armies to rise against them and destroy them, had their conversion to prophetic religion been thorough instead of superficial, what a different sequel their history might have had!

It could not be. Man was still too low in the scale of evolution to act rationally in the mass. Rome was doomed to perish, for lack of vision. Its people's gift for administrative organization, which might have enabled them to establish the empire as a voluntary association of equal self-governing provinces, retaining the *pax Romana,* but without fear of the sword, was wasted in a futile effort to maintain the dominion of an effete, otiose people consumed by wealth and luxury over powerful, unspoiled, rugged barbarians and provincials. The abolition of provincial tributes might have depopulated the Imperial City; it might have emptied its slums; it might have removed some vain fopperies from the palaces. But the Empire would have been founded on a rock, European civilization would have escaped the eclipse of the Dark Ages, and the world would have been spared the pains of death and rebirth.

As it happened, the Palestinian academies, which failed to save civilization, were ultimately the instruments of its restoration. What occurred should be a commonplace of popular historical knowledge; yet it is imperfectly realized by all but a few antiquarians. The Western Empire fell victim to the illiterate Vandals, who destroyed all semblance of its civilization; the Eastern Empire was overcome by an equally fatal obscurantism, which drove the philosophical schools from Greece to pagan Parthia. Slowly, all of Europe sank into the darkness of the sixth, the seventh and the eighth centuries. Writing became a rare skill; Charlemagne himself could not sign his name! Libraries were burned; works of art broken to fragments; roads torn up; palaces demolished; wealth destroyed. The world was thrown back two millennia; imperial government gave way to feudal anarchy.

That this confusion was ultimately dissipated and civilized life restored was due to the Church, the Caliphate and the rabbinical academies in Europe and Africa, all three of which had their ultimate sources in the inspiration of Palestine.

The Church remained the reservoir of what little learning survived in Western Europe after the fall of Rome. As at the beginning of history, the hierarchy—the priests and monks—became the world's only scholars and copyists. The use of the term clerk for both secretary and churchman is a permanent reminder of this fact. But these ecclesiastics had no access to the main body of Greek science and philosophy. A large part of it had been irrevocably lost; and the rest was to be found only outside of Christendom, under the rule of Persia.

Greek wisdom was brought back from its exile through the Eastern Renaissance—the rise of Islam and its Empire. The Arabs, stimulated into new life through the teachings which Mohammed brought to them out of Scripture, became apt disciples of the philosophers of Persia, and provided them with a wide field of influence, bringing their teachings to the gates of Europe.

That they passed those gates was due to the rabbinical academies of Spain, Italy, France, and the Rhine-country, whose existence was a distant result of Akiba's activity and courage. His insistence that study was a paramount duty, which must be observed even at the risk of one's life and in the face of the most brutal persecution, had prevented the disappearance of Jewish learning during the crucial period of Hadrianic oppression. Twenty years after his execution, his pupils established a new academy in Galilee, and this became the ancestor of other, equally distinguished schools, first in Babylonia, and then throughout the Jewish Dispersion.

In some of these schools, like those of Kairowan in North Africa and Otranto in Italy, the study of philosophy was encouraged. Their teachers became expert in astronomy, mathematics, medicine and other skills. But even the schools, like those of France and Germany, whose students were limited to rabbinic subjects, may have served as stimuli toward learning in the general community. It is a plausible surmise that the ability of the minority to maintain its schools, graduate its teachers, and perpetuate its learning, moved the majority to think also of *its* forgotten traditions. Thus not only the rabbinical scholars who, by their translations from Arabic into Latin, were the physical restorers of "lost" learning to Western Europe, but also those who, by their intellectual interests, exerted a less definable influence, must be credited with bringing about the first European Renaissance, that of the twelfth century. The founding of the Universities, which was one of the first signs of this re-awakening, marks the end of the Dark Ages.

It is an interesting, in some respects a melancholy, fact, which must be noted, that when the rabbinical schools had performed this function, they began to decline. Almost like flowers which have produced their seed, they lost their glory and withered away. They had escaped the desiccation of the Middle Ages just long enough to save the world. The civilization which they had helped to restore circumscribed their activities and threw them into the narrow confines of a physical and spiritual Ghetto. They gradually lost access to science and philosophy; and even in their own fields, their beauty faded. From the heights of the three great talmudic teachers of the eleventh century: Alfasi, in Spain, the most distinguished of codifiers (d. 1103); Nathan ben Yehiel, in Italy, still the foremost of talmudic lexicographers (d. 1106); and Rashi, in France, unsurpassed as talmudic commentator (d. 1105); we descend step by step to the mediocre authorities of the fifteenth and sixteenth centuries.

Not before the end of the eighteenth century did the darkness which had settled on them begin to lift and the renaissance which the mediaeval rabbis had helped bring to the world come to their own descendants. With the enlightenment and the emancipation a new epoch opens both in the history of Israel and in the history of the world. Whether we are moving to a brighter noon, or having passed the zenith of our civilization are to experience once more the darkness of medievalism, none can as yet dare say. Whatever be in store for civilization in the immediate future, its ultimate destiny undoubtedly depends on the preservation of intellectual life. This may involve conflicts, perhaps martyrdoms, on a scale far wider than that which Akiba dealt with or could have envisaged. Yet who can doubt the validity of his doctrine, even when applied to this worldwide field.

It is with much pleasure that I acknowledge the assistance rendered me by a number of scholars and other friends in the preparation of this work. Those to whom I turned with specific questions are mentioned in connection with the replies I quote from them. I have received more general help from my wife who, reading the proofs of the book, made a number of valuable suggestions, and from Doctor Solomon Goldman, my friend since childhood days. The manuscript was read in its entirety by Doctor Cyrus Adler, who gave me many detailed criticisms, and who was particularly responsible for my writing the second chapter. Mr. Maurice Samuel, with characteristic generosity, devoted a considerable part of the summer of 1935 to a study of the manuscript, as far as it was then completed. With unwearying patience, he went over the work with me, contributing greatly to its improvement in content and style. Finally I must record that the work could not have been produced in its present form without the generous assistance of the librarians of the Jewish Theological Seminary of America, Union Theological Seminary, Hebrew Union College, Jewish Institute of Religion, Dropsie College and Columbia University.

AKIBA

I. THE GRAVE ON THE HILLTOP

IN the year 26 c.e., not long before he executed John the
Baptist, Herod Antipas, the son of Herod the Great, built
at the southern end of the beautiful Sea of Galilee a health
resort which he named Tiberias, after his patron, the second
Roman Emperor.[1] For reasons which are no longer clear, the
Pharisees declared a boycott against the place, claiming that
at least part of it was an ancient cemetery, and therefore a
defilement to priest and layman alike! Neither the Idumean
tyrant nor his fiery antagonists foresaw that within two
centuries the accursed spot would become a haven of refuge
for Jewish learning and that it would remain a center of
rabbinical scholarship for almost a millennium, a longer time
than any other Palestinian city, save perhaps Jerusalem itself.
The prohibition was officially removed when, toward the end
of the second century, Simeon ben Yohai identified the actual
burial places and thus localized the defilement.[2] But in our
own times, Tiberias stands again under the sign of its tombs.
One tradition, certainly inaccurate, places the grave of Akiba
on a neighboring hilltop;[3] another, more reliable, puts that of
Maimonides in the city itself. Two such memorials in one
small locality turn our thoughts to the dead rather than the
living.

It was perhaps a curious fancy which associated the hilltop
with the memory of the illustrious Akiba ben Joseph. As
Moses is said to keep watch over Palestine from the southern
height of Mount Nebo, so Akiba, who in popular fancy and

in legend came nearest to being a reincarnation of the first lawgiver, has set his guard on a northern hill, overlooking the entrance to the valley of Jezreel. In our modern minds another symbolism might apply to the grave on the hilltop: the life of the man who is said to sleep there was one long and painful ascent, ended—and crowned—by his magnificent death. Though for a symbolism more in keeping with his austere and rugged greatness we should look not to the hills about Tiberias, but to the wild and snow-covered heights of Hermon itself.

No other talmudic teacher impresses himself on our minds so indelibly. Most of the great sages of the following generation were his disciples, and an authority of the third century informs us that the Mishna, the Tosefta, the Sifra and the Sifre—those ancient compilations of rabbinic thought which have survived until our own time—all had their origin in his scholarly activity.[4] The dialectic which he developed became basic to all later rabbinic reasoning, and as we turn the folios of the massive tomes of the Talmud we come everywhere upon traces of his remarkable influence on the subsequent systems of Jewish law, ethics and theology.

Of his physical characteristics, the rabbinic sages, always contemptuous of accidental trivialities, record only his exceptional stature and his baldness.[5] In this instance, however, we may regret their almost otherworldly indifference to the body. Surely the strange blend of humor and pathos, of rigor and mercy, of practical good sense and sentimental mysticism, which characterized the man, must have found some expression in the cheek, the forehead and the eye. There must have been something singular and arresting in the contrast between the intellectual preoccupation of the statesman-scholar, and the powerful physique of the one-time shepherd. But the

Talmud records nothing of this. We are left to re-create Akiba in our imagination out of his pithy maxims, his witty answers, his ingenious arguments, his penetrating decisions, his mature theology, his pedagogic method and the memorable events of his life: his romantic marriage, the catastrophic incident of his conversion, his rapid rise to leadership, his guidance of his people and his martyr's death. Whether the personality, if not the appearance, of Akiba can be reconstructed out of these materials must be demonstrated in the following pages.

II. IN THE DEPTHS

AKIBA'S permanent significance to his people and the world derives largely from the extraordinary character of the age in which he lived. Intellectually and spiritually it was one of the most productive periods in history. It was marked by new thoughts, widening horizons, reborn ideals, daring adventures, creative personalities, heroic martyrs and memorable teachers. In little more than a century tiny Palestine produced the twin religions of rabbinic Judaism and Christianity, the one destined to serve the world, the other also to conquer it.

These supreme contributions to civilization would be remarkable under any circumstances; they become amazing, even unbelievable, in view of the political decline, social disintegration and economic impoverishment of the times. When Akiba was born, about the year 40, the last Jewish ruler, Agrippa I, the grandson of Herod, still sat on the throne of Judea. The country had reached the highest point in its prosperity. Pilgrims flocked to Jerusalem from all parts of the Roman Empire. In the words of Agrippa himself, Jerusalem had become the metropolis not only of Judea, but also of many other countries "by reason of the colonies which it has sent out from time to time." [1] The income of the Temple was so great that it could not be utilized in routine expenses, and accumulated surpluses were each year set aside as invested capital.[2] The market place of Jerusalem was equally affluent. Without placing too heavy burdens on the people, the gov-

6

ernment could undertake vast building operations, support public games in foreign cities like Athens and pay enormous tributes to the Empire. Prosperity brought with it an era of unprecedented good feeling. The partisan divisions, which had torn the Jewish body politic for centuries and had even led to civil war, lost their bitterness. The Pharisees, representing the masses of the people, tolerated the appointment of a high priest from the opposing party without fear that he might violate the precepts of their sect.[3]

Within their own ranks, factional differences had been composed; and instead of the double leadership which had become traditional among them, they had one head, Gamaliel, called the First, to distinguish him from his grandson who bore the same name and who was destined to be one of Akiba's chief adversaries. In recognition of Gamaliel's great achievements and his high prestige, a new title was invented for him: *Rabban,* "our master." The universal respect in which he was held in Palestine, and the friendship which Agrippa showed him, gave him influence also in the Diaspora. The high priest still remained the nominal head of the nation's supreme council, the Sanhedrin, which combined in itself the functions of legislature and supreme court; but the real president was Gamaliel. It was Gamaliel and his associates who regulated the calendar, the one phase of Jewish life which united all Israel. He issued his edicts to the various provinces of Palestine, Lower Galilee, Upper Galilee and the South, as well as to distant Babylonia, Media and "all the other places of Jewish exile."[4] Both the scattered communities of the Roman Empire to the west and those of the Parthian Empire to the east, looked to him and the Sanhedrin for guidance in their internal, religious life. They sent funds to maintain his academy, just as they helped to support the

Temple. For the first and only time in their history, the Jews formed an *imperium in imperio,* a little empire, with Jerusalem as its capital, under the powerful aegis of the huge Roman dominion. The common central government provided a closer association between Palestine and the Roman Diaspora than had been possible while the little country was fully independent.

Gamaliel, who was the center of this whole system, was fortunately a statesman of the first order and knew how to exercise authority with wisdom and restraint. He introduced important reforms in the judicial procedure, encouraged the schools of learning, won the support of the king and the high priests, and meted out careful and generous justice to the lowly and oppressed.

His task was made easier by King Agrippa's obvious anxiety to win the affection of the people. The grandson of Herod knew how profoundly the masses hated his family, the descendants of the Idumean upstart who had slaughtered the last scions of the noble Hasmoneans. He realized too that his foreign ancestry and his Hellenized life before he became king made the people look on him as a stranger, who had no right to sit on the throne of David. It was with especial diligence therefore that, after he ascended the throne, he avoided any infringement of the law. So careful were both he and the queen with regard to ritual observances that it was said, "The King is guided by the Queen, and the Queen is guided by Gamaliel"! [5] In the festive procession of the pilgrims bearing the new fruit to the Temple, Agrippa could be seen with his basket on his shoulder, side by side with the lowliest plebeian of the kingdom.[6] When, walking through the streets with his retinue, he noticed that a bridal procession had stopped to let him pass, he halted and bade it take precedence.[7]

These fine gestures achieved their purpose. At the Sukkot festival in the year 41, which was the seventh of the Sabbatical cycle, the King, in accordance with the prescriptions of the Bible, read the Book of Deuteronomy in public. When he came to the verse, "One from among thy brethren shalt thou set king over thee; thou mayest not put a foreigner over thee, who is not thy brother" (Deut. 17:15), he suddenly remembered that in the opinion of many present the law barred him from the throne, and he burst into tears.. But the sages, led by Gamaliel, consoled him, calling out, "Fear not, Agrippa, fear not! Thou art our brother!" [8]

Gamaliel extended the same tolerance to the small, rising sect of Christians. Less than a decade had passed since the crucifixion of Jesus, and the Church was still in its infancy, when Peter the Apostle was brought before the High Court on the charge of heresy. For a little time, the leader of the apostles stood in danger of severe punishment—of scourging, perhaps death. But Gamaliel, who was no less adamant than his colleagues in his rejection of the new doctrine, saw little danger in it. Peter and his fellow Christians still observed every iota of Jewish law. They had not even broken with rabbinic theology. They disagreed with the other Pharisees only in their assertion that the Messiah had already appeared in the person of Jesus of Nazareth and in their claim to miraculous healing powers. Gamaliel could easily dismiss the first doctrine as meaningless, since Jesus was no longer living; and whether the expected Messiah, in whom all the Pharisees believed, returned under one name or another, was obviously immaterial. The therapeutic activity of the Apostles must have seemed equally harmless to a teacher who did not regard their sect as in itself dangerous. Moreover, Gamaliel probably realized that persecution would only strengthen the new group and drive it permanently out of the ranks of standard Pharisaism. At any rate, he was determined that no one should be punished with his consent, merely for teaching an unpopular doctrine. His faith in God convinced him that falsehood would fall of its own weight and that the truth could not be conquered. Anticipating the modern advocates of freedom of the press and freedom of speech, he held that the Sanhedrin was without authority to punish expressions of opinion; it was concerned only with action, not with words. And at his insistence, Peter was freed.[9]

Agrippa's sudden death in the year 44 brought an end to this happy era. From that day onward disaster followed disaster. The Roman procurators who succeeded Agrippa as rulers of the country were entirely without interest in the welfare of the land they governed. They did not even seek the gratitude or respect of its people. Their only purpose in coming to Palestine was to enrich themselves so that they might return to a life of greater luxury and power in Rome. Their avarice, their tyranny, their lack of any sense of responsibility, are described in vivid colors by Josephus who, certainly, was not inclined to do them any injustice. Appeals to their superiors in Syria and in Rome were of no avail; the Roman bureaucracy, like every other, defended the misdeeds of underlings even when they were most patent. The result was what might have been expected. Within a century Jerusalem had become a heap of cinders, Judea was utterly devastated, the Temple was plowed over and hundreds of thousands of people had been slaughtered, sold as slaves or driven into foreign lands.

The events which led to this final catastrophe followed one another with the inexorable logic of Greek tragedy. Given the character and position of the two opposing peoples, the one obstinately idealistic, deeply religious and firm in its faith, but without knowledge of strategy or military force; the other arrogant, aggressive, well-organized and utterly ruthless, the end could hardly be other than it was. Before Akiba was thirty years old, the ultra-nationalists of Judea, maddened by the oppression of the Roman procurators, had persuaded their brethren to undertake a hopeless rebellion which culminated in the capture of Jerusulem and the burning of the Temple. Half a century later, a second rebellion broke out, because Trajan violated his pledge to restore the Temple and Jerusalem; and then, after another seventeen years, came the final catastrophe of the Bar Kokba rebellion and its aftermath of unforgettable destruction. Each of these conflicts cost the little country treasures of wealth as well as thousands of lives. Trade was interrupted, cities were burned and lands were confiscated.

In the end, the straggling bands of Judean refugees who made their way into Galilee, the northern province of Palestine, were brought to the nadir of economic life. Six people had to cover themselves with a single blanket; [10] children of seven or under had to be put to work to earn their food; [11] men lay about in the streets, swollen with hunger, though grain could be had at the low price of four *seahs* for a *sela* (about a bushel and a half for a dollar); "none had even that much." [12]

It is difficult to think of another period in history when such spiritual gains were made in the midst of progressive decline and disintegration. The political and economic decadence of Rome was accompanied by a darkening of its intellectual horizons; the impoverishment of the Middle Ages put an end to the development of science; the splendor of Arabic culture disappeared with the retrogression of the caliphate. The Romans might well have thought that the destruction of Judea would end the spiritual life of its people. But the very opposite happened. Judea died, but she died in childbirth.

The most remarkable phase of this spiritual revolution was its occurrence where it might least have been expected—in the lethargic Palestinian countryside.

Jewish thought had made memorable advances long before the time of Akiba. There was a world of difference between the simple faith of Elijah and the complicated theology and ethics of Ezekiel, Deutero-Isaiah, and the author of Job. But this development had been essentially a product of city life, primarily the life of Jerusalem. For eight centuries that great capital had been the center of Jewish spiritual energy: a creative dynamo in a dormant world. The sharp contrasts and glaring inconsistencies which marked its activity, like that of other metropolitan centers, stimulated thought, especially in ethical and religious lines. Its numerous visitors, merchants, pilgrims, travelers, soldiers, diplomats and statesmen brought to it cosmopolitan ideas, challenging and widening its inherited conceptions. There Isaiah announced his epoch-making conceptions of world peace, international justice, the saved remnant, the inviolability of Zion and the Holy One of Israel; there Jeremiah struggled for a formula which would combine the traditional belief in divine providence with the newly discovered doctrine of free will; there Habakkuk first questioned the justice of the universe and Zephaniah proclaimed his enduring faith in the poor of the land. It was the descendants of the artisans and traders of Jerusalem who preserved and expanded the prophetic teaching during the Exile. Among them arose Ezekiel with his mature teachings of individual responsibility and human equality, and his powerful denunciation of imperial arrogance. Restored, Jerusalem produced the eloquent skepticism of Job and the convincing replies of the Hasideans. The beliefs in resurrection and immortality as religious ideals became fully developed; the moral responsibility of the individual was most emphatically asserted; the invigorating doctrine of the Oral Law took form; and the paradox of faith plus freedom was fully recognized and accepted.

The country had resisted these teachings from beginning until the end. The same conservatism which made the Jewish husbandman of the first century an almost exact replica of his Amoritic predecessor of Abraham's time and, except for change of language, indistinguishable from his modern successor, the Arabic-speaking *fellah,* prevented the provinces from contributing new ideas to the thought or theology of the people. The provincial peasant of Akiba's day still carried about bones of the deceased as charms; he still poured out drops of his wine to satisfy the greed and envy of the evil spirits; he still ate enormous meals on the ninth of Tishri in commemoration of forgotten Canaanite rites.

This was especially true in the province of Galilee which, being farthest from Jerusalem, had been least affected by it. Whatever light had pierced the darkness of the peasant mentality of this district had come from the Pharisaic teachers, the scribes of Jerusalem. Their disciples had brought the conceptions of the resurrection and immortality, of individual responsibility and human worth, to the remotest corners of the land. But even when the Galilean accepted these teachings, he transformed them into ideals more in keeping with his own simplicity and naïveté. The doctrine of the resurrection ceased to be the robust prop of the downtrodden, enabling them to face transient sufferings with equanimity, and became a romantic call to deny the world and to live only for a future life. The paradoxical combination of worldliness and otherworldliness, of idealism and practical common sense, which is basic to Pharisaism, was too complicated for the husbandman. Accepting the doctrines of Jerusalem, he followed them to their logical conclusions. If God is the Healer, why call on a physician? If the soul is immortal, why shun death? Thus the faith which had enabled the plebeian of Jerusalem to live, moved the Galilean peasant to die. The provincial Pharisees became either zealots burning with desire to usher in the Divine Kingdom through force of arms, or Christians holding that only faith was needed to put an end to the Roman dominion. Both peasant groups agreed that the Kingdom of God was at hand and that everyone ought to *act* on that premise. The zealot became a soldier, ready to die on the battlefield; the Christian gave his all to the poor, and prepared for martyrdom.

The sudden acquisition of creative power by the intellectually backward countryside can be explained, in part, by the increased influence of the scholars of Jerusalem during this period. As the doom of the great metropolis became evident, many of them fled to the province as well as to the Diaspora, hoping to save the ideals of their ancestors from destruction. Certainly it was some such thought which motivated the high priest Joshua ben Gamala in establishing the first provincial school system during the last decade of the Temple's existence.[13] And certainly, too, it was this conviction which turned the minds of the apostles from Jerusalem and Palestine to the Diaspora for converts to their faith.

But no less important than these social forces was the influence exercised by the two dominating personalities of the age, Akiba ben Joseph among the rabbis, and Paul of

Tarsus among the apostles. Laboring in different fields and with different methods, the two teachers achieved varying results. Yet in the perspective of history it is clear that both contributed to the miracle of turning destruction into creation and death into life. There is a remarkable correspondence in the life history of the two men which, seen against the background of their magnificent but tragic age, ceases to be a coincidence and becomes typical of it. Both of them in middle life underwent conversions to causes which until then they had hated and persecuted; both emerged as central figures in their respective faiths; both undertook reformulations of the traditions which they had accepted and struggled unremittingly for the acceptance of their doctrines; both sought to universalize the teachings of their colleagues and to impose philosophic breadth and order on their religions; and finally, both crowned their careers with the martyr's death. Considered in the light of these similarities, the two picturesque figures appear almost as personifications of their time, with its readiness for radical change, its impatience with tradition, its wide interest in humanity, its restless search for new truths, its desire for reformulation and systemization and its willingness to perish for its ideals.

True, Paul died before the year 70, and Akiba after the year 130; Paul taught the abrogation of the Law, Akiba its perpetuation; Paul gave himself to the Gentiles, Akiba to his own people; Paul became a Christian, Akiba remained a Jew. These wide divergences only emphasize their amazing similarities in life and circumstance.

Perhaps indeed, their peculiar histories contain the secret of Akiba's and Paul's enduring influence. The chaotic times in which they lived demanded leadership which was free from the trammels of tradition and precedent. The Palestinian world was ready for fundamental changes; its teachers, reared in their respective faiths, could offer it no guidance. Among the Christians, the daring rejection of the Law by which the Founder had lived could be proposed by no one who had known him and followed him. Only Paul, who had undergone a complete transformation in his own life and who, being without personal knowledge of Jesus, could reconstruct him freely in his imagination, could tear the Church from its pristine moorings. Similarly Akiba, brought into the Rabbinic world in middle age, could view it and criticize it freely. Overwhelmed at first by the grandeur of rabbinic Law, he was later able to detect the flaws and weaknesses of its complicated structure. The habits of thought and argument which his older colleagues accepted without question because they had grown up in them, aroused in him antagonism and opposition.

It is not surprising that the transformation of rabbinic Judaism was less radical, and occurred half a century later, than that of Christianity. The difference was not due merely to the accident of Akiba's later birth. Conceivably rabbinic Judaism might have produced an Akiba in the year 50, had the times been ripe for him. The fact is, however, that the deeper foundations of rabbinic Judaism made fundamental change in it far more difficult than in the new religion. Paul had to contend with traditions which were only twenty or thirty years old; those which Akiba undertook to recast had the authority of centuries. In the year 50, Christianity was still entirely fluid; even the Founder's sayings had probably not been collected into fixed booklets. The Oral Law, with which Akiba had to deal, had been handed down by a chain of teachers which reached back beyond the beginnings of Pharisaism, and indeed antedated the origins of the Second

Commonwealth. To effect even a moderate change in so ancient a system required extraordinary genius, as well as extraordinary experiences.

The extent of the metamorphosis which Akiba underwent in preparation for his task becomes apparent only when we consider the surroundings in which he was reared. He was born in southwestern Palestine, probably in the vicinity of Ludd, the modern Lydda, in the low-lying plain near the coast of the Mediterranean. The warm semi-tropical climate of the district, the character of its soil and the abundance of subterranean waters seeping down from the hilltops, makes it, in spite of the comparatively small rain supply, one of the most productive parts of the country. To this day, the fertility of this coastal plain is three or four times as great as that of the Judean hill country.[14] It was there that Isaac received returns of a hundredfold (Gen. 26:12); and it is only there and in the Jordan Valley that such fertility is recorded today. No wonder that this part of Palestine was settled long before the rest;[15] and no wonder, too, that at all times the powerful and wealthy landowners sought control of this plain, forcing the weaker and the poorer farmers into the less productive hills.[16] Archaeological discoveries prove that long before the advent of the Hebrews there was a definite economic division between the wealthy low country and the poor plateau, corresponding to that between the *pediakoi* and the *diakrioi* of Attica.[17] The pre-Israelite people who dwelt in the mountain differed from the Canaanite who lived by the sea, not in language, or in culture, or in form of government, but in riches and power. The Hebrews who invaded Palestine in the fourteenth century B.C.E. found little difficulty in conquering the weakly fortified cities on the mountains, but for centuries they could not drive out the Canaanites who held the plain, "for they had iron chariots," not to speak of superior organization and military technique. When, finally, the Hebrews with their superior numbers did force their way into the plain, the land was, as a matter of course, seized by the patrician leaders of the army; and the natural division between the lowland and the highland was emphasized by the difference in the social status of its new owners.

Thus it came about that in the time of Akiba the upper country was divided into a large number of small holdings, each barely sufficient to maintain its owner and his family; while the lowland, in which he was born, was entirely under the control of wealthy landowners, whose far flung estates were tilled by slaves or hirelings.[18] Only in Jerusalem could there be found wider differences in wealth and status than were apparent in this coastal plain. The mighty patricians who owned the soil lived in fine, well-built mansions, with many rooms, even with upper stories. The walls might be built of hewn stone or marble; the windows and doors, of cedar or olive wood; there might even be found inlays of ivory and coverings of beaten gold.[19]

But it was not in such a palatial home that Akiba was born and reared. His father, Joseph, was a poor, landless peasant, a laborer on the estate of a rich neighbor. It was with unconscious irony that these people were called *am ha-arez,* men of the soil, for their lack of landed possessions was the fundamental characteristic of their existence. But the term had long lost its honorific connotations, and now meant nothing but "boor" and "ignoramus"; and in these senses it could be applied to Joseph with absolute precision. He knew nothing and cared nothing about the national literature of his people or the learned traditions of the Scribes. Probably he could neither read nor write; he was, furthermore, unconscious of any void in his life because he lacked these skills.

The house in which Joseph lived had no hewn stone or marble or wood of any kind. It was similar to that still to be found among the Arabic *fellaheen* of the district. The walls were built of sunburned bricks, unprotected by any cement or plaster, and uninterrupted by any opening for light or air. The roof, held up by sundry branches and boughs, consisted of a mixture of clay, straw and earth, sufficient to keep out the sun in the summer, and all but the worse rain in the winter. Nothing but straw mats covered the bare earth, protecting the inhabitants and their clothes from contact with the soil when they went to sleep. If Joseph was removed from the lowest strata of pauperdom, he may have possessed such luxuries as a bed, a table, some chairs and an earthenware lamp. More probably, however, he, like the rest of the poor husbandmen, went to bed as soon as the sun set and worried little about household furnishings.

The food of these peasants was of the simplest. Some barley bread with cabbage, turnip, or perhaps garlic in the morning, and the same in the evening, was all they could afford. The scarcity of fuel made it difficult to cook even these vegetables. To prepare them in some degree, they would obtain a jug of hot water from a rich neighbor, or perhaps from a central village supply, and dip the vegetables into it.[20] They regarded this life as entirely natural, and considered it contumacy on the part of their ancestors to have asked Moses for such delicacies as leeks, cucumbers, and fish (Num. 11:5). It did not seem to them at all grotesque that people who demanded meat should have been punished by an unnatural death for their inordinate appetite. They probably agreed with the scholar of the period who declared it sinful to eat meat unless one owned herds of sheep and oxen.[21] To purchase it in the market was almost profligacy. According to this sage, a man must accumulate a capital of no less than ten mina (five times the dower right of a virgin) before he may indulge in cooked vegetables every day.[22] If he has twenty mina, he may eat fish; if he has fifty mina, he may eat meat once a week, on the Sabbath; but not until he possesses a hundred mina may he eat meat every day!

Since Akiba's father possessed far less than even one mina, he must have contented himself and his family with the simplest possible fare. Yet the delight of these meals, frugal as they were, was never forgotten. Long afterward, when he could afford to buy any food he desired, Akiba still insisted that the meals he ate as a child were proper subjects for gratitude to God. "He who eats but a little herb, provided it be his regular meal, must recite the full grace after it," he said.[23]

Such was the poverty of the husbandmen in this rich wine country, that most of them knew no other drink than water. Many of them, making a virtue out of necessity, declared the use of wine degrading and harmful. One of the scholars who derived from this class used to say that the four cups of wine which he drank, in accordance with the ritual, on the Passover eve gave him a headache until Pentecost.[24] Akiba himself, though he did not entirely abstain from wine in later years, never outgrew his prejudice against it.

Clothes were as simple as food, drink or shelter. The fine, multi-colored garments of imported linen and dyed wool which were used by the wealthy were quite unknown among the poor. Next to the body one wore a tight-fitting linen tunic, and above it threw a rectangular piece of woolen cloth, the prototype of the modern prayer shawl, which did service as cloak by day and blanket at night. Many had to use linen sheets as substitutes for this woolen garment.[25] Other families possessed a single woolen garment which was used by husband and wife in turn, when they had occasion to leave the house.[26] Special rules had to be made permitting the woman remaining at home, only partly dressed, to recite the prayers and benedictions.[27]

It would be an error to infer from what has been said that Akiba's childhood was unhappy. He knew hunger, he knew toil, he knew exposure, and he doubtless was accustomed to severe punishment. But the ancient Palestinian child had also his games, his fun and his holidays. Like children of other ages, he imitated in play what he saw his father or neighbor do seriously. At harvest time, the boys would garner sand instead of wheat, and could be seen measuring out little nutshells of their "produce" as ecclesiastical gifts to the "priest," the "Levite," and the "poor." [28] Like his father, Akiba was out of doors most of the day, and could enjoy the bright sunlight and the country air. Living in the fertile coastal plain, he could look to the east and see the beauty of the Judean hills, he could enjoy the wonder of the starlit, Mediterranean sky, and when he stole away to the sea which lay only a few miles off, he could let his imagination roam over the dark mysteries of its unmeasured distances.

It was impossible for him, however, to receive any book learning. Twenty years were to elapse before Joshua ben Gamala was to establish his first system of general rural education for Judea. At that time children could learn only from their parents, and Akiba could get from his father nothing more than the simple technique of sheep tending.[29] Presumably he was set to work at the same early age as other plebeian children and, before long, apprenticed to one of the large sheep-owners of the neighborhood, in return for food, clothing and shelter.

The rabbinic maxim, "marriage at eighteen," [30] would have sounded like mockery to him. It was meant for the affluent, among whom the father, according to ancient custom, provided a house for his son on his marriage.[31] Among the poor, a man usually passed his thirtieth year before he could think of taking a wife.[32]

Condemned to the companionship of animals, and of peasants who were hardly more articulate, Akiba hated those to whom he should rightly have belonged; and his hatred was the more violent because his awareness of his rights was confined to his subconscious mind. "When I was an *am ha-arez,*" he reported in later years, "I used to say, 'Would that I had a scholar in my hands and I should bite him like an ass.' " [33] Those who knew Akiba in his older, mellow days, when he had attained profound learning, social charm and gentle manners, could scarcely have credited his words. To us, they are evidence of the fierce intellectual energies which, imprisoned beneath an uncouth pastoral exterior and denied their proper expression, broke forth in hatred and envy.

From this pit of perdition Akiba was fortunately saved by the love of the woman, Rachel, who became his wife.[34] Who she was, and by what genius she was able to penetrate so graceless an exterior and see the immense potentialities within, we do not know. Cimabue found an untutored boy drawing sheep by the roadside and launched the great Giotto on his career; Johanan ben Zakkai, Akiba's older contemporary, might have engaged the unlettered Judean shepherd in conversation and out of the fullness of his wisdom and experience recognized a potential equal. But how came a young and inexperienced Palestinian maiden, of whom it is not even recorded whether she was literate, to perform this miracle? Legend describes her as the daughter of Ben Kalba Sabua, one of the three richest men in Jerusalem at the time. But this is probably moralistic fiction. Nothing is really known with definiteness about her identity or origin, and in a case so extraordinary anything may have been true. The only reliable record which has been preserved concerning her forebears indicates that they were neither famous nor wealthy; for it cites a tradition in the name of "Johanan, son of Joshua, son of Akiba's father-in-law." [35] It is quite inconceivable that so important and distinguished a person as Ben Kalba Sabua should be referred to without the mention of his name, but merely as related to Akiba. However, daughter of scholarship and opulence, or of poverty and ignorance, she must be recognized as one of the most remarkable women in the whole of Jewish tradition. Throughout his life Akiba insisted that he owed everything to her. "Whatever you have achieved, and whatever I have achieved," he said to his disciples when they gathered in hosts to greet him, "belong to her"! [36]

That this was neither modesty nor generosity nor pose, but the plain truth, we know from the observations of Akiba's colleagues. When one of the wealthier among them was upbraided by his wife because he did not give her as fine presents as Rachel received from her poor husband, he remarked with more candor than tact, "Had you done for me what she did for him, I should have given you, too, a headdress of gold"! [37] To recognize the potential Akiba in the *am ha-arez,* required insight of a high order; to accomplish the transformation, needed character of equal distinction. Rachel persuaded Akiba to leave his goats and sheep and become a pupil of the scholars whom he envied and loathed. This decision made, they were married, and entered together on the struggle for his education.

Numerous stories are current about the discouragements which Akiba met and overcame in his first efforts to learn how to read and write. His wife's father, who had opposed the match from the beginning, refused to admit the poor, ignorant shepherd into his home; and Akiba had no house to which he and Rachel might go. His toil barely provided enough for the family to eat. Added to these economic troubles, were the disappointments of his student life. Apparently he found his studies so difficult that more than once he was ready to return to his sheep and his ignorance. And, in truth, the system of education then in vogue was hardly adapted to the needs of an alert, mature mind.

When the pupil had mastered the alphabet and was able to read Hebrew texts, he was introduced not to the fascinating narratives of Genesis, but to the incredibly difficult and technical laws of sacrifice which are found in the Book of Leviticus.[38] This curriculum had originated centuries earlier in the first public schools of Palestine, established by the priests to train their children for Temple worship. In those early times the priests had been the only people who could afford the luxury of professional teachers and at the same time had some interest in book learning. The other important social group, the lay patrician landowners, like the barons of medieval Europe, considered ignorance not only blessed but ennobling; while the plebeians had to do their own teaching, as they did their own mending, baking, cleaning and other household chores.

When, ultimately, economic improvement of Jerusalem's market place brought a new, learned, and more prosperous plebeian class into being, the system of education had become fixed and unchangeable. Indeed, the Book of Leviticus was so firmly established as the foundation of Jewish education that even in medieval Germany, a thousand years after the time of Akiba, a child was taught the first chapter of Leviticus before he was permitted to read Genesis.[39] In Akiba's time, not merely one chapter had to be mastered, but the whole book, with its successive regulations for whole burnt offerings, peace offerings, sin offerings and guilt offerings; its detailed analysis of the laws of purity; its enumeration of the various symptoms of skin and sexual disease; its description of the service on the Day of Atonement; and its list of the marriages prohibited as incestuous. Akiba, unaccustomed to the discipline of book learning, and free to study only after the fatigue of a day's labor, must have found it difficult to keep awake as he struggled to remember which offering was sacrificed in the north and which at the door of the sanctuary; whether the sin-offering of the high priest was a bullock or a ram; whether the presence of yellow hair on a leprous person was a sign of impurity and disease or of purity and healing. His teacher, probably a country sage whose mentality and learning were just sufficient to meet the needs of six- and seven-year-old pupils, could have been of little help to Akiba, who apparently found the effort so unpleasant and discouraging that despite his promise to Rachel he sank back to his earlier life as a contented and carefree *am ha-arez*.

Meanwhile, Rachel had given birth to a child. The affectionate shepherd's heart, already lacerated with his disappointment in himself, must have been torn as he asked himself whether his child too was destined to remain an *am ha-arez*. The first gurgles of the infant, his attempts to walk and speak, his rapid assimilation of new ideas, his ready adjustment to changed circumstances: what chords, which

Akiba might have preferred to keep silent, they struck in his very soul. Never had he been so conscious of latent abilities; never so envious of those who had been trained in the Torah. Brooding and ruminating over his unhappy lot, Akiba came one day, it is said, to a spring, where for the first time he noticed the deep groove which the falling waters had cut into the rock. As frequently happens to a highly gifted and imaginative person, the commonplace sight produced on him an effect altogether unpredictable and quite incommensurate with itself. The spring became for him what the almond tree had been for Jeremiah and the sight of the Temple for Isaiah, the catalytic agent of his conversion. Suddenly his thoughts crystallized, his mind became clear, his purpose assumed definite shape.

He took his child, then a lad of four or five, to a teacher of children. "My master, instruct us," he said. The middle-aged father and the little boy sat down, side by side, before their teacher, who wrote an alphabet for them. Akiba took hold of the tablet by one end, gave the other to his son, and they followed the lesson together. "This," the teacher said, "is an *aleph,* this a *bet,* this a *gimmel,*" and so on through the whole series of twenty-two letters.

Akiba easily recalled his forgotten studies and repeated the lesson to the boy, watching with delight the response of the immature mind to the strange creation of human artifice. How the little fellow's eyes brightened when at last he could recognize the letters himself, and how happy he was in his father's evident satisfaction and pride. In the effort to help the boy, Akiba found his own learning less tedious and painful. He was now amused rather than chagrined at the simplicity of the teacher who, fixed in his routine habits, insisted on making him follow a technique fit for infants. When they could recite and recognize the letters as they had been arranged in the first place, the master wrote them again in reverse, and then in confused, order. Only when they had finally demonstrated to his satisfaction that they could recognize each individual letter, no matter where it was placed, were they admitted into the stately, forbidding portals of Leviticus.

This time Akiba did not falter. What was hard to learn, was easy to teach. He mastered Leviticus, and then the other books which had legalistic significance: Exodus, Numbers and Deuteronomy. Genesis, which contained only a few laws, and was full of stories, was apparently not studied in the regular curriculum. Yet Akiba, preparing for advanced rabbinic studies, mastered this too, as well as the prophets and the hagiographa. He had now far outstripped his little boy, and was ready to apply for admission into the rabbinical academy.[40]

This was about the year 80. Akiba, approaching his fortieth year, the age when most people of promise have already achieved some distinction in their chosen fields, had not yet entered on his career. But his work was being prepared for him. The momentous transformation in his private life had synchronized with even more fundamental changes in the structure of the body politic. The double process of decay and growth characteristic of the period had already set in.

* * * * *

While Akiba was still in his infancy, Agrippa's glorious reign had come to an end, giving way to years of tumult and rebellion, cruel hatreds, unjust denunciations and bitter strife. The ancient struggles between the Pharisees and the Sadducees, and among the various Pharisaic factions, had broken

out anew, and with redoubled vigor. Public arguments between the opposing sects were of daily occurrence, and at
least on one occasion a Sadducean high priest suffered physical
injury because he refused to follow the Pharisaic interpretation of the Law. One of the usually calm, peace-loving Hillelite sages nipped his ear, thereby rendering him permanently
unfit for high priestly service.[41] Among the Pharisees themselves, there were equally bitter quarrels. United as they were
when their common doctrines were attacked, their various
factions were well-nigh at war with one another.

This clash of social forces, which was to affect Akiba's
public activity so intimately, becomes fully intelligible only
in its historical perspective. The fundamental class division
in Palestine was that between the semi-nomadic landless shepherds and the landowning farmers.[42] The conflict between
these groups antedated the appearance of the Israelites in the
Holy Land by more than a millennium, and is allegorized in
the biblical story of Cain and Abel (Gen. 4:2). Almost
equally ancient, and in part related to it, already described,[43]
was the struggle between the small farmers of the stony hill
country and the wealthy patricians of the fertile valleys.
Both of these class conflicts persisted after the Hebrew inva-
sion of the land, merely taking on new forms. It is no mere
chance, for instance, that the first king of Israel, Saul, was a
farmer of the tribe of Benjamin, while the second king was
a shepherd from the semi-nomadic hill country of Judah. Nor
is it strange that Jeroboam, when he rebelled against the
Judean dynasty, should have rebelled against the calendar as
well (I Kings 12:32). For Jeroboam drew his support largely
from the lowland farmers, and when the autumn festival was
being celebrated on the highlands of Jerusalem in the month
of September, he and his class were still enjoying summer.[44]

But neither the shepherds nor the small peasants of the hills could offer effective resistance to the great patrician landowners who dominated Palestinian culture and politics. They lacked organization, a program and class consciousness; it was only in the city that the plebeians achieved partial victory. Here they were massed by tens of thousands; here contact with each other and with visitors to their markets developed in them a sophisticated outlook; here, finally, the class divisions, which had been partially concealed by the simple life of the country, took on sharpness and clarity. Moreover, it was from the two extremes of the social system that the city recruited its population: the landowner rich enough to appoint an overseer, and the *fellah* whose land he had acquired. The former sought the court, the latter a job.[45]

In the Second Book of Samuel (19: 39), for instance, we are told how David persuades Chimham, the son of the rich Barzillai, to leave his home in Transjordan and seek his fortune in Jerusalem; while in Genesis (4: 17.22) we read how the clans of itinerant smiths gave up their nomadic life and settled in the cities to enter the employ of the patricians.

By the second century B.C.E., the Holy City had attained a population of more than seventy-five thousand, swelled in times of pilgrimage to thrice that number. This offered an unprecedented opportunity for plebeian organization and education. The market place of Jerusalem became the cornerstone of the whole plebeian edifice, and it was here that the successive plebeian factions—the Hasideans, the Pharisees, and the Hillelites—had their beginning and their inspiration.

The social cleavage was, however, most clearly visible in the sanctuary. The lower class of Temple servants, the Levites, who were the singers and the gate-keepers, made common cause with their fellow plebeians throughout the coun-

try. The community of interest between these groups was
strengthened by the fact that the priests, who claimed descent from Aaron the brother of Moses, were actually the
most powerful landowning group in the country. "Most
priests are men of wealth," was a current proverb.[46] Moreover, the differences of station, imperceptible in the country
but pronounced in city, were incontinently emphasized in the
sanctuary. The wealthy noble and the harassed artisan of
Jerusalem met only by accident, in the street; the great landowner of Ludd never saw the peasant of Tekoa; but priest and
Levite were always together. The Levite was essentially the
menial of the Temple, yet the majesty of the God whom he
served in common with the priest made him, in his own eyes,
the equal of the latter. The struggle became all the more
fierce because in the Temple social and political groups were
hardened into castes. There was nothing to prevent a fortunate
peasant from acquiring large estates; and some able merchants
had hewn their way into nobility; but never could a Levite, or
his descendants, become a priest.

Hence it came about that the most acrimonious class struggle in ancient Palestine involved not the largest class of the
underprivileged, the small farmers; nor even the city proletariat, who were also quite numerous; but the tiny group of
Temple Levites. In their championship of these oppressed
ecclesiastics many lay scholars found compensation for their
ineffectual efforts on behalf of the vastly larger sections whose
complicated problems defied any efforts at remedy. Nevertheless, the wide plebeian interests appear from time to time in
the opposition platforms; they are especially evident, as we
shall see, in Akiba's juristic system. Within his wide range of
sympathies he included the struggle of the shepherd against
the farmer, the highland against the valley, the town against

the country, the artisan against the noble; and the Levite against the priest.

During the First Commonwealth the defense of the plebeians had been conducted largely by the prophets; in the Second Commonwealth, the prophet was replaced by the scholar, whose forum was his school room. Here the humble teacher would interpret the Law, applying it to new situations as they arose, and demonstrating that its spirit was one of human equality, merciful justice and universal peace. His words had, of course, no immediate practical significance, for he had no share in the government of the community. The control of both the religious and civil life of the people was vested in a Gerousia or Council of Elders, the patrician "heads of the families," who qualified by lineage rather than accomplishment. Even the high priests, who presided over this Gerousia, stood generally on no higher intellectual or cultural level than the other members. The decisions of the Gerousia in religious and ceremonial, as well as civil, questions, were based entirely on observed practice or precedent fixed by earlier patrician landowners.

The objections of the plebeian scholars or scribes remained unheard in the counsels of the great. But they were not forgotten. They were handed down as dissenting opinions from teacher to pupil, generation by generation. In time they formed a body of traditions which, unrecognized and rejected by the rulers of the people, were yet accepted as authoritative by large masses. This was the Oral Law. Some of it had doubtless originated in hoary antiquity, in the days when the prophets of God struggled against the worship of Baal. But the newer additions of later times were accepted by the plebeians as equally authoritative with the older elements. The whole Oral Law, they said, had come down "from master to master" along a chain of tradition which led back to Moses on the summit of Mount Sinai.[47]

From time to time, plebeian teachers, who, like the author of Psalm 119, were especially vociferous in their denunciation of their opponents, suffered persecution for their ideals. More generally the movement was dismissed with contemptuous tolerance, as doomed to a speedy end.

How long would people continue, the men of power must have reasoned with themselves, to study as the word of God an Oral Law which the high priests declared an imposture and which was daily violated in the Temple? And, indeed, it is difficult to see how plebeian scholarship could have survived the fourth century B.C.E., had it not received new life and energy from a totally unexpected source—the rise of Hellenism.

The advent of Alexander the Great, and the ease with which he demolished the great Persian Empire, had wrought a spiritual revolution, in Judea as well as in the rest of the Near East, without parallel in the history of this world. The patricians, who had always been inclined to imitate the ways of their imperialist masters, were carried away by their admiration for the Greeks. They desired for themselves nothing better than to be called Hellenes.

But, as usual, it was only the externalities of the new civilization which attracted them; they had no mind for its intellectual attainments or spiritual ideals. There were no students of Homer or Plato among them; no disciples of Euripides or Aristophanes. They produced no mathematicians, philosophers or physicians. Their Hellenism consisted in attempting to adopt Greek sports rather than in studying the products of Greek intellect. They liked to give themselves Greek names. But the names they chose were not those of

Thales and Anaximander, the heroes of the Greek mind, but of Jason, Menelaus, and Alexander, the foremost examples of physical prowess. They made pathetic attempts to stammer Greek, but succeeded only in forgetting their Hebrew. Young priests, dressed in Athenian garments, could be seen rushing from the altar, where they had offered sacrifices to the God of Israel, to the gymnasium, where they disported themselves naked in accordance with the pagan custom. Living in a Jewish land, many of them felt a sense of shame in the sign of the Abrahamitic covenant, and underwent painful operations to conceal it.

From the distance of centuries these attempts of the patricians to remake themselves as Greeks must seem both comical and pathetic. But to the contemporary plebeians, they were tragic. The scholars realized that much more than class interest was at stake in the conflict between them and the patricians. The whole Jewish tradition was likely to be swept away by the flood of Hellenization.

Determined to save their religion, they borrowed a weapon from the civilization which they were so stoutly opposing. During all the centuries of conflict which had passed, the prophets and the scholars had had a following, but no organization. The plebeians listened to their words, obeyed their instructions, memorized their teachings and handed down their traditions. But it did not occur to either leaders or followers to establish a plebeian party. It was the rise of Alexander which first taught the Orient what power inhered in ordered and united action. The Macedonian phalanxes had won their victories not through superior numbers but by better organization. They had torn through the Persian armies like a well-aimed dart through the flesh of a large beast. The lesson was not wasted, at least so far as the plebeians of

Jerusalem were concerned. For the first time in history they organized themselves as an active opposition—the Hasideans, or pietists.

No less important than this discovery of the meaning of organization was the substitution of the national for the class interest. So long as the plebeians had merely demanded new rights and recognition for their own customs, they found the patrician group united against them. But when they threw themselves into the breach to oppose the flood of Hellenism, they gained support from many members of the aristocracy. The high priesthood, which had so long condemned the scholars, realized at last what peril of widespread apostasy was facing the whole faith.

The foremost of the converts to the plebeian cause was the distinguished statesman-ecclesiastic, Simeon the Righteous.[48] He, more clearly than anyone else in his generation, saw that the future of Judaism depended on study rather than on worship. Priest as he was, he formulated the position of the scholars better than anyone of them had done. "The spiritual world depends," he said, "on three things; the Torah, the ritual, and acts of lovingkindness." [49] The Torah came first; ritual was second. The assertion was as significant and revolutionary in its day as King Josiah's acceptance of the prophetic teaching had been in his. The foremost patrician had given recognition to the plebeians, and had himself placed learning above lineage.

Acting on the principle he had formulated, Simeon convoked a Great Assembly to discuss the problems confronting the people and their faith. Such assemblies had been called before, in times of great emergency. They consisted not of patricians alone, but also of representative plebeians. Artisans and traders, priests and Levites, landowners and shepherds, townsmen and provincials, aristocrats and common people, all sat together in the national council. Led by the high priest, who presided, the Assembly reached a number of decisions which became of historic importance. They closed the prophetic canon; they formulated the prayer service of the synagogue; they prepared a ritual for the Grace After Meat. But the most important decision was of a constitutional nature: they replaced the ancient Gerousia with a new Sanhedrin, which was to include in its membership plebeian scribes as well as patrician elders.[50]

The admission of the plebeian scholars into the Sanhedrin, and the open adherence of Simeon the high priest to their cause, gave them new prestige and standing. The high priest's example was followed by other, lesser aristocrats, especially among the younger men. The most prominent of these were doubtless Jeshua ben Sira, the author of *Ecclesiasticus,* and Antigonus of Socho, who in the next generation became the leader of the Hasidean movement. There were doubtless others, whose names have been forgotten, who were equally talented and devoted. The Oral Law had ceased to be the possession of a class; it had become "the inheritance of the community of Jacob."

To those who regard the Hebraic-Christian-Moslem tradition of ethical monotheism as fundamental to western civilization, Simeon's action must appear of universal, rather than purely national, importance. It was one of those critical moments in history when the future really rests in the hands of an individual. The tide of Hellenization could not indeed be stopped, but it could be directed. Simeon the Righteous, making plans both for the immediate and the distant future, compelled the mighty force to flow and do its work in the channels which he had dug for it. Had Simeon been an assimilator, like his immediate predecessors and successors, the victory of the decadent Syrian Hellenism over Judaism could not have been prevented. The Jewish tradition would have disappeared as completely as that of the Edomites, the Phœnicians, and the other small near-eastern peoples. The two magnificent syntheses of the Hebraism and higher Hellenism, rabbinic Judaism and Christianity, would have perished before they were born.

Yet, naturally, it is in the history of Jewish thought that Simeon's activity looms especially large. For four centuries after him, patricians and plebeians continued to sit together in the Sanhedrin—studying, arguing and at times quarreling. The continuous discussions between the parties clarified their opinions, sharpened their dialectical methods and amplified the legal system. But most important of all, it brought the different factions of the people into a body where they could arrive at mutual understanding, if not common agreement. At last, the conflict of classes had been brought into the Council Chamber where it belonged.

The full measure of Simeon's influence becomes apparent in the light of the curious and instructive history of the century following his death. The Syrian government, watching the struggle between the Hellenists and Hasideans in Palestine, finally became impatient of the slow process of natural assimilation, and undertook to force the people into apostasy. Antiochus IV, Epiphanes, King of Syria and thereby ruler of Palestine, issued edicts in the year 168 B.C.E. transforming the sanctuary in Jerusalem into a heathen Temple, and prohibiting the study or practice of the Jewish faith in his domains.

What followed forms one of the most amazing chronicles in all human history. Were the events less well documented, or had they occurred half a millennium earlier, they would be dismissed as myths. But their historicity is beyond doubt. The Jews, undisciplined, unorganized, impoverished, few in number and divided in counsel, rose in revolt against the mighty Syrian Empire, with its well-trained armies, its enormous wealth and its excellent organization. Led by a family of provincial priests from Modin, the Maccabees or Hasmoneans, the Hasidean pietists showed themselves indomitable soldiers and heroes, as well as learned saints and pious martyrs. "The high praises of the Lord were in their mouths, and a two-edged sword was in their hands."

But the diplomatic astuteness of these plebeians and peasants is even more remarkable than their military skill. Their most significant victories were won not on the battlefield but in peace conferences. Playing off the rival empires and claimants for the various thrones against one another, they obtained greater and greater concessions, until they achieved absolute self-government and freedom. The Maccabees, who had led them both in the war and in the negotiations for peace, became their high priests, replacing the old Zadokite dynasty which had been in control of the Temple for almost eight centuries. Together with this ecclesiastical authority, the Maccabees obtained also complete temporal power. They were to be the heirs of David as well as of Aaron. Yet they did not dare to establish an absolute monarchy. They constituted the executive branch of the infant government; its legislative and judicial functions were vested in the Sanhedrin.

For a time it appeared as if the Messianic era had burst on Palestine; there was complete harmony between rulers and people, the land was prosperous, the study of the Torah was making rapid progress. As in the days of Agrippa, so then, prosperity was helping to break down partisan barriers. The

Hasidean party disappeared; the whole country was one united theocracy. But this Golden Age endured for no more than three decades. Within that time the history of the Hasmoneans was to demonstrate that the Hellenism of the earlier high priesthood had not been the result of willfulness or inner depravity; but was the natural concomitant of their exalted, social position. A definite sociological law makes the leaders of small peoples especially subject to influences emanating from neighboring empires. No matter what their personal background might be, the rulers of Palestine in every age tended to emulate the nobility of larger nations.

This division had been evident long before the time of the Hellenists; indeed, it could be perceived as early as the first days of Israel's entrance into Canaan. The defection of the patricians to Baal worship, the attempts of Ahab and Jezebel to foist the Phœnician gods on the people of Samaria, the imitation of the Babylonian altars and ritual by Ahaz, the wearing of foreign apparel by the princes whom Zephaniah denounced, were all part of the same innate tendency of the Palestinian nobility toward assimilation. No sooner had the Maccabees placed themselves in the seats of the mighty than they became subject to the same influences; they too became Hellenists and assimilators.

Never was the futility of violent revolutions more cogently demonstrated; never were the effects of social position more clearly exhibited. The grandchildren of the men who had given their lives for the Torah became willing apostates; they were called by Greek names, Aristobulus, Alexander, and the like; [51] they neglected the Jewish tradition; they hated and persecuted the scholars. In the eyes of the plebeians their Hellenism was, if anything, baser than that of their predecessors, for their acceptance of the pagan civilization did not prevent them from becoming political and military chauvinists and imperialists. Cultural apostasy and national ambition —the combination seemed most hateful of all to the peace-loving pietists.

It was at this time that the full effects of the activity of Simeon the Righteous were felt. Half a century after his death, his influence was still sufficiently potent to hold in check the tendency toward assimilation and to save at least some of the patricians for the Torah. The imperialistic, assimilated Maccabees had to wage their struggle not with a submerged class of plebeian traders, but with the combined forces of all scholars and teachers.

The two groups of pietists, those of the urban market place and those of the landed estates, united to form a single order, replacing the forgotten Hasideans, calling themselves *Haberim,* "comrades" or "friends." The outer world, however, came to know them as *Pharisees,* "separatists," or "purists." In response to this unified opposition, the groups sympathetic to the high priesthood, too, organized. Since the Maccabees now regarded themselves as descended from Zadok, the party was called Zadokim or Sadducees. From that time onward there was a double social struggle in Judaism: that between the organized patricians or Sadducees and the scholars or Pharisees; and that within the Pharisaic party itself, between the faction which derived from the patricians and provincials, and that which derived from the plebeians.

The name Pharisee was most appropriate to the order of the scholars. Their basic principles were exactly what those of the Hasideans had been. They believed in the resurrection of the dead, the existence of angels, providential control of human decisions and, above all, in the divinity of the Oral Law. But what especially impressed their contemporaries was their insistence on the observance of every iota of the Law, especially that section of it which dealt with the rules of Levitical impurity.

Few modern students of Scripture take the trouble to read the part of Leviticus dealing with these ceremonial regulations; those who do readily dismiss these rules as taboos, similar to those current among most primitive peoples. To the ancient Jews, however, they were of transcending importance. One-sixth of the Mishna, the basic code of Jewish Law, is devoted to their exposition and elucidation. They affected the daily life of the observant Jew more than any other part of his religion. They regulated the type of food he could eat, the clothes he could wear, the houses he could enter, and the friends he could make; they fixed the time and manner of his washing and of his bathing, and even of his relations with his wife. Contact with the dead, or with persons suffering from various sexual or skin diseases, or with menstrual women, and a dozen other "sources of impurity" defiled him. Once unclean, he could not touch ordinary food or vessels, lest he contaminate them. In fact, he had to leave his house, and remain outside of the "camp" or city until he became pure. In cases of minor defilement, this might be the same evening, after he had bathed; for a major defilement, like that arising from contact with a corpse or with persons suffering from sexual disorders, a more elaborate ceremony was necessary, involving visits to the Temple, sprinkling with the ashes of the red heifer, or the sacrifice of two pigeons.

The Law, intended to make of the Jewish people a "kingdom of priests and a holy nation," was too rigorous for universal observance. People living at a distance from Jerusalem could not resort to the Temple for purification every time they attended a funeral. Peasants could not accept a law which barred them from their house for a whole day every time they spoke to a person suspected of "suffering with a flow." They justified and rationalized their impiety, however, on the ground that the laws were not intended for general practice. The rules applied only, the provincials argued, to people who frequented the sanctuary. They were quite willing to "purify" themselves when about to go on a pilgrimage; but otherwise they practically ignored the law.

The pietists of Jerusalem could not accept this lenient interpretation. They considered the law of purity as binding as any other part of the Pentateuch, and carried out its precepts to the minutest detail. The provincials who refused to be bound by the Levitical Law were in their opinion perpetually "impure"; contact with them or their possessions was defiling. The merest drops of spittle which came from their mouths when speaking carried contamination to the person they addressed. It was for this reason the Pharisees were so amazed when Jesus sat down to eat with publicans. As an observant member of their sect, he could have had no commerce whatever with the defiled.

The Pharisees *were* "separatists," and this is the more remarkable because they were altogether unaware of the broad, human, hygienic significance of the Law they observed. They intended only to do the word of God; they actually preserved the health of men.[52] The careful washings, ablutions and bathings, the insistence on separateness from any contact with the dead, the quarantine of those afflicted with sexual or skin ailments, were important prophylactics against disease. They were especially necessary in Jerusalem, where the large aggregation of people, the crowded streets and houses, above all, the massing of the pilgrims in the Temple, might lead to the rapid spread of epidemics. That Jerusalem remained a healthful city and, indeed, that the Jews in later ages were, in spite of persecution, impoverization, and ghetto life, free from many communicable diseases, was due in large measure to the Pharisaic insistence on the observance of their sanitary regulations. The "separation" of the Pharisees from the rest of the people thus implied neither snobbery, nor bigotry nor self-righteousness.

There has never been a religious movement more enlightened or broadminded or tolerant of differences than this ancient sect. From the first, its adherents continued to worship in the Temple, though the high priest and most of his associates belonged to the opposing group, the Sadducees. More than that, the composite character of their own order compelled the Pharisees to tolerate differences of opinion and to encourage the preservation of variant rituals. The plebeian and patrician members were agreed on a few fundamental principles of belief and practice, but they were divided regarding a whole series of ceremonial detail. For generations neither group made any attempt to foist its system on the other. Even disagreements regarding the laws of marriage, involving the most intimate concerns of the members of each group, did not lead to a break. The rules of each group were recognized as binding and authoritative for its own members. "Although," the Mishna says, "one group permitted marriages which the other prohibited, and declared pure what the other considered defiled, they freely intermarried and permitted food to be prepared in common." [53] "Both traditions are the words of Living God," [54] the scholars taught, with their usual daring inconsistency and their fearless love of paradox.

To emphasize the equality of the two groups within Pharisaism, a system of dual leadership was arranged, giving each equal representation. If the first sage (later called the

Nasi or president) was a patrician, the second or associate sage (later called *Ab Bet Din,* or head of the court) had to be a plebeian, and vice versa.[55]

For many generations the two groups worked together without the encumbrance of separate organizations. But the long reign of Herod, with its bitterness, its absolutism and its subservience to Rome, aroused the dormant nationalism of the provincials and lower patricians. Acting on the principle established by his Roman masters, *divide et impera,* the astute King showed special favor to the peace-loving plebeians, fomenting dissension between them and their patrician colleagues.

The factional quarrel became more bitter when, immediately after the death of Herod, the nationalists sought to destroy his dynasty. He had designated his son, Archelaus, as his successor, but before the new king could go to Rome for confirmation by the Caesar, the pilgrims, who had gathered in Jerusalem for the Passover celebration, declared a revolt against him. They encamped in tents about the Temple, controlled the entrances to it, and were obviously preparing to seize the city. For a day or two Archelaus could not make up his mind. To begin his reign with bloodshed might cost him the permanent affection of the people; to show any weakness might prevent his confirmation in Rome. In the end he placed his faith in the Caesar. He sent his whole army against the rebels, killing three thousand of them and dispersing the rest to their homes.[56] Having apparently settled the rebellion with this decisive blow, Archelaus sailed for the imperial capital with a light heart. Little did he realize the depth of the resentment against his father's house. His absence enabled the nationalists to increase their forces and prepare better plans. Their boldness rose with their enthusiasm. They would drive from the country not only the Herodian, but his Roman masters. They would restore the glorious days of the Maccabean theocracy. Their war-fever infected even the Sanhedrin, which now voted for war. "On that day, Hillel sat bent before Shammai, like one of the disciples," records the Talmud; "and," the pacifist chronicler adds, "it was as grave a catastrophe for Israel as when they made the Golden Calf." [57]

Shammai, however, did not content himself with the victory for his foreign policy; he took advantage of the situation, as party men are wont to do, to force also the acceptance of his social and ceremonial program. "If you anger me, I will declare impurity also against the gathering of olives," [58] he cried out to Hillel, who had apparently been outvoted, if not temporarily removed from office. Such strong words could come only from a man who felt certain of his control of the Sanhedrin; a control which Shammai, as second to Hillel, never possessed in normal times, and gained at the moment only as a result of the nationalist excitement.

It was probably during this Passover, while the nationalists controlled the approaches to the Temple, that there occurred the almost incredible incident of Hillel's narrow escape from physical violence at the hands of the enthusiastic Shammaites. The old sage had brought a whole burnt offering to the Temple on a festival day, and had put his hands on its head in accordance with the usual custom. In the eyes of the Shammaites, his action constituted a double offense. It was first of all forbidden, in their opinion, to sacrifice a whole burnt offering on a holiday; and it was additional transgression to lay one's hands on it. Being apparently in control of the outer courts of the sanctuary, the excited partisans of Shammai gathered about Hillel threateningly when they saw him violate their traditions. To understand fully the significance of the incident, we must bear in mind that usually it was left to the individual's conscience to accept the views of either faction on the disputed question. But apparently the Shammaites were tired of tolerance, and determined to enforce their views even against the leader of the opposing faction.

Seeing his danger, Hillel resorted to stratagem. "It is not a whole burnt offering," he said, "but a peace offering." This mitigated the offense, and during the discussion which ensued about the other half of the charge, Hillel made his way to safety. Yet the next day the Shammaites gathered in the Sanhedrin and endeavored to outlaw formally the Hillelite practice which had always been permitted to those who adhered to it. They would have succeeded had not one of their foremost leaders, Baba ben Buta, a man equally noted for his piety, wealth, prudence and dignity, and a personal friend to Hillel, dissuaded them.[59]

Encouraged and strengthened by their victory in the Sanhedrin, the nationalists gathered in hosts for the next pilgrimage, that of the Pentecost, which occurs six weeks after the end of Passover. They seized the Temple mount, which was situated to the east of Jerusalem, and the Upper City, which covered the western hills; thus completely surrounding the Roman garrison in the center. A terrific battle ensued, in which hundreds of nationalists were slain, the cloisters surrounding the temple courts were burned, and the festival celebration was broken up. Yet the uprising was not crushed until Varus, Governor of Syria, came into the country with two additional legions, burned several important towns, entered Jerusalem and crucified two thousand rebels.

This ended the disturbance. The Hillelite members of the Sanhedrin who had so suddenly become converted to the nationalist cause returned to the fold, and Hillel was once more the recognized Nasi. But the extremists were not so easily reconciled. The provincial and patrician Pharisees honored the dead rebels as heroes; the peace-loving plebeians denounced them as traitors. This controversy could not be conducted with the calm, judicial patience and tolerance which had become the rule in disagreements regarding ceremonial. The fierce passions of the nationalists, clamoring for war, and the eagerness of the plebeians to maintain peace at all costs, left no room for an academic, rational approach. A bitter quarrel arose within the Pharisaic order, and the two wings established themselves as separate and opposing schools. The patricians became known as the Shammaites; the plebeians as the Hillelites, after their respective leaders, Shammai and Hillel.

During the reign of Agrippa, and under the leadership of Gamaliel, who was Hillel's grandson, the breach was temporarily healed, as we have already observed. But as soon as Gamaliel died, it reappeared. The Shammaites continued to gain new strength from the rebellious mood of the people, who resented the insolence and the exactions of the Roman procurators. Hundreds, perhaps thousands, who had no interest in the patrician interpretation of the Law, joined the School of Shammai, as a protest against the Roman rule, and an expression of their desire to take forcible action. The most notable of these converts was no less a person than Simeon ben Gamaliel, the son of the late Nasi, and the great-grandson of Hillel, the founder of the plebeian school.

The defection of this scion of the House of Hillel to the teaching of the Shammaites was as characteristic of that agitated period as the conversion of Akiba to scholarship and the apostasy of Paul to Christianity. But to his contemporaries it was vastly more significant. It must have struck dismay

deep into the hearts of the Hillelites. It was as though their
foremost prop had been taken away from them. True, Simeon
ben Gamaliel was, by reason of his wealth, no longer a
plebeian. The fortunes of the House of Hillel had improved
considerably during the preceding generation. Its founder
had been a poor artisan; Gamaliel had become wealthy;
Simeon had been born into affluence and power. Yet the
plebeians, remembering how recent was the family's advent
into better circumstances, could not but count him as their
own. Alas, they did not realize that it was his humble descent
which was driving him from them. Simeon the Righteous, a
born patrician, tracing his descent to Zadok and Aaron, could
join the plebeians without fear; Simeon ben Gamaliel could
remain with them only at the risk of losing his social position.

Social position meant everything to Simeon ben Gamaliel,
and he could not bear to risk its loss. His abandonment of the
Hillelite School was not merely formal and outward; it was
inner and complete. He had inherited the mind of his ancestors but not their spirit, their shrewdness but not their
understanding, their keen insight but not their broad sympathies and social conscience. He could foretell as well as
Hillel or Gamaliel might have done the probable results of
his actions; but this prescience did not deter him from taking
steps certain to cause widespread suffering. Above all, he had
lost that fundamental quality of self-effacement, which had
made the House of Hillel universally revered. He could never
forget himself. Vain, pompous and egotistical, conscious of
scholarly inferiority among the Hillelites and of social inferiority among the Shammaites, he found his greatest delight in dramatic exhibitions of personal authority. It was
this love of showmanship which led him into actions involving danger to others. Unusual ability, especially among his

subordinates, evoked in him both terror and jealousy. "Come and see," the Talmud remarks, when it compares him with his noble father, "the difference between the humility of the former generation which was strong, and the arrogance of the later generation, which was weak." [60]

Everything that Simeon ben Gamaliel did reflected his social ambitions. He lived in a fashionable court, where his nearest neighbor was a Sadducee.[61] He gave one of his daughters in marriage to Eliezer ben Hyrkanos, one of the wealthiest of the young scholars, whose father was a provincial landowner in the coastal plain.[62] More amazingly, he married a second daughter to Simeon ben Nethanel, an ignorant but extremely wealthy *am ha-arez* who, refusing to accept the Pharisaic rules of purity, had to be bound in the marriage contract not to interfere with his wife's observances.[63] Finally, his respect for office led him to adopt as his third son-in-law an illiterate peasant, Phineas the son of Samuel of the village of Aphtha, perhaps the only person in history to attain fame, position and immortality *in a lottery*.[64] This man knew nothing of the traditions of his people, or even the forms and ritual of the Temple. Of the same social rank and intellectual attainments as Akiba's father, he was working as a stone cutter in a quarry when the revolution against Rome broke out. The extreme revolutionaries, who were then in power, impatient of the lukewarm support their cause was receiving from the recognized Temple authorities, decided to replace the officiating high priest with someone to be chosen by lot from among all the descendants of Aaron. When, to the surprise of everyone, the choice fell on the poor stone cutter of Aphtha, Simeon ben Gamaliel, who had bitterly opposed the proceedings, admitted the new high priest into his family.

Even in his daily life, Simeon followed Shammaitic rules

of conduct rather than those in which he had been reared.[65] Worse still, he opposed the fundamental plebeian principle of the primacy of learning in Judaism. It was the recognition of this principle which had first stamped Simeon the Righteous as a Hasid; its rejection necessarily classified Simeon ben Gamaliel as a patrician. This did not necessarily involve his resignation from the Pharisaic order. Difference of opinion on this subject was permitted, for the patrician scholars had long become wary of the endless legal arguments of the plebeians. They had not, indeed, reversed Simeon the Righteous; they still agreed that the School took precedence over the Temple. But they held that general ceremonial practice was more important than either. "Say little and do much," was a favorite maxim of Shammai, the founder of their school.[66] Simeon ben Gamaliel's doctrine, "Not the study but the practice of the Law is essential," [67] expressed the thought more clearly and unequivocally.

With the usual zeal of the neophyte, Simeon out-Shammaited the Shammaites. Not only did he affect to despise argument in the Law, but he made no effort to teach at all. Alone among all the famous rabbinic scholars, whether patrician or plebeian, he had no disciples. His own sons-in-law had to join the plebeian school in order to master the Law. More than that, this child of the most culturally distinguished family in Judaism tried to assume the manners of the backward provincial and patrician landowners. He acted as though, like them, he found conversation difficult, and feigned to despise it as an art. With unparalleled effrontery, he asserted that he had learned this from the experience of his father's house. "All my life have I grown up among the sages," he said, "and I have found nothing of greater benefit to one's body than silence. Whoever is profuse in words causes sin."[68]

Whether Simeon's conversion to the patrician party helped him in his obvious desire to succeed his father is uncertain. The advance of the nationalist cause by the time of Gamaliel's death (about the year 50 c.e.) may have placed its adherents once more in control of the Sanhedrin. More probably, they were still in a minority. But apparently the plebeians could not bring themselves to oppose the election of the scion of Hillel and Gamaliel. His desertion of their group had been a severe blow to their pride. But it was easy to attribute it to ardent youth and to hope that with age Simeon would achieve the mellow wisdom of his ancestors.

Nevertheless, the Hillelites were not prepared to vest the sole leadership in Simeon; they insisted that the bipartisan government, traditional among the Pharisees for two centuries, be restored. Simeon ben Gamaliel was chosen as Nasi; Johanan ben Zakkai, a tradesman who had become a scholar and acknowledged leader of the Hillelites, was made his Ab Bet Din. Perhaps the Hillelites deluded themselves with the thought that this arrangement gave them a double advantage. Johanan ben Zakkai was theirs already; Simeon would join them when he matured. In any event, their special relation to him and his family would give them preponderant influence not only in the Sanhedrin but also in the councils of the opposing faction. With a scion of Hillel at the head of the Shammaites any threatened rift in Pharisaism would be averted.

If such were the thoughts of the Hillelites, they were doomed to disappointment. The new Nasi had become a convinced Shammaite and nationalist; nothing could bring him back. His leaning toward the provincials involved graver consequences than the acceptance of their ceremonial practices and the establishment of a new ethics based on their rural ideas. In fact, he was so completely estranged from the life of Jerusalem that he ceased to have any understanding of the city's problems. On no other basis can we explain the utter irresponsibility which led him to render a decision certain to bring ruin on a large section of the traders of Jerusalem, and to aggravate the evil by the selection of a most inopportune moment, as well as a most precipitate manner, for the announcement.

It happened that as Passover approached there was a great demand for pigeons in Jerusalem. They were needed for various sacrifices of purification, but more especially for the childbirth sacrifices of the women, which were usually offered at the pilgrimage season. Some people were required to offer as many as five or six pairs of pigeons at the altar. The increased demand for these birds naturally raised their price. Without consulting his associates or giving any intimation of the action he planned, Simeon waited until the prices reached their peak, then suddenly announced that, in his opinion, no one had to offer more than a single pair of pigeons. The validity of the Nasi's opinion was, of course, unquestioned, and the unexpected shrinkage in the demand for pigeons caused a panic on the market. A pair of birds which cost a golden dinar (about six dollars) on the morning of that fateful day could be purchased in the evening for half a silver dinar (about twelve cents). Simeon had displayed his power; he had brought disaster on the pigeon-dealers.[69]

Simeon's impetuosity, his failure to warn the traders of this imminent decision, and his utter unconcern for what happened to them, were not an indication of legislative short-sightedness. Josephus, who certainly bore him no good will, speaks of him as "a man highly gifted with intelligence and judgment." [70] He knew what would be the results of his

announcement, and he welcomed them. It did not occur to
him that, having failed to give his judgment before the
traders prepared for market day, he was no longer free to
offer it at a critical moment when his words meant ruin to
them. He saw the situation only from the point of view of the
countryside: the sellers of doves were profiteers who ought to
be destroyed.

Even more revealing, and of more enduring interest, was
the effort he made to crush Josephus in the year 67 when that
future historian was a young general in the revolutionary
army. The insurrection had broken out the previous year
when the corruption and misgovernment of Florus, the last
of the Roman procurators, had culminated in his seizure of
seventeen talents from the Temple treasury. Some wags had
derisively passed baskets about the streets of Jerusalem, feign-
ing to beg alms for their impecunious ruler. This insult had
brought retaliations which further aroused the people, leading finally to the interruption of the daily sacrifices on behalf
of the Emperor—a virtual declaration of war.

In vain did the men of rank and position, who had everything to lose and nothing to gain in a war, urge the people
to be calm. Agrippa II, the nominal king of the country
(whose only prerogative consisted in his right to appoint the
high priest), spoke for the Herodians; Hanan, the high priest,
spoke for the Sadducees and the authorities of the Temple;
Josephus, who had just returned from Rome, described what
endless resources the Empire could command, how hopeless
it was for Judea to measure its strength against the world;
Johanan ben Zakkai headed the traditional plebeian lovers
of peace. All arguments were futile. The maddened people
could not be dissuaded. The Roman soldiers were driven out
of Jerusalem; and when Cestius Gallus, Governor of Syria,

and his army invaded the country, they were met, surrounded and put to ignominious flight. The impossible had happened; a Roman army had suffered defeat at the hands of the Jews.

The victory was fatal. Even sober men like Hanan and Josephus were carried away by the overwhelming enthusiasm. Ever opportunistic, they deserted their teachings of peace as soon as war seemed likely to achieve desirable results. The fever infected even the more idealistic lovers of peace, who thought the Messianic age was at hand. The pacifist faction virtually ceased to exist. It was reduced to a few Romanophile Herodians, like Agrippa II and his followers, who joined the Roman army; and to Johanan ben Zakkai and his extremist Hillelite colleagues who, refusing to desert the Sanhedrin and yet unable conscientiously to join in the war, strove to maintain a doubly perilous, almost impossible neutrality.

Once more, as immediately after Herod's reign, the Shammaites were in complete control of the Sanhedrin. Again they took advantage of the nationalist fervor to impose not only their political, but also a large part of their social and religious program on the people. They organized the government of the infant rebel state, giving the most important posts to the priests who dominated their faction;[71] they made preparations for the oncoming struggle; and, finally, they voted a series of eighteen decrees which both in their form and content opened a new epoch in the development of Jewish law.[72] For the first time in history a gathering of Jewish teachers arrogated to itself the right to add ceremonial restrictions to those found in Scripture. Departing from the precedent which required scriptural authority for new decrees, the Sanhedrin frankly declared itself a religious legislature as well as judiciary. And, indeed, it would have been difficult to find any basis in Scripture for some of the rules which were established, such as those prohibiting the purchase of wine, oil, cheese or bread from the Romans, or the sale to them of land or of animals to till the land.

Simeon ben Gamaliel, as president of the Sanhedrin, and Hanan, the high priest, were recognized apparently as the two chief officers of the State.[73] Among the priests who were given responsible positions under them was Josephus, then a young man of thirty, who was despatched as a member of a commission of three to bring the Galilean zealots under the control of the newly organized government and also, perhaps, to prepare for the defense of Galilee.

It was almost inevitable that a bitter quarrel should ensue between Simeon ben Gamaliel and Josephus. The two men were so similar in ability and character that their minds were open books to one another. Equally matched in personal charm, mental alertness, intellectual subtlety, in physical as well as spiritual courage, they easily won the affection and confidence both of prominent individuals and of the general populace. Simeon attained the presidency of the Sanhedrin and, when the revolution came, was able to place his chair above that of the high priest. He achieved such popular acclaim that when in the third year of the war the extremist Galilean revolutionaries overthrew the government of the Sanhedrin and slew most of the earlier leaders, he continued to hold his own. Similarly, Josephus, who on his arrival in Galilee was the youngest and least recognized of the Commission of Three, became in a few months the most widely beloved hero of the province. When captured by the Romans, he, a rebel general and a prisoner of war, made his way to the hearts of such men as Vespasian and Titus.

The curious involutions and twistings of the young general's mind, the conflict between his youthful idealism and his growing opportunism, the hesitations and inconsistencies resulting from his fluctuating desires for temporal power and eternal life, were all transparent to the older, more experienced head of the Sanhedrin. Simeon knew that Josephus's conversion to the rebel cause was incomplete, that he wavered between a hope for Jewish independence and a conviction that it was unattainable.

Josephus, on the other hand, realized that the Nasi discerned his inner difficulty, and feared the consequences of entrusting to such a man the responsibility for the defense of Galilee. For, whatever might be Simeon's deficiencies of spirit, he was thoroughly sincere both in his piety and in his patriotism. That his conversion to Shammaism had been caused by social prejudice, he was unaware. He believed that both the Shammaitic interpretation of the law and their political ideals were valid. Faith in God implied for him willingness to die for the independence of Judea.

Josephus understood the sterling quality of Simeon's faith; he also realized how completely he himself lacked it. He had a deep love for the Jewish people and considered them in many respects unique among the nations of the world; even as apostate in Rome he could write warmly in their defense. He knew, however, that if ever he should be confronted with a choice between loyalty to his people and the satisfaction of his ambition, he would not hesitate; he would reject his people and follow his career. Josephus could not doubt that the keen and discerning president of the Sanhedrin was aware both of his inner vacillation and of the probable outcome.

The battle between the two men forms one of the most interesting chapters in Josephus's autobiography. It is a pity that, not having his opponent's account of the proceedings, we must rely altogether on the colored, *ex parte* statement

of one, of the contenders. Yet the main facts emerge with
sufficient clarity.

When Josephus arrived in Galilee, he was determined to
rid himself of his two colleagues. To accomplish this purpose
he practiced the most careful self-abnegation, while they in-
dulged in self-enrichment. As priests, they accepted the tithes
of the produce; he refused to do so.[74] He would not accept
even gifts. Rather amazingly, he takes the trouble to inform
us that "he preserved every woman's honor." The result was
that he was soon in a position to dismiss his fellow commissioners, send them back to Jerusalem and install himself as
sole governor of Galilee.

His remarkable administrative and organizing ability soon
won him the loyalty of the whole countryside; and he might
have begun to give his attention to his chief duty, resistance to
the approaching Roman legions, had he not been worried
about one man, John, son of Levi, of Gishcala. This wealthy
oil merchant, a personal friend of Simeon ben Gamaliel,[75]
submitted outwardly to Josephus but mistrusted him in his
heart. Perhaps he resented the intrusion of the priest of Jerusalem into the affairs of his province. A native of Galilee, he
may have felt that neither he nor his fellow provincials
needed the guidance of a townsman; indeed, he may even
have aspired to the governorship. True, he had opposed the
revolution at first; but so had Josephus and so had the high
priest, Hanan. Having joined the revolution, *he* was prepared
to risk everything for its success. He was not so certain about
Josephus and Hanan. The metropolitan townsmen, notor-
iously able to conceal their feelings, were always more than a
match for a simple Galilean.

John decided to oppose Josephus by force. With his usual
wit and courage Josephus escaped him; and John appealed to

his friend, Simeon ben Gamaliel, as head of the Sanhedrin, charging that Josephus planned to become dictator.

Simeon, who had watched the growth of Josephus's authority and popularity with anxiety and fear, was only too ready to interfere. What if the governor of Galilee should decide to march on Jerusalem instead of against the Romans? He could easily impose his terms on the Sanhedrin; and, ambitious as he was, he might demand supreme power. He might declare himself a second Maccabee. Whether he could defeat the Romans was problematical, but there could be no question of his success against his superiors. When Simeon approached the high priest Hanan with John's appeal for intervention, tribal loyalty asserted itself and Hanan refused to participate in action against his fellow-priest. Simeon outwardly accepted Hanan's view but secretly contrived with John's brother to win Hanan to their side by a display of special friendship. Before long Hanan the high priest had agreed to send a commission composed of two patricians and two plebeians to examine the charges against Josephus and ultimately, doubtless, to supersede him.

The mission was futile. Had Simeon himself come, he might have beaten Josephus at this game. His agents, acting under directions which could not provide for every contingency, were powerless before the daring and shrewd young governor. Their first letter to him was a hypocritical invitation to join them for a consultation regarding John of Gischala. But Josephus plied the messenger with drink, learned the true purpose of the commission, replied courteously but firmly that he could not leave his post, and invited the Commission to come to him. Simeon failed, apparently, to foresee and plan for such an eventuality. Left to their own initiative, the commissioners dropped all pretense and dispatched a peremptory order to Josephus to appear before them. The history of the following months is one of foxy schemes, strange adventures, and hairbreadth escapes.

On one occasion the commissioners proclaimed a fast day, and lured Josephus with but two guards into a synagogue. When he was attacked, a tumult arose and he fled into the street, only to meet John of Gishcala and his troops. Josephus would have met his death then and there had he not quickly discerned a passage through the crowded houses and rushed to the Sea of Galilee where, seizing a boat, he escaped to a friendly village. In the end, Josephus managed to get the commissioners into his power and then, with a characteristic gesture, he sent them back to Jerusalem under the "protection" of five hundred soldiers.

In the meantime, his own agents had been active in Jerusalem. Simeon and Hanan were accused of usurpation of authority in sending the commission without consulting the Sanhedrin. Josephus was vindicated, the dismissal of his colleague was approved, and he became *de jure* as well as *de facto* sole governor of Galilee—to justify in the fullness of time every accusation which John of Gishcala had made against him!

The story is soon told. Vespasian invaded Galilee, lured Josephus into the fortified town of Jotapata, which he then besieged and captured. Josephus and forty soldiers took refuge in a cave where, realizing the hopelessness of their situation, they decided to kill one another and cast lots for the order of precedence in death. Josephus, as he shamelessly records, so managed the lots that he was one of the last pair and then, persuading his comrade of the folly of self-imposed death, yielded to the Romans. Hearing that he was to be sent to Nero in chains, he claimed the gift of prophecy and foretold

Vespasian's election as Emperor of Rome. When in the course of two years his words were fulfilled, he became the intimate friend both of the new Emperor and of his son, Titus. Throughout their lives he remained their companion, their favorite and their tool. He was awarded the rights of a Roman citizen, given a lodging in the former palace of Vespasian, and provided with a pension, as well as a considerable estate in conquered Judea. Josephus, in turn, undertook to write a history of the triumph of the Flavians over his people. First in Aramaic, "to deter," as he himself remarks, "others who may be tempted to revolt"; [76] and then in Greek, "thinking it monstrous . . . that while Parthians and Babylonians and the most remote tribes of Arabia, along with our own countrymen beyond the Euphrates, and the inhabitants of Adiabene were through my assiduity accurately acquainted with the origin of the war, the various phases through which it passed and its conclusion, the Greeks and such Romans as were not engaged in the contest should remain in ignorance of these matters." [77] It is to this work that we owe our detailed knowledge of his people's calamity and his own perfidy.

For the moment, however, all this was part of the unborn future. The result of the struggle between Simeon and Josephus was a draw. Simeon had been unable to oust Josephus, but he had retained his own position. There was only one loser: the Jewish people and the revolutionary government. While the leaders were quarreling with one another, the Romans were advancing and precious time was being lost. Whether the Jews could have been victorious against Rome under any conditions is more than doubtful. But certainly harmonious coöperation of the saner elements might have prevented the most violent extremists from gaining control in the course of the following year, and might even have led to some understanding with Vespasian.

During all this time, Johanan ben Zakkai remained in Jerusalem as head of the vanishing peace party. He was as near to the spirit of Hillel and Gamaliel as Simeon was removed from them. A tradesman by vocation,[78] a scholar by training, he brought into public life the pragmatic wisdom of the market place and the theoretical insight and idealism of the academy. But the two were not separate in his mind. His idealism was permeated with practical understanding; his practical endeavors were motivated by the highest ideals. An erudite and ingenious student, a resourceful and determined executive, an inspiring teacher, a stirring orator, a farsighted statesman, an able judge, it was he who contributed more than any other single individual to preserve rabbinic Judaism when the Temple was destroyed.

He had demonstrated both his brilliance and his courage when, as a young student not yet ordained, he had through ingenious cross-examination of witnesses persuaded the Sanhedrin to acquit a man about to be convicted of murder. The case was recorded as a precedent, and is preserved to this day in the Mishna.[79]

The fundamental principle of Johanan's policy as Ab Bet Din was the maintenance of peace and the development of Jewish learning. Never did he waver, even for a moment, in his opposition to the rebellion, which he felt was destined to bring destruction on the people, the sanctuary, and the land. The romantic nationalism which was moving men to unheard-of deeds of heroism and self-sacrifice appeared to him altogether evil and irrational. Messianism was useful as a consolatory doctrine; it was pernicious as a guide to practical policy. He put this thought in vivid, concrete terms which even the simplest peasant could understand. "If you are about to plant a tree," he said, "and someone tells you that the Messiah has come, finish your work and then go forth to meet the Messiah"! [80]

When, heedless of the sage's advice, the people rushed head-long into war, he warned them to be in no hurry to wreak their vengeance on the Roman sanctuaries. "Do not destroy the heathen temples," he said, "lest it turn out that you are actually building them. You destroy temples of brick, and will be required to restore them with stone; you destroy temples of stone, and will be required to restore them with wood." [81] He was vehement against those super-patriots who tried to compel the unwilling to join the army. Military courage, he held, was a virtue hardly commended in Scripture. The faint-hearted is not only excused from battle, "but in order to shield him from any possible insult, others are sent home with him—the newly married, he who has just purchased a house, and he who has recently planted a vineyard." [82]

Johanan's opposition to war had nothing in common either with Agrippa's admiration for the Romans, or Josephus's and Hanan's fear of them. He loved his people with as much fervor as Simeon ben Gamaliel himself; and he was as firm in his faith as the most devoted zealot. It seemed to him, however, that the aims of the revolution were irrelevant to life. Anticipating one of Akiba's fundamental teachings,[83] Johanan held that the most important aspect of living was the study of the Torah. And he could not see how that could be better promoted in an independent state than in a Roman province.

He realized, of course, that his devotion to the Torah was in a sense a flight from the troubles of the world. It was not,

however, an escape from reality into dreams, but rather from
dreams and shadows into the only reality. "If you have studied
much Torah," he remarked to his disciples, "take no pride,
for study is the purpose of your creation." [84] When a priestly
family whose members were dying in their youth asked for
his advice and help, he hinted that avarice might be the cause
of their troubles and suggested that they could find healing in devotion to the Torah. Recalling that the sons of Eli,
the famous priest of Shiloh, were denounced for their greed,
he said to them, "Perhaps you come from the same family;
study the Torah, and you will live." [85] There could be no
more thorough cure for mundane ambition than study.

Realizing how urgent was the need for learning in the
provinces, Johanan settled in Galilee, where for eighteen years
he struggled to establish an academy. But his rationalism
evoked no response in the Galileans. His appeal to study the
Torah seemed as irrelevant to them as their Messianic dreams
to him. In despair he returned to Jerusalem, foretelling in his
last address to the provincials the outbreak of the revolution
and its disastrous consequences. "Galilee, Galilee," he said,
"thou dost hate the Torah; thy end will be seizure by the
Romans." [86]

The Ab Bet Din met no obstacles in establishing a school
for advanced studies in Jerusalem. All the younger men
flocked to him for instruction. Shammaites no less than Hillelites attended his lectures and came under his influence. Indeed, almost all the prominent scholars of the next generation
were his disciples.[87] In addition to the academy, where he met
the future teachers, he established a forum of public lectures
for the general populace. This lyceum attracted such large
audiences that they could meet only on the Temple mount,

finding protection from the hot and dazzling Palestinian sun in the shade of the vast Temple porticoes.[88]

Some of the fragments of Johanan's addresses were memorized by the hearers and preserved for future generations. On one occasion he asked: "Why is it forbidden to use iron in the preparation of the stones of the altar? Because iron is the element out of which the sword, the instrument of human suffering, is forged, while the altar is the instrument of human reconciliation with God. It is not fit that the sword should have power over the altar. Consider then," he continued, "if the stones of the altar, which can neither see, nor hear, nor speak, are protected from the sword because they serve to reconcile Israel to God, how much more will those who study the Law be free from all evil?" [89]

The further development of both the academy and the lyceum was interrupted by the outbreak of the revolution in the year 66. Johanan was already an old man.[90] He had attained such a position in the community that his pacifist teachings were heard with tolerance and even respect, though they ran counter to the waves of popular emotion. No one dared injure or repress him. The Herodian Romanophiles were in peril of their lives from the beginning of the insurrection; the moderate leaders of the war party, like Hanan the high priest, met their death when the extremists came into power; but Johanan was left unmolested. Everyone knew that there was nothing selfish in his opposition to the struggle; his courage, his patriotism and his willingness to suffer death for his country were unquestioned. His devotion to the Torah might be rejected as the eccentric vagary of an impractical academician; yet even in the moment of their severest condemnation of his ideas the people must have felt instinctively that there was truth in them.

Finally, in the summer of the year 68, Vespasian, having conducted a typical colonial war against the Jews, reducing their cities one by one, was ready to lay siege to Jerusalem, their sole remaining stronghold. The conditions in the city were indescribably bad. Two years of nervous strain had robbed both the masses and their leaders of reason and self-control. With their common enemy almost at the walls, the factions fought one another, destroying the treasures of food essential to protect the city against the siege, slaying able leaders and condemning as traitors all who violated the least of their regulations. The astute Roman, realizing what strife was raging in the capital, had purposely delayed his attack, lest he force the enemies to unite against him. He was quite willing that the Jews should work havoc with one another and spare his legions the trouble of destroying them. When, however, the news arrived of a revolt against Nero in the west, Vespasian, mindful of Josephus's prophecy and his own secret ambition, decided to end the Palestinian war with all possible speed. He encircled Jerusalem, cut off all its commerce with the rest of the country and prepared to starve the inhabitants into submission.

This was a difficult moment for Johanan ben Zakkai and his colleagues. They had hitherto abstained from active participation in the rebellion, and had also refused to hold any communication with the Romans. But now a new situation confronted them. The city could not be saved. Even if the Romans should fail to make a breach in its walls, famine and thirst must ultimately compel surrender. And then what would happen? Destruction and rapine, cruelty and violence, slaughter of the men, violation of the women and enslavement of children. The horrible aftermath of a prolonged siege when the soldiers, finally liberated from their discipline and restraint, would be permitted to do their will in the city was only too vivid in the minds of all the people. Could anything be done to avert the fearful disaster?

Johanan called a secret conference of his nephew, Ben Betiah, one of the revolutionary leaders, and his two foremost disciples, Eliezer ben Hyrkanos, a nationalist, and Joshua ben Hananya, a peace lover.[91] Ben Betiah admitted the desperateness of the situation, but he could do nothing. He and his colleagues were enmeshed in a net of their own weaving. They had stimulated the mob spirit with their demagogic, warlike harangues until the frenzied people would no longer listen to the sober truth. If anyone were to reveal the futility of further struggle against the Romans, he would be repaid for his trouble with instant execution. Even those who knew the facts would join in stoning such a candid and realistic adviser. Josephus had been almost slain when he suggested to his fellow captives that they surrender to the Romans; what would happen to the leaders of Jerusalem if they made such a proposal?

Since the earlier foolhardiness and the present timidity of the rebel chieftains had sealed the doom of Jerusalem, there was but one thing to do—to save the Torah. A plan was evolved requiring utmost courage and almost unbelievable self-control. Johanan was to feign illness, then death; and to be taken out of the city by his disciples, as if for burial. He was then to seek out Vespasian and obtain permission to establish a new academy in one of the provincial cities already under Roman control.

The scheme was full of dangers. The revolutionaries were on guard against any attempt to desert to the Romans. They permitted no one to leave the city even to bury the dead. "For burying a relative, as for desertion, the punishment was death;

and one who granted this boon to another instantly stood in need of it himself." [92] The bodies were, presumably, thrown immediately outside the walls and left there to putrefy in the hot Palestinian sun. Special permission might, probably, be obtained for the interment of so great a sage as Johanan ben Zakkai. But would not the revolutionaries want to make certain of his death?

In spite of all perils the plan was carried out with the utmost precision and success. No one but Johanan's two disciples, Eliezer and Joshua, were permitted to approach him during his "illness" or to tend the body after "death." He was placed on a bier (coffins were not used for interment in ancient Palestine) hidden from the eyes of the guards only by the death clothes, which completely covered every part of his body, including the face. Lest the absence of the odor of death, especially noticeable in the warm Palestinian climate, arouse suspicion, a piece of animal meat was hidden under the shroud.

Thus Johanan was borne through the narrow streets—prone, motionless, hardly daring to breathe. Days of practice had given him control of every muscle; even his eyelids did not betray the slightest quiver. Followed by wailing crowds, Eliezer and Joshua, who carried the bier, made their way to the city gate nearest the cemetery. No one interfered with them until they tried to pass the guards. Wondering, perhaps, at the temerity of the disciples who were willing to expose themselves to Roman missiles in order to bury their master, and wishing to make sure that death was not feigned, the soldiers said to Ben Betiah, "Let us stab him."

"How can you?" he replied. "People will say, 'The revolutionaries have violated the body of the Master.'"

"Let us at least push him," they said.

"People will still say, 'The revolutionaries have pushed the body of the Master.'"

Ben Betiah's apparent sincerity convinced the guardsmen, and the bier was allowed to pass through the gate.

Once out of the city, Johanan was removed from the bier, and he made his way to the Roman commander. In spite of his keen insight, Johanan could hardly have realized what importance Vespasian attached to his surrender. Roman imperial policy demanded not merely the subjugation of the Jews but also their reconciliation. Palestine lay within striking distance of Rome's traditional enemy, the Parthian Empire, and in even closer proximity to the restive tribes of Arabia, Mesopotamia and Armenia. There were widely scattered Jewish communities throughout the Roman Empire. Any disturbance in Judea might lead to repercussions, the ultimate results of which could hardly be foretold. Indeed, it was the likelihood of such widespread riots which had encouraged the rebels. "The whole of the Eastern Empire," Josephus tells us, "was in the balance."[93] It was essential that the Romans regain the sincere loyalty of the defeated people and that they separate Palestine from the Diaspora. How better could the Romans achieve this double purpose than by a demonstration of respect for Judaism at the moment when they were crushing the rebellion?

These considerations explain Titus's concern for the sacrificial worship during the siege of Jerusalem and his anxiety to spare the Temple when the city fell into his hands.[94] A declaration of allegiance by a leading rabbinical sage was certainly an asset which the Romans could not afford to despise. Vespasian must have known enough of Jewish life to be able to distinguish between the pro-Romanism of Agrippa II, the opportunism of Josephus and the idealism of Johanan; and to realize that of the three only Johanan could exert any widespread pacific influence.

Unaware of the full extent of his power, Johanan dared not ask too much of the Roman commander. When Vespasian asked, "What shall I give thee?" he was, doubtless, amazed to hear that the aged scholar had undergone all his trials and risked his life for no greater boon than permission to establish an academy! The modest request was immediately granted.

Johanan decided to establish his academy at Yabneh, a city on the Mediterranean coast which Vespasian had already begun to populate with deserters from the Jewish ranks. Never had Johanan shown himself a more clear-sighted statesman than in making this choice.

The city consisted of two parts, a port and an inland borough. It was an important commercial center; but what was even more significant, it lay in the richest part of Judea, the district to which many refugees from Jerusalem would inevitably turn when their city was destroyed. They could expect to find little help in the hill country, where the farmers were barely able to subsist. Some would rush to foreign lands, such as Egypt and Babylonia, and to Galilee; but most of them would seek the nearer coastal plain. Within a short distance from Yabneh, was the city of Ludd, where many might find employment; there were the neighboring villages of Gimzo, Bene Berak, and Emmaus, where they could obtain some shelter. It was obvious that this district was destined to be the future center of Judea, and necessarily, therefore, of Judaism.

In this warm and beautiful coast country there was no need for a building to house the proposed academy; Johanan either purchased or obtained a vineyard as a meeting place. When, two years later, Jerusalem fell into the hands of the besiegers, the school at Yabneh was ready to receive the refugee students and teachers. Johanan's position of favor with the Roman generals made his school a safe retreat; he alone had a workable program for reconstruction. Above all, time had vindicated his views, and pointed to him as the spiritual guide of the generation. Simeon ben Gamaliel had died during the last year of the war and many of the other Shammaites had gone into retirement. But a number joined the Hillelites and became followers of Johanan.

Johanan was now ready for a more daring step. He declared the assemblage at Yabneh the true Sanhedrin of all Israel, the authorized successor of the body which had met for centuries in the "Chamber of Hewn Stones." Characteristically, he made this momentous announcement not in any formal legislative or executive decree, but judicially, in connection with a practical issue. The question before him concerned the ancient ritual of sounding a ram's horn (*shofar*) on New Year's Day. This ceremony had been observed for centuries both at the Temple and in the synagogues. There was this difference, however; the Temple ritual was carried out whether New Year's Day occurred on Sabbath or week days; the synagogue service of the ram's horn could be observed only if New Year's Day occurred during the week.

It happened that at the time when Johanan was looking about for some dramatic method of establishing the prestige of Yabneh, New Year's Day fell on a Sabbath. Johanan immediately recognized the opportunity. If the *shofar* were sounded at the New Year's services, as had been done at Jerusalem, that would be a formal declaration that Yabneh had succeeded Jerusalem as the center of the Jewish world. He made the necessary preparations for the ceremony. When, on New Year's Day, the priests who were jealous of the prerogatives of the destroyed Temple raised objections to his plans, he refused to argue with them until the services were concluded. "We will sound the *shofar,* and then we will discuss the Law," he said. When they tried to open the argument after the services, he said, "The *shofar* has been sounded in Yabneh; a precedent has been established; there is no further room for discussion." [95]

And indeed this was no time for academic debate. The survival of rabbinic Judaism depended in large measure on the recognition of Yabneh, and this recognition could not be demonstrated more effectively and dramatically than by endowing the new academy with the ritual prerogative of the old Sanhedrin. It was not, however, the clever retort that won the day, but Johanan's immense spiritual power.

The "Vineyard of Yabneh," in which the conclave met, became as famous and important as the "Chamber of Hewn Stones." Though the conclave was destined to meet there for only sixty years, while other centers of learning persisted for centuries, the Vineyard of Yabneh holds a permanent, and unequaled, place in Jewish tradition, for it was there that Judaism was saved in its direst crisis. Although Johanan apparently refused to accept the title of Nasi and remained merely Ab Bet Din, he came to occupy the position which had been held by Gamaliel I. He, too, was given the title Rabban. He guided the people through the difficult period of the reconstruction, carrying on negotiations with Rome and maintaining the loyalty of the scattered Jewish communities. Under him, as in the time of Agrippa and the Maccabees, factionalism once more disappeared. Only now it was not the common prosperity, but the common adversity, that made the people forget their quarrels.

Curiously, Johanan was apparently dissatisfied with his achievements. Like other intellectually creative personalities, he considered his practical endeavors unsuccessful. He did not realize the full significance of the academy he had founded, and the conclave he had reorganized. He could not foresee that these institutions were destined to more enduring glories than the Temple had achieved. Indeed when one of his disciples asked him how Israel could obtain forgiveness from God, now that it had lost its Temple, he no longer mentioned study. "There is another means of atonement," he replied, "lovingkindness, for it is written, 'I desire lovingkindness rather than sacrifice.' " [96] He was approaching his ninetieth year, he would soon have to give an account to God for his lifework. Had he fulfilled his mission? Repeatedly he asked himself whether more determined efforts to prevent the rebellion, or more urgent appeals to Vespasian during the war, might not have saved the country and the Temple. He recalled with bitter pangs of conscience the remarkable story of Hezekiah and Isaiah, in whose time Jerusalem was saved from the Assyrian, and wondered why he and his colleagues had been unable to save it from the Roman. Was he less righteous than Hezekiah had been? Had he prayed less fervently? Had he acted less wisely, or less energetically?

When he fell into his last illness these painful thoughts brought tears to his fading eyes. His disciples, seeing him weep, cried out, "Light of Israel, Pillar of Strength, Mighty Anvil, why dost thou weep?"

"Alas," he replied, "if I were being taken for judgment before a mortal human king, who could only be angry with me, or imprison me, or kill me for a time, I should weep; how much more reason have I to weep when I am about to appear for judgment before the Holy One, blessed be He, the King of kings, who can impose anger, imprisonment and death for all eternity." [97]

Suddenly a new radiance came over his face. The tears ceased and he smiled happily. All was well. His work had been approved. Before him, regal and majestic, happy and welcoming, he saw the very king whom he had so long wished he might have emulated—Hezekiah himself! Those who stood about Johanan and watched him focus his gaze on vacancy must have thought his mind was wandering. They were wrong; he was as lucid and practical as ever. He calmly made the necessary preparations for the end. "Remove the vessels from the house so that they may not be defiled when I die," he said. And then, in the same clear tones, "Set a chair for Hezekiah, King of Judah, who has arrived." [98]

It was shortly after this event that Akiba appeared at the Vineyard of Yabneh, seeking higher rabbinic instruction.

III. AMONG THE FOOTHILLS

WHEN Akiba came to Yabneh, Johanan's place was still vacant.[1] Yet so firmly had the academy been established that there was no interruption in its activity. Nor had Johanan's death brought any diminution to its prestige. On the contrary, its position seemed higher than that of any earlier council. Its predecessor, the Sanhedrin of the "Chamber of Hewn Stones," had always stood below the Temple in its influence on the people, both within Palestine and outside of it. The destruction of the Temple and, with it, the last vestiges of hereditary ecclesiastical authority, had enabled the scholars to come into their own. Jewish learning offered its devotees not only the deferred rewards of Paradise, but immediate returns of honor, prestige and influence. The dangers of earthly temptation were recognized by the teachers. They said: "Perhaps you may say, 'I will study that I may become wealthy, or that I may be called Master, or that I may receive divine reward'; therefore Scripture commands you to *love* the Lord thy God." [2]

The warning may have been needed by disciples; it was altogether unnecessary for the sages. Nowhere, certainly, could selfless love for God and the Torah be found in such measure as among these scholars and teachers. Neither material rewards nor the promise of glory could move them from the path which they had set before themselves: the interpretation of the Law according to their best understanding. In many respects they formed the most brilliant and illustrious

73

governing body the Jewish people ever possessed. Never before
or since, have so much erudition and acumen, such a mixture
of statesmanship and scholarship, been found in any single
group. The assembly of the scholars had become a Jewish
senate, a far more spiritual replica of the mighty Roman legislature. Judaism, which Simeon the Righteous, had transformed
from an aristocracy into a nomocracy, had reached the form
it was to keep for a thousand years, a sophocracy or government by sages.

It was easy to enter the Vineyard where the scholars
gathered for their deliberations. There were no guards at the
gate; the sessions were held in public; the discussions were
open. When questions of grave importance arose, requiring
an executive session, the scholars would meet in the mansion
of one of the wealthy members of the community, preferably
in an upper chamber, where their deliberations could not be
overheard. But such occasions were unusual; most frequently
the scholars took both the contemporary community and
future generations into their confidence. Differences of opinion
were announced and remembered; opposing arguments were
heard and refuted. The tone of the discussions was generally
calm. Indeed it was customary for the presiding officer or
lecturer to speak in so low a whisper that an attendant, standing by him, had to repeat his words aloud for the benefit of
the audience. But sometimes the sages would forget themselves; the debate would become heated, and even personal.
This was specially true when the provincial scholars, accustomed to instant obedience in their homes, had to defend their
views against the better-mannered and more completely controlled plebeians.

It must have been with a surging and violently beating
heart that Akiba approached the gate behind which the con-

clave sat. Within a few hours' journey of that Vineyard, his former colleagues, the shepherds, were still watching their flocks. He was about to leave them forever, to pass into a new and unknown world, the world of the men whom only half a dozen years earlier he had bitterly hated.

We may imagine what humility and bewilderment seized him as he entered the enclosure and viewed the scene before him. With their backs toward him sat rows upon rows of students and disciples, most of them far younger than himself, listening intently and trying to memorize each argument and decision. Farther in front, in a wide semi-circle, facing the audience and himself, sat the great sages, the foremost leaders of his people, the authoritative interpreters of God's will to man. Akiba could hardly have been conscious of them as separate individuals; all he could discern was a series of keen, intelligent faces. Some were clean shaven, some were bearded; of the latter, most were gray, a few were still black-haired. Above each forehead could be seen the huge, black, cubical phylactery which, projecting vertically upward and glistening in the semi-tropical sun, overshadowed all the natural features by its prominence and gave the whole face a spiritual, other-worldly appearance. The rest of the sages' bodies were swathed and enshrouded in their characteristic garments, the rabbinic *Gulta,* a vast, striped, rectangular woolen cloak, covering the head, hanging loosely over the shoulders and extending to the very sandals on the feet, its blue and white fringes trailing from its four corners in easy disarray.

As Akiba gazed on these men, in wonder and admiration, it must have seemed to him that they looked less like living men than like sacred embodiments of the Law. Yet a few moments' observation showed the great diversity and contrast to be found in this world in miniature.

Here were wealthy landowners and halfstarved artisans, ambitious careerists and self-denying saints, ardent patriots and cosmopolitan internationalists, uncouth peasants and polished townsmen. There were among them Tarfon, the wealthy, good-humored humanitarian, but direct and brusque priest, who in a year of famine betrothed himself to three hundred women so that he might enable them to share in his ecclesiastical emoluments;[3] Samuel the Little, whose epitaph was to be that he was fit for prophecy;[4] Jose Ha-Kohen, whose extravagant saintliness (fortunately overridden by his colleagues) forbade him to attend his wife's funeral which occurred on the eve of Passover, lest, becoming defiled, he should be unable to offer the paschal sacrifice;[5] Zadok, the wealthy ascetic, who had fasted daily for forty years to obtain Divine pardon for the Temple, and who achieved subsidiary fame as the man who always chose the severer forms of a disputed ritual;[6] Nahum of Gimzo, equally famous for his learning, his poverty and his cheerful resignation in the face of the most dreadful personal disasters;[7] Pappias ben Judah, that strange mixture of simplicity and worldliness, whose anthropomorphic ideas of God Akiba was destined to denounce, and who, in turn, advised Akiba against undergoing the risk of martyrdom for the sake of the Torah;[8] Judah ben Baba, the sickly, perhaps tubercular, saint, whose only sin consisted in the possession of a goat (an animal forbidden in the country as an omnivorous pest) which he needed to supply him with warm milk.[9] There were others, of inferior reputation, but not of inferior interest, such as Judah the Baker, Huzpit the Announcer, and Yeshebab the Scribe. There may even have been present some of the Galilean scholars like Hanina ben Teradyon, and Halafta, the father of the more famous Jose ben Halafta, who, living in the distant province, undoubtedly attended some of the more important meetings of the conclave.

Obscure among the others were to be recognized Gamaliel, the son of the late Simeon ben Gamaliel, whom the conclave wished to elect as Nasi, and his brother-in-law, Simeon ben Nethanel, the illiterate *am ha-arez,* who had finally decided to enter the academy out of respect for his wife's family. Two younger men who were to play an important role in Akiba's life were probably still among the pupils: Eleazar ben Azariah, the charming, polished and eloquent aristocrat who traced his ancestry back to Ezra the Scribe; [10] and Elisha ben Abuyah, destined to achieve unique and hateful preëminence as scholar, apostate and traitor.[11]

In the center of the whole magnificent group sat the two men who had helped Johanan ben Zakkai found the academy: Eliezer ben Hyrkanos and Joshua ben Hananya. Nothing could more dramatically have illustrated the composite nature of Pharisaism and the Sanhedrin than the juxtaposition of these two leaders, alike in their erudition and piety, but differing from one another in every other aspect of material and spiritual life. Eliezer, the foppish, rich landowner who, reared as an *am ha-arez,* had fled from his father's house in order to study the Torah, and had finally attained such proficiency that Johanan had compared him to "a well-lined cistern which never loses a drop"; and Joshua ben Hananya, ungainly in form and plain of face but possessed of remarkable wit and a melodious voice, a temple singer who, when Jerusalem was destroyed, became a needle-maker, and in the midst of direst poverty, in a soot-covered hovel, pursued his studies until he had mastered not only Jewish learning but the secular sciences of mathematics and astronomy.

Recent events had impressed on this gathering of types so

varied in their gifts, proclivities, temperaments and social standing the supreme necessity of union. Nevertheless, the cleavage between the patrician and the plebeian traditions, which had been sharply marked in Jerusalem before its destruction, was bound to persist in the new center. For the second reading of the *Shema* (the scriptural passages prescribed for morning and evening recitation), Eleazar ben Azariah and Tarfon reclined; their colleagues did not.[12] Eliezer ben Hyrkanos insisted that if a circumcision occurred on the Sabbath, the necessary utensils could be prepared on the very day; Joshua ben Hananya maintained that they had to be made ready on Friday.[13] Gamaliel would not send his clothes to a pagan launderer after Wednesday, lest they be washed on the Sabbath; the other Sages considered this to be over-fastidious.[14]

The apparent triviality of these differences should not mislead us into disregard of the social interests to which they owed their origin. Lying down to read the Shema was a custom which grew naturally out of the rural habit of early bedtime; it was carried into the city by the landowning patricians. The patricians, who permitted the preparation of utensils for circumcision on the Sabbath, followed the precedent set by the priests in the temple service and opposed by the plebeians for many generations. The objection to sending one's clothes to a pagan launderer who might wash them on the Sabbath involved a conception of property and personality which was abhorrent to the free proletariat.[15] It implied that one's possessions were in a mysterious way a part of oneself, and that if one's garment was being cleaned on the Sabbath, it was as though one were oneself engaged in labor. One extremist patrician was so fastidious with regard to such considerations that he never intrusted a letter to anyone but a Jew, lest it be carried or delivered on the Sabbath! The plebeians might have raised no objection to this pedantry had it been limited to rules about clothes and the Sabbath.[16] Unfortunately the division of outlook applied also to living property, especially slaves, as extensions of the personality of the owner.[17] In the eyes of the plebeians such a doctrine was shockingly foreign to the assertions of human equality and freedom, which they considered an integral part of Judaism.[18]

In this tumultuous and dazzling assembly at Yabneh, Akiba turned first, we gather, to Eliezer ben Hyrkanos, perhaps because he too had entered on his studies when he was a mature man. If this was the reason for Akiba's choice, it was a pitiful miscalculation. For, then as now, opinion was divided on the spiritual privileges which ought to be accorded to the poor. With the Shammaitic school, whose traditions Eliezer followed, it was a cardinal principle that the poor ought not to be taught the Law;[19] that was a perquisite of affluence. At any rate, Eliezer held that just as God had given the Law to a generation which was fed with manna, so later teachers should accept as pupils only those who had no economic worries to distract them.[20] The man whom Eliezer rejected, received, like many others before him, a warm welcome from the poor Joshua ben Hananya. Joshua, however, could hardly spare sufficient time for the beginner, and therefore sent him to Tarfon, who was of Akiba's own age and who became his closest friend.[21]

Legends are current concerning the privations which Akiba and Rachel suffered during those first difficult years. For a time, Akiba hired himself out as a laborer for part of the day. But his meager earnings did not cover the barest necessities, and on one occasion, her own and her husband's hunger drove Rachel to sacrifice her hair for food.[22] Finally, they decided to live apart, presumably because Rachel was able to obtain employment elsewhere. This separation, doubtless the most difficult of their trials, lasted several years.[23]

Akiba may thus be regarded as the founder of the peculiar institution of married "monasticism" which, while it never became very popular in Judaism, has exerted an influence throughout the centuries. Many of Akiba's pupils followed his example, and hardly more than a generation ago there were groups of people in the small Lithuanian communities, called *perushim* (separatists), who resurrected the ancient custom.[24] After marriage, they would devote themselves completely to their studies while their wives supported them. Rightly or wrongly, the talmudists believed that as married men, students were less open to temptation than as celibates. "He who has bread in his basket," they said in a rather coarse metaphor, "is safer than he who lacks it." [25] Projecting their manners into more ancient times, they described Moses himself as living apart from Zipporah, his wife, and they asserted that the slighting remarks for which Miriam was punished concerned this marital separation.[26]

Akiba was earning his livelihood at the time, according to the popular story, by gathering pieces of wood, half of which he sold for his food, using the remainder for fuel. When his neighbors, who were annoyed by the smoke, offered to buy all the wood so that he could provide himself with oil, he declined to sell it. "The wood is of great benefit to me," he said, "I study by its light, I am warmed by its heat and I use it as a pillow." [27]

When, in the day of final judgment, God tries the poor for their failure to study the Torah, he will point, the sages say, to the example of Akiba. If the poor protest that they had to support their families, God will remind them that Akiba too had a wife and child and yet he studied. But the severity is mitigated toward the end: the poor will be able to offer as defense that their wives were not like Rachel! [28]

Tarfon, who was both wealthy and generous, would gladly have supported Akiba, but the latter was either too proud or too pious to accept from his teachers anything but instruction. Anxious to be of help, Tarfon at last offered him a loan for investment in a field. Akiba, instead of buying the field, distributed the money among others who were more needy.

When, some months later, Tarfon said to him, "Have you bought the property?" Akiba replied, "Certainly." "Did you get a deed?" "Yes, and here it is," Akiba continued, as he opened a book of Psalms and pointed to the verse: "He hath dispersed, he hath given to the needy, his righteousness endureth forever" (Ps. 112:9).[29]

It speaks much for the good-nature of Tarfon, and his affection for Akiba, that he does not seem to have been annoyed at the generosity which Akiba practiced at his expense.

The super-piety which Akiba displayed in this incident was characteristic of him during this early period of his student days. Unable as yet to grasp the spirit of the Law, and yet anxious to observe its last letter, he sometimes found himself guilty of transgression through his ignorance. Once, for instance, he found a dead body by the road. Having learned enough to know that any passerby is under obligation to provide proper burial for an unidentified corpse, he lifted it up and carried it four miles to the academy. When Eliezer and Joshua saw him approach with his burden, they rebuked him: "For every step you are guilty as though you had shed blood," they said. "A dead body must be buried where it is found, not carried along the road to a more convenient place." [30]

When the news of his father's death reached him, he re-

fused to follow the usual custom of mourners, to bare their
shoulders as a sign of grief. Even in bereavement, and
although others present followed the rule out of respect
for him, in accordance with the general custom, he retained
his garments as they had been, and declined to follow their
example.[31]

In general, Akiba declined to avail himself, at this time, of
any lenient interpretations of the Law. He always accepted
the severer view, whether it had been handed down by the
Shammaites or the Hillelites.[32] Later scholars, receiving this
tradition, were amazed, for in their time such practice was
condemned as unnecessary and unwarranted obscurantism.
They failed to recognize that the stories belong to the initial
stage of Akiba's student days, when he possessed the piety,
but not the learning, of the rabbi.

Tarfon's love for Akiba was the more remarkable because
it soon became evident that the disciple was destined to out-
rank the master. Early in his studies, Akiba uncovered an
intuitive feeling for the correct interpretation of Scripture and
tradition which amazed his colleagues. On one occasion he
maintained that priests with a physical blemish were not permitted to sound the trumpet in the Temple. Hearing this,
Tarfon lost his temper and cried out, "Akiba, how long will
you continue to pervert the plain meaning of the Scriptures?
I distinctly remember seeing my uncle, who was a lame priest,
sound the trumpet in the Temple."

"Perhaps, my master," Akiba said, "that happened during
the informal Sukkot celebration, which was not part of the
regular service?"

Tarfon, suddenly reminded of the true circumstances, could
not restrain his admiration. "I swear by the Temple service,
that you are right. Happy may Abraham be that he has such

a descendant as Akiba. Tarfon saw the event and forgot;
Akiba interprets the verse and arrives at the truth. Oh, Akiba,
whosoever parts from thee, parts from life itself!" [33]

On another occasion, Tarfon cried out, "Akiba, to thee may
be applied the verse, 'He bindeth the streams that they trickle
not, and the thing that is hid bringeth he forth to light' (Job
28:11). The things which are hidden from the children of
men Akiba has brought into the light." [34]

A certain rough playfulness which Akiba still retained out
of his untutored youth was forgiven him by most of his colleagues because of his brilliance. It seems that the young
scholar-priest, Eleazar ben Azariah, following the usual custom of his class, had been receiving the tithes which Scripture
specifically reserved for the Levites (Num. 18:21). The priests
justified this perversion of the Law by the claim that as
descendants of Aaron, who was a great-grandson of Levi,
they were also Levites, and entitled to Levitical emoluments
as well as to their own. The controversy had been argued with
much bitterness for centuries. So large was the income involved, and so determined were the priests to retain it, that
some of them had not hesitated to mutilate the text of a passage in Nehemiah,[35] by adding a phrase asserting their right
to the tithe.

The Hasmoneans, whose victories over the Syrians had put
them into control of the government, naturally endeavored to
assist their fellow-priests in the assertion of these rights. But
in spite of the prestige and power of the family, the Levites
would not yield. Assisted by some of the plebeian scholars,
they denied that the priests could justly demand this special
Levitical tax. God had given them their own ecclesiastical
emoluments, the heave offering, universally paid, which constituted an average tax of 2.5 per cent of all Palestinian

products; the redemption money for all firstborn male children; the firstlings of cattle; the first shearings of sheep; parts of most sacrifices, and of every animal slaughtered for profane use; and numerous gifts which reverted to them from the Temple.[36] These protests were, however, ignored by the richer and more powerful priests. Josephus, for instance, being a priest, takes it for granted that the tithe must be paid to his fellows, and repeatedly states this as the law.[37]

Eleazar was thus following group precedent in his actions. In vain did Joshua, who was a Levite, argue with him. Rich as Eleazar was, and little as he needed this additional income, he continued to collect the tithe, holding it a matter of loyalty to his fellow-priests as well as an assertion of his own rights. Akiba considered this procedure as unethical as it was unscholarly. He resorted to direct action. He had noticed that one of the fields from which Eleazar received tithes had two approaches, one leading to another field and a second opening into a cemetery. When the time for tithing arrived, Akiba simply closed the usual gate, and opened that leading into the cemetery path. This effectually prevented Eleazar from coming into the field, for as a priest he dared not enter a cemetery.[38]

Eleazar did not resent this trick; he told the story in the academy, laughing at his own discomfiture. "Akiba walks about with his tools, and how shall I get my living!" he cried.[39]

The tradition as he received it from Tarfon did not, however, satisfy Akiba. Tarfon, as we have seen, was really a member of the patrician wing of the Pharisees, while Akiba's sympathies were with the plebeian group.[40] When purely humanitarian questions arose, the two scholars were generally in agreement. They both said, for instance, that had they sat in the Sanhedrin when it possessed the right of capital punishment, they would never have condemned a man to death.[41] But when questions arose which involved social and economic issues, the two men parted ways.

Perennial interest attaches to some of the questions which divided the ancient scholars, even though they involve situations far removed from our times and activities. They offer us the most vivid insight into the daily life of the ancients, permitting us to see them at their work, at their play, in their homes and in their houses of worship. Like archaeological remains, they help us re-create the whole of a forgotten age. When we analyze their arguments we realize, what must concern us more nearly, how easy it is to create a façade of rationalization about our personal prejudices and immediate concerns, and we begin to wonder how much of our own discussion is pure logic and how much is mere baroque. The ancients, like ourselves, were entirely convinced that they were proceeding objectively and with unerring dialectic; it never occurred to them that, since the same dialectic led different people to opposing conclusions, there was need for looking beneath the surface of the argument into the opposing interests which evoked it.

Tarfon taught, for example, that olive oil, like wine, may be offered to the Temple as a voluntary gift without an accompanying sacrifice either of grain or animal.[42] This may seem a reasonable rule to us, but in its own setting it involved a social conflict. For while the vine could be grown by any Palestinian farmer, rich or poor, the olive with its wide-spreading roots could be cultivated economically only on large holdings. This, and not any special fitness of the soil, accounts for the fact that Galilee, which in the Second Commonwealth as in the First was the home of vast estates, became famous for its olives.[43] A century before Tarfon's time this class interest in olives had led to bitter controversies between the Pharisaic factions. The Hillelites had openly accused the Shammaites of unfair and illegal leniency toward the rich. "Why," the usually pacific Hillel had demanded of Shammai, "do you insist that grapegatherers must be pure, and impose no such restriction on olivegatherers?" [44] Shammai's reply was not an argument, but a threat. Indeed, he had no logical reason to offer, for his interpretation of the Law was, in this instance, based not on logic but on the inherited custom of his followers.

Tarfon, who was quite unaware of the deeper prejudices which prompted his interpretation of the Law, showed equal partiality for the olive in his halakic decisions. He held, for instance, that only olive oil might be used for the Sabbath eve lights.[45] When he announced this rule in the academy, Johanan ben Nuri, who was himself a Galilean and friendly to the patricians, but remembered the days of his own poor youth when oil was an expensive luxury, sprang to his feet and cried: "What shall the Babylonian Jews do, who have nothing but the oil of mustard seeds? What shall the Median Jews do, who have nothing but the oil of nuts? What shall the Alexandrian Jews do, who derive their oil from radishes? And what shall the Cappadocian Jews do, who have no vegetable oils at all, but only naphtha?"

It is against this background that we must envisage Akiba's impatience with what seemed to him Tarfon's partiality to the rich and their olive oil. It was well enough to permit a poor man who wanted to bring a gift to God, but could not afford a cow or a sheep, to send his wine instead; but a farmer, who had room enough on his estates to raise olives, should send a more suitable sacrifice than some oil.

A second disagreement arose from the habit of some priests, who could not use all the heave offering they received, to plant the remainder. According to rabbinic law, whatever grew from such seeds inherited their sacredness and could therefore be eaten only by priests. Hence, Tarfon argued that the gleanings of these fields could be gathered only by poor priests. Akiba, however, maintained that this was a denial of the just rights of the other poor, who were in the vast majority. They could gather these gleanings, he said, and sell them to priests.[46]

Tarfon's special interest in the priests and the heave offering led to another controversy between the two scholars. Rabbinical Law provides that if a woman who has gone abroad with her husband returns and says that he died, her word is accepted and she is permitted to remarry. If, however, the man had several wives, this permission does not apply to those who have no direct and personal knowledge of his death. Since these other wives may not marry, Tarfon holds that they may continue to eat the heave offering if the husband was a priest. Akiba, however, insists that since the husband is probably dead, none of the wives may eat the heave offering, the use of which the Law limits exclusively to priests and their families.[47]

These controversies are typical. Perhaps, however, one other should be mentioned because it concerned the rights of the Temple, which was no longer in existence.

The Law provides that a person who unwittingly uses anything belonging to the sanctuary must make restitution according to the benefit he received, adding, however, one-fifth as fine, and bringing a ram, worth two silver pieces, as sacrifice of atonement (Lev. 5:15 ff). There were, however, occasions when people were not clear in their own minds whether they had transgressed the Law at all. Perhaps they had two oxen in their fields, one their own, the other the Temple's, and they could not recollect which animal they had yoked to the plow. Tarfon maintained that since there was some possibility that Temple property had been employed profanely, the usual payment, fine and sacrifice were obligatory. Akiba denied this.[48]

Joshua, to whom Akiba would naturally have turned for further guidance, was too much the pacifist and compromiser for the ardent student who at forty was still young to the world. Frequently when Akiba thought the plebeian view should be stated with vigor, Joshua would equivocate, compromise or yield to the powerful patrician teachers.[49] Joshua must have shocked the plebeians, for instance, when he publicly declared that only wealthy men could be entrusted with judicial office. He found support for this truly remarkable opinion in the phrase, "men of might," used by Jethro in his enumeration of the essential qualifications for judges (Exod. 18:21). " 'Men of might,' " he said, "means, 'men of property.' " Eleazar of Modin, priest and patrician as he was, protested against such an anti-Pharisaic interpretation of the Law. "The expression means only 'trustworthy people,' " [50] he maintained. We may be sure that it gave the plebeians little pleasure to hear themselves defended by one of their opponents and maligned by their own leader. Moreover, Joshua relied almost entirely on tradition for his views and hesitated to establish new plebeian principles of law; Akiba sought a comprehensive statement of the plebeian philosophy which could be applied to new cases as they arose.

Finding himself in fundamental disagreement with Tarfon on the social issues of the day, and unable to follow the slow-moving, good-humored, half cynical, easily satisfied Joshua,

Akiba turned for inspiration to the brilliant, but comparatively unknown, Nahum of Gimzo, who owes his fame almost entirely to the greatness of his illustrious pupil. Nahum's value to Akiba lay less in his inherited traditions than in the new method of interpretation which he himself had developed.

According to Nahum's system, every word in Scripture, and indeed every letter, has significance. Even the particle *et* which indicates the accusative in Hebrew (but which sometimes has the meaning "with") must be explained wherever it occurs. Thus when Scripture says that God created the heavens (*et hashamayim*) we must infer from that particle that other objects or beings, unmentioned in the text, were created at the same time. This principle was in later times taken over from Akiba by his famous disciple, Aquila the Proselyte, who renders each *et* in Scripture by the Greek preposition *syn* (with), even when that makes no sense.

Absurd as this must seem to us, it appeared altogether logical to Nahum, Akiba, and their followers, who could not attribute to the Scriptures anything less than perfect economy of expression. In this they represented the plebeian tradition of the day and the mental bias of the trading groups, which, true to type, placed high value on the virtues of thrift, craftsmanship and efficiency. When Akiba once derived from an unnecessary *Vav* (the sixth letter in the Hebrew alphabet) that the daughter of the priest who commits adultery should be executed by burning, one of his colleagues cried out, "Shall we burn this woman because you must find an interpretation for your *Vav?*" [51] Perhaps the accusation was unjust; for Akiba had common sense, and juristic reasons for his opinions, and only used the superfluous letters as pegs on which to hang his views.

There was one verse which puzzled Nahum so much that

he almost abandoned the whole method he had developed. This was the verse, "Thou shalt fear the Lord (*et YHWH*) thy God." (Deut. 6.5) According to the system, the particle *et* preceding the divine name in this sentence, signified that some other being, too, ought to be feared, and yet who could deserve equal reverence with God? The very suggestion was heretical, and at the moment especially so because the Christians, a rapidly multiplying sect, were actually teaching that their Messiah was God's equal. Painful as it must have been for him, Nahum decided to reject the whole method. "Just as I pleased God with my interpretations, so I will please Him with my rejection of them," he said to his colleagues and pupils. It was precisely at this time that Akiba came forward, ready to save the verse and the method and pure monotheism. "The particle *et* in this verse," he explained, "refers to the scholars, who must be paid as much reverence as is due to God Himself." [52]

Akiba's association with Nahum continued for twenty-two years. Long after he had become an illustrious scholar, he would travel forth and back between the village of Gimzo and the city of Yabneh, bringing to the sick old man the news of the conclave, and taking back to his colleagues ideas born out of these fleeting contacts.

Having mastered the plebeian doctrines of Joshua and Nahum, Akiba decided to return to Eliezer, who had rejected him in the first place. In this, he was moved by a number of considerations. True, Eliezer was a patrician like Tarfon, and indeed one of the bitterest partisans of that faction. But he was everywhere recognized as the foremost talmudist of the age, and Akiba could not consider his education complete until he had studied under him. Moreover, since Akiba began to study, he had been living in Ludd, the city of his first master, Tarfon; and there Eliezer, too, resided. The great sage was thus easier to approach than he could have been in some other town. Eliezer, who must have heard of Akiba's brilliance and promise, did not this time refuse to admit him, but neither did he "recognize" him. He taught him, together with the other pupils, and listened to his arguments with what patience he could muster. He refused, however, to take special pains with him or to assign him any important place in the school. Akiba, who never resented any personal affront, sometimes lost patience with his intransigeant, traditionalist master's unwillingness to hear an argument. He would then rush to Pekiin, where Joshua lived, to pour out his complaints and explain his views.[53] But the prudent, cautious sage would give him only partial encouragement. He praised Akiba's dialectic, but frequently supported Eliezer's decisions. "Your reasoning is right," he would say, "but what can we do since the tradition is fixed?"

We do not know how long Akiba remained associated with Eliezer in this way. But it is said that after he had spent thirteen years in study under his various masters, he decided openly to challenge the patrician traditions of the Shammaites, although his new master, Eliezer, was their foremost exponent in the conclave.

IV. THE STEEP ASCENT

THE day had opened in its usual fashion in the conclave at Yabneh. Eliezer had offered an opinion, and Joshua had raised an objection. There was nothing to indicate that the occasion would assume historical importance until Akiba, still comparatively unknown outside the limited circle of his teachers and their immediate acquaintances, stood up to oppose the man who, according to Johanan ben Zakkai, outweighed in learning the entire host of his contemporaries. What followed has become a saga of scholarship, and the arguments, even the invectives, used by the protagonists still echo wherever the Jewish tradition is studied.

Characteristically, the question which precipitated the combat was of purely academic interest at the moment. The Law required certain sacrifices to be offered on Sabbaths and holidays, and it had always been agreed that the performance of the labor connected with these duties necessarily superseded the Sabbath and festival prohibitions. The priests maintained further that not only was the actual work of sacrifice permitted, but with it also all ancillary activities, such as sharpening knives and preparing fuel. This the plebeians vigorously denied. The Temple had been in ruins for almost a quarter of a century when Eliezer mentioned the priestly tradition and defended it in the academy. He urged that since slaughtering an animal—a major activity—was permitted, sharpening a knife—a minor activity—must, by implication, certainly be permitted. Joshua made a feeble attempt to answer this argument but, in his usual fashion, was about to retire from the field, when Akiba stood up to voice his opinion.

It was probably expected that a single word from the master would rout the beginner; to the amazement of the assembly, Akiba gave as well as he got. Joshua, watching the fray from the sidelines, could not resist the impulse to call out the verse from Judges (9:38), "Behold the people whom thou didst despise, go out, I pray thee, and make war against them!"

Eliezer fought back vigorously and ingeniously. "Does not the Bible say," he shouted, " *'In its season'* (Num. 28:1)? And does that not mean that sacrifices must be brought at their specified times whether on the Sabbath or on week days?"

"Indeed," Akiba replied, "but show me where it says that knives must be sharpened in the appointed seasons."

To this there was no possible response, and Eliezer, seeing himself refuted, could only cry out: "Akiba, you have refuted me from the laws of slaughter, by slaughter shall you meet your death!"

Akiba replied simply, "My master, you yourself have taught me that purification, which is also a minor activity, must not be done on the Sabbath; and I infer from your words that the same law applies to other activities which are ancillary to the sacrifice." [1]

We may conjecture, with much plausibility, that this first public argument won Akiba his ordination and, with that, full membership in the conclave. Surely the scholar who could refute Eliezer ben Hyrkanos in debate could no longer be called a pupil; he was a Master of the Law. By virtue of his new status, he was not only a recognized authority on all ceremonial questions; he could also sit as judge in matters of civil law, which were usually presented before three ordained teachers. He could also act as member of a court to exercise criminal jurisprudence in so far as the Romans permitted the Jewish community to enforce its law.

Both Akiba and Eliezer must have realized that this discussion was only an opening skirmish in the long-drawn-out battle which life was forcing upon them. With unwearying persistence, Akiba returned to the struggle each day, lying in wait for any expression of Shammaitic opinion which he might need to refute.[2] More than once when Joshua, the titular leader of the plebeians, had yielded to Eliezer, Akiba "sprang up" (the expression commonly applied to his action at this time) to repulse the attack.[3] Whether the issue was one of civil law or ceremonial observance, theological belief or simple exegesis, the vigilance of Akiba was quick to perceive the implication of opposed class interest behind the academic façade.

During the eight or ten years which Akiba spent under the tutelage of Joshua ben Hananya and Nahum of Gimzo, he had become completely transformed; his interests now transcended his provincial origin; he had absorbed the whole plebeian outlook on life, in the form which centuries of Hasidean, Pharisaic, and Hillelite thought had stamped upon it. His manners were those of a polished gentleman; his speech that of a cultivated townsman. His legislation protected plebeian interests, but it was expressed in terms of concrete legal rules and healthy, mature, sophisticated, urban idealism. His political and theological ideals may be studied with profit, in our own times, which, *mutatis mutandis,* have so much in common with his.

Yet running through all which is permanently significant in his thought, we continually find legal opinions which could have no other aim than the increased prosperity of Jerusalem, and especially of its workers and artisans. In his discussion of such matters, Akiba exhibited a remarkable feeling and understanding for the economic interests of the capital which no longer existed. Nothing can better illustrate the curious time-lag of human thinking than the devotion of this scholar, and even some of his later disciples, to needs which had disappeared and might never again be recreated. True, Akiba expected Jerusalem's speedy restoration, but the vision of the future metropolis could hardly explain the passion with which he came to the defense of positions traditionally held by the plebeians of Jerusalem and yet were of no significance in his own time.

In one of these discussions, Akiba endeavored to protect Jerusalem's vested interest in the visiting crowds of pilgrims which had contributed so greatly to its prosperity. Three feasts brought into the sacred city tens of thousands of Jews from every part of the world. Biblical law demands that every Israelite present himself at the Temple thrice a year, but the emphasis has always been on the Passover pilgrimage. Anyone failing to come then is threatened with the penalty of being cut off from his people (Num. 9:13), which was understood in rabbinic times to mean early death without issue. It is expressly stated, however, that the punishment does not apply to such as live far from Jerusalem; they are still under obligation to come, but are not to be "cut off" if they fail to do so. But, how far must one be from Jerusalem to be exempt? The question had doubtless been debated while the Temple still existed. The farmers who found the annual pilgrimage a heavy burden were inclined to limit the zone. The Temple priests, who gained little from the crowds who came into the sanctuary, and who were wearied to death by the endless series of sacrifices to be offered, agreed with them. So did the patrician nobles of Jerusalem, who would have liked a quiet,

dignified festival at the Temple. The workers and the merchants, however, who needed the custom of the pilgrims, were
moved to extend the obligation as far as possible. Eliezer,
reflecting the ancient rural and patrician view, maintained the
extreme opinion that "Only a person who is within the
Temple area and yet declines to offer the Passover sacrifice is
under the penalty of the Law." Akiba, whose sympathies were
entirely with the plebeians and the metropolitan traders and
artisans who had been associated with them, said that anyone
living within a radius of fifteen miles from the Temple must
attend.[4] Eliezer applied the same lenient principle, of course,
also to other festival pilgrimages, which he indeed practically
abolished. "I give praise," he said, "to the lazy men who do
not leave their homes during the festival periods, for it is
written, 'And thou shalt rejoice, thou and thy household' "
(Deut. 14:26).[5]

A second argument between Akiba and Eliezer gives us a
curious insight into the different materials used for writing
by the wealthy and the poor of Judea. Every Pharisee wore
on his head and on his arm, black leather phylacteries
(tephilin), containing little scrolls on which were inscribed
the four chapters of Scripture mentioning this rite. The most
pious and learned wore these phylacteries all day; others put
them on only for prayer.

The plebeians, who could afford only inferior grades of
ink and parchment for their tephilin, had to examine the
contents each year to be sure the writing had not faded. The
patricians used better and more durable materials, and could
dispense with these repeated inspections. From this difference
in circumstance emerged two views of the Law; the Hillelite
plebeians insisted that the tephilin must be examined once a
year, no matter what the materials used; the Shammaites

denied this. The subject had been debated in the Sanhedrin as early as the time of Hillel and Shammai, and in the course of the argument Shammai had exhibited his own phylacteries, which he said he had inherited from his grandfather, as proof of the durability of good ink and parchment. The issue had remained unsettled at the time; now Akiba claimed that a specific verse in Scripture corroborated the plebeian view. For the Bible says: "And it shall be for a sign unto thee, upon thine hand, and for a memorial between thine eyes, that the Law of the Lord may be in thy mouth, for with a strong hand hath the Lord brought thee out of Egypt. *Thou shalt therefore keep this ordinance in its season from year to year*" (Exod. 13:9).[6]

"The passage can only mean," said Akiba, "that the phylacteries, which are the sign upon the hand and the memorial between the eyes, must be examined each year in the proper season."

Eliezer, representing the view of the Shammaites, said, "No, the verse deals only with the observance of the Passover which is the main subject of the chapter."[7]

The difference between rich and poor with regard to their writing materials was perhaps less important than with regard to their landed property. The interest of the patricians in the cultivation of olives, which had led to one of Akiba's earliest controversies with Tarfon, formed the basis of an even more prolonged and bitter discussion with Eliezer. Since the olive had become the fruit par excellence of Galilee,[8] the production of its oil in the prescribed "purity" involved serious difficulties. Living at a distance from Jerusalem and the Temple, the Galileans could hardly arrange to "cleanse" themselves when they became defiled by contact with the dead; for that particular form of "impurity" could be removed only

with the ashes of the red heifer which were kept in the
Sanctuary (Num. 19:1 ff). The Galileans, apparently, did
bathe to wash away minor impurities,[9] but in the eyes of the
scholars this did not mitigate the effects of the major impurity. Legally they were "impure" and their touch con-
taminated. What, then, was to be done about the olives which
they garnered? The Shammaites, who were especially concerned with this question, had an easy solution. They pointed
to the verse in Leviticus (11:34) which denies that food can
become impure unless it is moistened. The plucked olives
were moist only with their own juice and, said the Shammaites, that liquid is not sufficient to render them susceptible
to impurity. The Hillelites asked why the juice of grapes and
all other fruits should be considered "preparation" for defilement and not the juice of olives. No satisfactory answer was
given to this question, but the Shammaites insisted on their
position.[10]

This convenient rule did not, however, solve the whole
problem. What was the status of the oil derived from the
olives? The question was not merely academic and theoretical; nor did it concern only the super-pious who observed
the laws of purity after the Temple was destroyed. It had a
very practical importance, and involved vast property interests.
The heave offering which every Jewish farmer in Palestine
gave to the priest could be eaten only if it was pure. Obviously, if it was held that most of the olive oil produced in
Galilee was impure, the priests would lose a large fraction of
their income.

The situation was aggravated rather than mitigated by the
destruction of the Temple. While the ashes of the last red
heifer had somehow been saved and were available for purification, they could be used only sparingly. Levitical impurity

thus became so widespread that the priests had to reconsider the status of the heave offering of wine and other fruit juices, as well as of olives.

Eliezer solved the whole problem with a sweeping declaration that "liquids are not susceptible to any form of impurity." [11] The urgency which led to this decision is obvious from the fact that it runs counter to a specific statement in Scripture (Lev. 11:34) and certainly was opposed to the tradition of the day. It is especially noteworthy that Eliezer ben Hyrkanos, who boasted that he never gave an opinion which he had not received from his masters,[12] should have been the author of this remarkable, and in a sense revolutionary, innovation. The proof he offered as basis for his interpretation of the Law effectually refutes him, as he himself must have recognized. He maintained that his rule was a corollary of a pronouncement made more than two hundred years earlier by Jose ben Joezer, one of the earliest Pharisaic teachers, who declared that the "liquids of the Temple slaughter-house are pure." [13] Eliezer insisted that legally no distinction could be drawn between the liquids which Jose ben Joezer mentioned and others; if the old Pharisaic sage was correct so far as his rule went, then all liquids were pure.

It is obvious that an opponent of Eliezer might argue with equal, if not with greater, cogency that Jose ben Joezer's words imply that other liquids *are* impure. But Eliezer, like the earlier Shammaites, did not listen to objections. Convinced, doubtless, that the ruling was indispensable and justified, he offered it to those who would follow him.

Akiba, however, was unmoved by the plight of priest or provincial farmer. He knew that liquids had always been considered impure, and he could see no good reason for making a change in the tradition. On the contrary, he opposed even the attempt made by his colleagues to effect a compromise declaring liquids subject only to "rabbinical impurity."

An important difference regarding civil law had its origin in the same opposition of interests. If a lender, having taken a pledge for a loan, loses it, he can nevertheless, according to Eliezer, recover the money due him by taking an oath to the facts. Akiba insists that the pledge is not merely a token; the borrower can say, "You lent me the money only on the surety of the pledge; give me the pledge, and I will pay the loan." [14] It must be borne in mind in justice to Eliezer that loans in ancient Israel were not profit-making transactions; they were simply favors. Yet Akiba holds that the poor borrower obviously ought not to be compelled to pay a debt when his pledge has disappeared.

A whole series of controversies had its origin apparently in nothing more significant than the difference in bedtime between town and country. City people who in ancient times, as today, usually remained awake long after provincials had gone to bed, were prepared to observe the Passover celebration at a correspondingly late hour. The Book of Jubilees which, in part, represents peasant opinion, demands that the Passover celebration be completed by the end of the first watch in the night, i.e. before 10 p.m. [15] Eleazar ben Azariah and other patricians of his day were willing to extend the period until midnight. [16] But Joshua, Akiba and their plebeian followers saw nothing wrong in continuing the festival through the night into the morning. An interesting incident recorded in rabbinic tradition, and nowadays repeated each year at the Passover service, tells how once Eliezer, Joshua, Eleazar ben Azariah, Akiba and Tarfon spent the Passover evening together, and so engrossed did even the patrician members of the group become in the conversation which ensued that they forgot their early-to-bed principles, and remained awake until they were called to the morning service! [17]

Applying the same rule to the time for reading the evening *Shema,* Eliezer limits it to the first watch of the night, but Akiba holds that it may be read at any time before dawn.[18]

Perhaps no controversy shows the different attitudes of these scholars more strikingly than that concerning the vineyard which produced only *olelot,* gleanings such as would ordinarily be given to the poor. Eliezer maintained that since the produce of the field was uniform, it all belonged to the owner. Akiba, defending as usual the interests of the poor, said the *olelot* belong to them; if there be no other fruit, the owner must suffer his loss.[19]

One of the most illuminating controversies between the two sages is that concerning the "captive woman." Eliezer's view is dominated by the social conditions of the patricians and provincials, who still practiced polygamy; Akiba's by that of the plebeians who had long been monogamists. The issue arose from the rule set down in Deuteronomy permitting an Israelite who finds a comely woman among the captives of the army to take her to his home and after a suitable time marry her. The Scriptures read: "Then shalt thou bring her home to thy house; and she shall shave her head and pare her nails; and she shall put the raiment of her captivity from off her, and shall remain in thy house, and bewail her father and mother a full month; and after that thou mayest go unto her, and be her husband, and she shall be thy wife" (Deut. 21:12). Eliezer's interpretation of the passage, or rather his literal acceptance of it, reflects the attitude of the patrician and rural circles, where polygamy was practiced and held justified. The feeling of the older wife or wives were not considered; there was no monopoly on the husband's affections.

But in the plebeian, monogamous circles, whose ideas Akiba had imbibed, there was less concern for the captive stranger than for the displaced wife. To Akiba it seemed that the delay which the Law required was intended to give the captor's first, legal wife an opportunity to win back her husband's affections. While, therefore, Eliezer leaves the sense of the passage unchanged, Akiba interprets it with some freedom. "By 'her father and mother,' her native idol-worship is intended," he says; "her nails are not to be pared, but rather permitted to grow; the time is not one month, but three months. . . . And why all these precautions? So that he may see his legal wife happy and properly adorned, and his new love continually in tears and in plain attire." [20]

Akiba did not confine his attention to these major issues of right and ceremonial; he was prepared to take up the slightest question of patrician exegesis. When, for instance, Eliezer made the innocent remark that the honey, which Scripture enumerates as one of Palestine's blessings, must mean the honey of dates, Akiba vigorously objected. He saw in this interpretation an attempt to enhance the prestige of the oasis of Jericho, the ancient home of aristocracy and the only part of Palestine where date palms grew. "No, it means the honey of the bees," he said; for that could be found in the plebeian upland country in even greater quantities than in the lowlands.[21]

When the verse was discussed, "In booths shall ye dwell seven days, for I caused the children of Israel to dwell in booths when I brought them forth from the land of Egypt" (Lev. 23:24), Eliezer commented that the booths of the wilderness were true bowers of leaves and branches.[22] Akiba, remembering that the booths erected by his poor plebeian followers for the festivals were greatly inferior to the leafy tabernacles of the wealthy patricians and rural farmers, saw in this interpretation an affront to his class. If the booths provided by God in the wilderness were actually covered with vegetable growths, then obviously such makeshifts as board-covered huts, rooms so tiny that they could only admit a man's head but not his body, tents built on the top of a wagon, or hovels of which one wall—for lack of boards—was a tethered ox or cow, and similar devices which the plebeians used, were objectionable, as the patricians maintained.[23] But, said Akiba, the booths of the wilderness were not of trees at all; they were the "clouds of honor" which followed the Israelites in their wanderings and, clearly, any covering could symbolize these thin sheets of aerial vapor.

A similar disagreement arose when the law of the unidentified slain person was debated. The Law provides that if a person be found murdered on the highway, and the assassin be not discovered, the nearest city must bring a calf as an atonement. But if the body be found midway between two cities, how exactly was the distance to be measured? Eliezer says, One must measure from the navel of the corpse. Akiba, however, insisted that this would be a derogation of man's dignity, which is expressed rather in his face, the Image of God. He therefore held that the measurement is made from his nose. Likewise, if the head is found at a distance from the body, Akiba said the trunk must be carried to the head, Eliezer said the head must be carried to the trunk.[24]

Sometimes Akiba would object to Eliezer's efforts to reinterpret the past from a pro-priestly or pro-patrician point of view, for, though no direct contemporary issues were involved, tradition always played a part in the accepted status of classes. The priests were particularly anxious to minimize the guilt ascribed to Nadab and Abihu in Scripture. According to the

story in Leviticus (10:1), the sons of Aaron actually attempted
to offer forbidden fire on the altar. This the later priests considered altogether incredible; and they were equally disturbed
by the story of the fire which came out "from before the
Lord" and killed these transgressors in the sanctuary. For
how could the bodies have been removed thence? No Levite
durst enter the sacred portals, and their brother-priests would
have been prevented from continuing the important dedica-
tion service by contact with the dead. Akiba answered simply:
an iron hook was thrown over their bodies, and with this
they were dragged into the open courts. Eliezer said, "Nay,
they died outside of the sanctuary's walls, where the Levites
could approach them." [25]

In several instances, however, Akiba disagreed not with
Eliezer's decision, but with his mode of interpretation.[26] The
disciple of Nahum was impatient with the intermediary steps
even when the conclusions to which they led agreed with his.

In spite of these continual controversies on questions of law
and public policy, Akiba managed to win Eliezer's affections
to an astonishing degree. Inevitably the icy reserve of the old
patrician yielded before the charm of the young, ardent disciple. None of the other sages, even those who had known
Eliezer from his earliest days at the academy, dared approach
him with the unrestrained freedom assumed by Akiba. The
former shepherd intuitively recognized that the brusqueness of the Master was nothing more than a mannerism;
underneath his superficial harshness Eliezer possessed a pathetic tenderness and hunger for affection. His vanity and
ill-temper rose from an inordinate, because thwarted, love of
praise, and not from native rancor. Few of his colleagues who
heard him bellow his legal opinions and personal insults in
the conclave would have credited him with the touching love

he could show in his family circle. A little niece who grew up in his home became so attached to him that when she reached the age of marriage and he urged her to accept a suitor she refused to do so. His mother, who realized how matters stood, urged him to marry the child. This he hesitated to do, partly because of the discrepancy in age, partly because she was his near relative. One day, however, when he spoke to her of marriage to someone, she replied, "I am your hand-maid, to wash the feet of your servants." [27] Hearing these words, Eliezer married her. A man who could inspire such devotion at home could not have been the ruthless tyrant his colleagues considered him.

Seeing deeper into the man, Akiba bore patiently with his outbursts. He was careful never to offend the Master, turning aside with some light remark any incident which might give pain. It happened, for instance, that once, during a drought, a fast was declared, and Eliezer was asked to lead the public prayers. He did so, "but there was no answer." At a second fast, observed a few days later in accordance with the pre-scribed ritual, Akiba officiated, and hardly had he begun the services with the improvised prayer, "Our Father, Our King, we have no King besides Thee. Our Father, our King, pity us for Thine own sake," when the rain came! The general astonishment at this miracle—for it was interpreted as nothing less—is indescribable. God had indicated his preference for Akiba. Of course, it could not be that the pupil was either more learned or more pious than the Master. But, it was widely held, the incident did prove that Akiba's kindliness and his readiness to condone the faults of others made him superior to Eliezer. Akiba himself paid no attention to the congratula-tions which were heaped upon him. He only hastened to mollify Eliezer. "My Master," he said, "what has occurred reminds me of the story of the king who had two daughters, one lovable and the other repulsive. When the lovable daughter appeared with some request, the king would be slow to grant it, for he wished to prolong the interview that he might hear the music of her voice and enjoy the wit of her conversation. But when he saw the unloved sister approach, he shouted to the servants and ministers, 'Give her anything she wants and let her go.' " [28]

It was Akiba's understanding affection which made it possible for the two men to live together in amity, notwithstanding their fundamental differences of philosophy, manner and opinion. No wonder that when Eliezer, being ill, was visited by several colleagues, he listened to all of them with impatience and, when they had done, cried out to his attendants, "Support me that I may hear the words of Akiba, my disciple." [29]

Meanwhile, Joshua watched the development of this prodigy, who had already outstripped Tarfon and gave promise of surpassing even him, with generous and unconcealed delight and admiration. Time and again when the old master reported traditions which he had received from Johanan ben Zakkai, with the admission, "I have heard these statements, but cannot explain them," Akiba would say, "I think I can explain them," and usually his interpretation was correct.[30]

Once Joshua was so moved by a demonstration which Akiba offered in support of an ancient plebeian rule that he cried, "Would that the dust might be uncovered from thy eyes, Johanan ben Zakkai, for thou didst say that in time the indirect defilement of a loaf of bread would be abolished because it cannot be inferred from the Law. Instead of which, thy pupil's pupil has done the impossible and has found its basis in the Law." [31]

On one occasion, which was long remembered in the academy, Akiba successfully opposed both of his masters— Eliezer, who defended the patrician position, and Joshua, who had proposed a compromise. The question arose out of the law requiring a man to marry the widow of a childless brother. This institution, called the Levirate marriage, had its origin, as the sages recognized, in the primitive law which deeds a man's wife or wives along with his other possessions, to his heirs. But while the Levirate marriage began as a privilege, it developed into a burden, for it would frequently happen in a relatively advanced state of society that an additional wife would be a liability rather than an asset. It is this situation which is envisaged in the Scripture (Gen. 38:9; Deut. 25:5). Yet among the patricians and provincials the earlier significance was not entirely forgotten.

As usual the conflicting conceptions found expression in a matter of technical, legal detail. The patricians insisted that even before the surviving brother takes the widow into his home she must be considered his wife, while the plebeians maintained that his rights over her begin only when he performs the marriage and receives her as his wife. One of a husband's prerogatives in Jewish law is that permitting him to annul his wife's vows. Eliezer, speaking for the patricians, maintains that as soon as one of the surviving brothers has indicated his intention of marrying the widow, he becomes authorized to annul her vows. Joshua, demurring from this extreme view, was ready to admit the rule when there was only one surviving brother and there could therefore be no question regarding the widow's destiny. But Akiba challenged the whole principle. What right did a man have to annul the vows of a woman to whom he was not yet married? The widow was not bound to her brother-in-law, he insisted, by any tie save that which forbade her to marry anyone else until certain ceremonies were performed. To make her his wife, automatically, on the death of her husband, was to accept as permanent law the primitive conception of the inheritance of wives. It was when he heard this argument that Ben Azzai, Akiba's close friend and admirer, called out, "Alas, that I did not have Akiba for a teacher!" [32]

So completely did Akiba win the hearts of both Eliezer and Joshua that when they traveled about the country to raise funds for the poor, they frequently invited him to join them. One of their most reliable contributors on such journeys was a certain Abba Judah of Antioch. In the course of time, it is told, this Abba Judah suffered reverses and once, when he heard that the scholars had arrived on their usual mission, he hid in his house so as to avoid them. His wife, noticing his embarrassment, said to him, "We still have one field left. Sell half of it and give them the proceeds." He did so. The scholars, unaware of the extent of his sacrifice, accepted his gift and blessed him.

When they returned to Antioch some time later, they found that he had regained his former wealth, and much beside. When they asked about him, people said, "Do you want to see Abba Judah? Who can call on him? He is Abba Judah the owner of oxen, the owner of camels, the owner of asses. Who can compare with Abba Judah?" When, however, he heard that the sages had arrived, he came to see them, "Your prayer has borne abundant fruit," he said to them, when they met. "Whereupon," the story continues, throwing a curious light on the relation of scholarship to affluence in those days, "they seated him next to themselves, and they applied to him the verse, 'A man's gifts make room for him' " [33] (Prov. 18:16).

Akiba tells us of one sea voyage which he took with his two masters during the Passover week. Though the occasion of the journey is not recorded, the matter which took them abroad was apparently of pressing importance, for otherwise they would hardly have left Palestine during the festival. Akiba merely recalled that he kneaded the unleavened cakes (*mazzot*) for Eliezer and Joshua, and since there was not enough water available on the ship, he was compelled to use fruit juices.[34]

Tarfon, who had always loved Akiba, now openly acknowledged him as master. Once the patrician sage rendered a wrong decision, declaring a cow, the womb of which had been removed, prohibited. The owner, accepting this opinion, fed the animal to the dogs. When the matter finally came before the conclave and Tarfon was adjudged in error, the wealthy sage listened to the judgment with his usual good-humor, merely saying, "Thine ass must be sold, Tarfon, to reimburse the owner of the cow." But Akiba said to him, "You are an expert judge, and are therefore free from liability for damages." [35]

A famous controversy between the two sages, which ultimately had to be referred to the conclave for adjudication, concerned the private pool of a man named Diskos in Yabneh. This pool, built into the cellar or *megaron* of the rich man's house, contained just enough water for ritual purification, namely twenty-four cubic feet. Naturally it was measured from time to time to determine its adequacy, and once it was found deficient. The question arose whether the people who had bathed in it since it was last known to have been full were pure. Tarfon maintained that they were. "The *mikveh* (pool for ritual purification) retains its approved status until it is demonstrated to be inadequate." Akiba, usually lenient in questions of Levitical purity, was in this instance inclined to be rigorous. He did not see any reason for establishing special rules for the benefit of those who were too proud to resort to the public pools which the community maintained at proper standards. Hence, he insisted that everyone who had used the bath since it was last known to have been full was impure. "The man who enters a bath is presumptively impure; he remains in that status until he is certain that he has bathed in an adequate amount of water," he said. After a long argument, the conclave voted to support Akiba.[36]

To those unacquainted with the development of Law in general it may seem strange that the extraneous considerations which apparently influenced Akiba in his stand on this question should possibly enter the mind of a jurist. But in justice to the interpreters of law we must bear in mind that only those questions are referred to them where precedent and established rule do not offer clear guidance. Obviously the technical arguments advanced by Akiba and Tarfon, in this instance as in others, were of equal weight. Under such circumstances, the judge's or the sage's decision must depend on what he regards as the social interest; this in turn will depend on his general point of view regarding the community in which he lives.

In his close friendship for Akiba, Tarfon frequently withdrew opinions to which he was already committed, when he heard that his former pupil disagreed with them. On the other hand, it is recorded that Akiba once, after defeating Tarfon in argument, reconsidered his position and accepted the views he had just rejected.[37]

Perhaps it was Akiba's sense of humor which more than anything else won the hearts of his masters and his colleagues. He soon outgrew the rough playfulness which had characterized him in his earlier days, but he never lost his ready wit. "Laughter protects one's honor," he used to say.[38]

Only one member of the conclave regarded Akiba's rise with ill favor: the patrician scholar, Elisha ben Abuyah. He was not generous enough to share Tarfon's joy in the phenomenal scholar, nor was he old enough to watch him with the secure detachment of Eliezer and Joshua. Akiba was his rival as well as his opponent. Neither Akiba's genius nor his humility made any impression on Elisha, who denied the existence of the one and despised what he called the affectation of the other. He could not believe that a man who had begun his studies in middle age, and who had spent so much of his time in earning his livelihood, could really attain to such eminence as was ascribed to Akiba.

"He who studies the Torah in his youth, absorbs it in his blood," he used to say, "and then the words of the Torah come from his mouth clearly and distinctly; but if a person begins his studies in advanced years, the words of the Torah are not absorbed in his blood, and do not come forth from his mouth clearly." Using another metaphor, he remarked, "He who studies in his youth is like unto ink written on new paper, while he who begins his studies in maturity is like ink written on used paper." Because Akiba did not observe the patrician rules, and frequently offered opinions which were revolutionary in their leniency, Elisha was led to say, "A man who has good deeds and then studies the Torah is like to a house which has foundations of rock and walls of brick. Even the approach of many waters will not harm it. But a man who studies the Torah, but has not good deeds, is like a house which has foundations of brick and walls of stone. Even a little water will wash it away." [39] One wonders whether he recalled these words when he became an apostate and traitor, the abject tool of the pagan oppressors.

Akiba could afford to ignore the envy of Elisha ben Abuyah; he could not dismiss as easily the tyranny of Gamaliel, whom the scholars had finally succeeded in making Nasi, or president.

The conclave was no longer the free forum it had been in the days when Akiba first came to it. Since Gamaliel was a patrician, it was considered proper to choose a plebeian, Joshua ben Hananya, as his associate, Ab Bet Din.[40] No sooner, however, had Gamaliel attained the powers he had coveted than he forgot the generous loyalty of the scholars who had raised him to the office of his ancestors. Neither Joshua, who was second to him, nor any other scholar, was permitted any freedom of action. He insisted that his colleagues, some of whom were older than he, treat him as their superior, and he was quick to show his displeasure when his dignities were affected.

"This was the custom of Rabban Gamaliel. When he entered the academy and said, 'Ask!' everyone knew that all was well. But if he entered the academy and failed to say, 'Ask!' people knew that there was some complaint."[41] We may imagine what terror fell on the assembled scholars as they waited for the morose, angry face to melt into something like a smile. Even those who had nothing to fear from him naturally fell under the spell of the common terror, as they waited impatiently for the magic *Shaalu,* "Ask," which opened the proceedings. No matter how urgent the business which the scholars had on hand, it could not be taken up before the formula had been spoken, and if the president was angry they would all have to sit in silence until he was appeased.

Frequently his surliness took harsher forms. In order to

complete his control of the conclave or the academy, he instituted supervisors who were to report to him all offences on the part of members. The first appointees were Eleazar Hisma and Johanan ben Nuri.[42]

Eleazar Hisma was an admirer and partisan of Akiba, who had helped and befriended him. It had happened, for instance, that once, on a visit to a certain town, Eleazar had been asked to lead the morning service, which in those days was recited by heart. When Eleazar, much embarrassed, admitted that he did not know the service well enough, the people cried, "Is this *Rabbi* Eleazar to whom we gave such a welcome? What right has he to the title of rabbi?" Whereupon Eleazar returned home, deeply ashamed and disgraced. Akiba, hearing the story, said to him, "Would you like to learn the service, my master?" And he taught it to him. In a short while Eleazar could go back to the community and redeem his reputation by reciting and chanting the whole of the service in excellent fashion.[43]

Since he sided with the plebeians, Eleazar did not have much to do in the office, which had been created primarily to hold them in check. But Johanan ben Nuri reports that he had frequent occasion to complain to Gamaliel of Akiba and that he *caused him to be publicly flogged five times!* [44] That such humiliating punishment should have been meted out to one of the foremost members of the academy—a man in his forties—would seem incredible, and indeed some copyists, out of respect for both Gamaliel and Akiba, have tried to soften the text. But the accuracy of Johanan's reports cannot really be doubted. We could only wish that he had described the derelictions for which Akiba was punished. They cannot have been infringements of the ceremonial law, for which the punishment would have been nothing less than expulsion from the academy. We must assume that some violation of academic rules was involved and that even this served only as a pretext; actually, Gamaliel could not forgive Akiba his frank and forcible championship of the plebeian cause. For Gamaliel, like his father, was really a Shammaite.[45] He observed Shammaitic rules in his household; he agreed with Eliezer, his brother-in-law, in a number of recorded Shammaitic decisions; and above all, he followed Shammaitic principles in closing the doors of the academy to the poor.[46]

Like most of the provincials and patricians of the day, he charged the urban plebeians and their descendants with hypocrisy. His dislike was probably based on other considerations. The plebeians already outnumbered the patricians in the academy, and the admission of scholars on the basis of ability would have emphasized the disproportion. He expressed his feeling about the poor scholars quite frankly when he said, "Students may be compared to four kinds of fish. There is the unclean fish, which is useless; and the pure fish, which is edible; there is the little river fish from the Jordan, and the great sea fish from the Mediterranean. The unclean fish corresponds to the impecunious student, who may have studied Scripture, Mishna, *halaka* and *aggada,* and will nevertheless remain without understanding; the pure fish corresponds to the wealthy student, who when he has mastered Scripture, Mishna, *halaka* and *aggada* will have understanding; the small Jordan fish is the student who having imbibed information cannot use it in argument; the great sea fish is he who having learned his fill can argue with his teachers."[47]

The coarseness of the similes betrays the prejudice of the patrician. The fact is that the Shammaitic scholars of the day were still not ready to accept the "scribes" or plebeian men of learning as their equals. Eliezer ben Hyrkanos definitely

distinguishes between the two classes; [48] and many passages
in the Gospels show that the Galileans, who were under the
influence of patrician conceptions, spoke of the "scribes *and*
the Pharisees."

Gamaliel's prejudice derived from the traditions of his class;
he therefore considered it sacred and, like all partisans, he
claimed to speak for the people as a whole. Able administrator
that he was, and belonging to a family which had been at
the helm of Jewish life for almost a century, he recognized
that many of the issues which divided the scholastic world
were in their ostensible substance unreal. He could not see
why, since the whole Jewish population had been reduced to
peasantry, the factional groupings which had originated in
the struggle between town and country should be preserved.
What he failed to realize was that Akiba and his fellow
plebeians were using the traditional party labels as a means
to obtain reforms which were still needed—now, perhaps,
more than before. Many of the ceremonial restrictions which
the Shammaites had established bore heavily on submerged
groups, such as the small farmers, the cattle-owners, the
women and the landless. This transferred significance is evident in some of Akiba's controversies with Eliezer, but it
became more fully apparent in the reforms which he introduced when he finally attained power. Gamaliel was quite
correct in his insistence that the struggle between Jerusalem
and the provinces was over; he was, of course, wrong when
he implied that there was no longer any social conflict
whatever. The fact is that both Akiba and Gamaliel wanted
national unity; but each on his own terms. As the event
proved, Gamaliel was in the weaker position because he
believed that the ceremonial differences had produced the factionalism, whereas the truth was that factionalism had produced the ceremonial differences.

The harshness which Gamaliel exhibited in the conflict was not inconsistent with the personal kindliness which characterized all the members of the Hillelite family whose lives have been recorded. We have observed that Eliezer at home was not the tyrant he became in the academy; this was even more emphatically true of Gamaliel. His relations with his servant, Tabbai, whom he treated like a son, prove this beyond question. "Have you noticed how well Tabbai knows the Law?" he remarked to his colleagues when the servant acted in accordance with the prescribed ritual. He taught him to wear phylacteries during prayer, although this was usually considered a special prerogative of freedom, and introduced him with such cordiality to the other scholars that they spoke of him as "one who ought to be ordained!" "Alas for Canaan," Eleazar ben Zadok once cried when Tabbai was waiting on them, "that he has brought the curse of slavery on all his descendants. It would be altogether logical that Tabbai should be sitting here, and I wait on him; but because of his descent from Ham, he must wait on me!" The children of his aristocratic house were trained to call the slave "Father Tabbai" and his wife "Mother Tabita." When the old slave died, Gamaliel sat in mourning for him as though he were a near relative.

"You have taught us, our Master," his colleagues protested, "that one must not observe mourning for a slave."

"Tabbai was different," answered Gamaliel, "he was a man of piety." [49]

His tenderness is perhaps best illustrated by the story which tells how for several days the students noticed that he came to the academy red-eyed with weeping, and when they investigated they found that he was awakened each night by the moaning of a widow who lived next door, and that he could not restrain his tears when he heard her. [50]

It was altogether natural that this sage should be the author of one of the finest ethical maxims in the whole rabbinical literature: "He who pities fellow creatures will obtain pity from God." [51]

In the academy, Gamaliel's surliness was probably the result of fear. With members of the opposition whom he did not consider dangerous his relations could be cordial. Samuel the Little, who was as much a plebeian as Akiba himself, exerted a deep influence on the Nasi. It is said that once Gamaliel invited seven scholars to join him in a Committee to decide the difficult question of calendar regulation. When he came to the meeting, he found eight men. Angry at this presumption, Gamaliel cried out: "Let him who has come uninvited, leave!" Samuel the Little, hearing these words, arose and made his way to the door. Gamaliel remembering that he had summoned him, immediately understood that the peace-loving plebeian was trying to shield the offender. He also recognized the implied reproach to himself, and at once calmed down. "Remain, my son, remain," he said. "It is altogether fitting that you should take part in this decision." [52]

But when he came face to face with energetic opposition, his whole personality changed. The kindly master and the tender-hearted neighbor was transformed into the rigorous disciplinarian and implacable tyrant. Then, like a general in battle, he considered tenderness to the enemy treachery to his people. There was an objective to be reached—the unification of Israel under patrician hegemony. Individuals and their feelings did not count. In line with this ruthless policy, Gamaliel even refused to ordain such plebeian scholars as had already been admitted. Among the scholars who were thus kept in the rank of students when their learning entitled them to seats in the conclave, were the three famous Simeons, ben

Azzai, ben Zoma and ben Nannos. Of these, Ben Azzai was particularly close to Akiba; but Akiba, helpless himself, could do nothing for his friend.

At last, weary of the continual struggle against Gamaliel and the other patricians, Akiba left Yabneh and settled as a village teacher in the small town of Zifron in Galilee.[53] He did not remain there long. The scholars who had taken him for granted while he sat with them in Yabneh suddenly realized all he had meant to them. "The Torah is outside," [54] they declared, referring to his absence from their discussions. Yielding ultimately to their clamor, Gamaliel invited him to return to the conclave.

It appears that, whatever the duration of the exile, it was of service to Akiba. His views crystallized, and many points regarding which he had been in doubt became clear to him. In any case, he returned strengthened in the struggle for the plebeian traditions and interpretations of the Law. But his determination did not blind him to the need for strategy; he bided his time for the opportunity to inflict a decisive defeat on the patrician rulers of the academy.

Akiba's chief support during these trying days was Joshua ben Hananya, who suffered almost equally with him. We are told of several encounters between Joshua and Gamaliel, each of which became of historic importance. The first difficulty arose out of a disagreement regarding the calendar.

It was the custom in those days for the scholars to fix the calendar not by calculation, but by the testimony of witnesses who had seen the new moon, and on the thirtieth day of each month the judges would sit in court waiting for personal reports. Two such witnesses marked that day as the beginning of a month. Of special importance was the new moon of the seventh month, which fixed the New Year's Day, Rosh Ha-

Shanah, a major holy day. Since no one could know before-hand whether witnesses would appear, it became the custom to observe the thirtieth day of Elul, the sixth month, as Rosh Ha-Shanah. If witnesses came to corroborate the assumption that the new moon had appeared, all was well. If they failed to come, then the next day was also observed as the second, and true, Rosh Ha-Shanah. Thus originated the double observance of Rosh Ha-Shanah.

It chanced once that two witnesses arrived in the morning, declaring that they had seen the new moon the evening before, and Gamaliel ordered the day to be proclaimed as "holy." That night, when the scholars looked to the west to see the thin crescent which should now have been higher in the heavens, visible to everyone, there was no sign of it. Clearly the witnesses had misled the court. What was to be done? The aged Dosa ben Arkenas, who had lived in retirement for many years, demanded that the court reverse itself. "How," he asked, "can witnesses testify that a baby has been born, when the next day the mother appears visibly pregnant?" Joshua ben Hananya announced that he agreed with Dosa. But Gamaliel would not admit his error. The day had been announced as New Year's Day in proper form and on evidence which the court had accepted. The matter was closed and could not be reopened.

Joshua, hearing this decision, prepared to observe the Day of Atonement, which occurs on the tenth of the month, according to his own calculation. Gamaliel, who had taken no action against Dosa, would, however, accept no such defiance from Joshua. "I command thee," he wrote his associate, "to appear before me with thy cane and thy purse, on the day which is the Day of Atonement according to *thy* reckoning." Only an observant Jew can appreciate the depth of

Joshua's horror at this order. The Day of Atonement is the most sacred day in the Jewish calendar and is entirely devoted to fasting and prayer. And yet Joshua was ordered to violate it by carrying his cane and his purse—two major transgressions.

It is highly suggestive for the position Akiba had attained that the old man went to him for advice. Akiba felt that in this instance Gamaliel was right. The decision which had been rendered had not been partisan; it had simply been based on misleading testimony. Akiba felt himself compelled to say, "I can prove to you that so far as the calendar is concerned, the judgment of the court is final; for it is written, 'These are the appointed seasons of the Lord, even holy convocations, which *ye shall proclaim* in their appointed season.' (Lev. 23:4). Whether they are announced properly or otherwise, the proclamation makes them holy."

Still dissatisfied, Joshua went to ask Dosa's advice. He too considered Gamaliel's decision valid. "If we are to review the decisions made by Gamaliel's court, we must also be prepared to reconsider every judgment which has been rendered from the days of Moses to our own."

Finding so little support for his views, Joshua took his cane and his money and came to Gamaliel on the day which, according to his calendar, should have been the Day of Atonement. The president could not repress the deep satisfaction he felt as he saw the black-visaged needle-maker approach. The authority of the Sanhedrin had been upheld. He rose from his chair, ran toward Joshua and kissed him fervently, saying, "Peace on thee, my master and my disciple: my master in learning, my disciple in obedience." [55]

Gamaliel's victory over Joshua mollified him for the moment, but it fed his arrogance. Once he actually threatened to expel Akiba not only from the conclave but from the Pharisaic order. This quarrel, too, had its origin in the ceremony of announcing the new moon, which Gamaliel considered especially important because it was a governmental function and a symbol of the authority of the conclave. Witnesses to the new moon were permitted, by Jewish tradition, to violate the Sabbath in order to reach the court, which was awaiting their evidence. On a certain Sabbath, more than forty pairs of witnesses appeared in Ludd on their way to Yabneh, to testify before Gamaliel. Akiba, seeing that a number of witnesses had already gone to the court, dissuaded the others from continuing on the journey. When Gamaliel heard of this, he wrote to Akiba: "If you interfere with these people, you will discourage them from doing their duty next time. And anyone who interferes with people about to fulfill a commandment deserves the punishment of excommunication." Not satisfied with this threat, yet fearful of taking extreme measures against Akiba, Gamaliel removed from office a petty official who, it seems, had been Akiba's agent in stopping the witnesses on their journey.[56] The redactor of the Mishna, Judah the Patriarch, respecting the memory of both Gamaliel, who was his grandfather, and Akiba, who was his teacher's teacher, omits from his record the story of the threat and the punishment of Akiba's agent. But other texts attest the fact, and there can be no doubt of its authenticity.

Gamaliel was fighting a losing battle, and Akiba knew it. Even in the presence of the Nasi, the younger scholar would follow the ceremonial tradition of the plebeians. Once on a visit to Jericho, the city of palms, the scholars ate some dates, after which, according to Gamaliel, a full Grace must be recited. Akiba and the majority of the sages considered an abbreviated Grace sufficient. While his colleagues were apparently wondering whether they ought to follow their own opinions or defer to Gamaliel's, since he was present, Akiba began to intone the short Grace.

"Akiba," Gamaliel cried, "why do you look for quarrels?"

"My master, you have taught us," answered Akiba, "that the decision of the majority is binding. Even though you have given your opinion, we must follow the majority." [57]

The repeated controversies sharpened the hostility of the two factions until the situation was as tense as it had been during the last decades of the Temple. The Nasi resented the obstreperousness of the plebeians; the plebeians objected to what they considered the insolence of the Nasi. Finally, Akiba and his colleagues decided that the time had come for a definitive test.

Unwilling to strike at the descendant of Hillel, the plebeians decided to make an example of his equally haughty brother-in-law, Eliezer, a leading patrician figure. To pick a quarrel with this scholar was not difficult. His insolent bluntness, his stubborn insistence on his own infallibility, his total disregard of the rights of others, made him, in spite of his brilliant record, especially vulnerable. The issue on which Joshua and Akiba, with their followers, finally decided to fight him, seemed incongruous even to the later talmudists. In spite of the tragedy in which the skirmish culminated, they saw its humor and entitled the narrative recording it, "The Stove of the Serpent Rings." [58]

Biblical law demands that earthenware pots and ovens which have become defiled, as, for instance, by contact with a dead insect, be broken (Lev. 11:33). To circumvent this law, the prosperous had invented a "serpent stove," i.e., an oven which—made of tiles, joined together by loose layers of earth—could be taken apart and put together again. This

procedure they called "breaking the oven." Eliezer, speaking
for the wealthy farmers, who could afford such complicated
utensils, defended the legal fiction. But the poorer scholars,
who had to be satisfied with ordinary ovens, resented the
subterfuge. They said that the oven would remain defiled
unless it was actually broken. This view was defended by
Joshua and adopted by the conclave. Eliezer continued to
declare these ovens pure.[59] When the conclave assembled to
hear charges against Eliezer, Gamaliel found himself in a
dilemma. He could not defend in his brother-in-law the
defiance he had repressed in others. Moreover, Eliezer made
no attempt to deny or mitigate the accusation; he merely
insisted that he was right and all the others were wrong.
Whatever may have been the original intention of Eliezer's
accusers, his attitude drove them into a frenzy of anger, and
they not only ousted him from the Sanhedrin, but expelled
him from the Pharisaic order. Not for half a century had this
punishment been meted out to a scholar.

The last to suffer it had been the famous Akabiah ben
Mahalalel, the colleague of Gamaliel's grandfather, who lived
about the year 40 C.E. That great teacher had steadfastly refused to recognize the authority of the Sanhedrin. "Renounce
the four teachings which you have rendered in violation of
our decision, and we will make you Ab Bet Din, the second
to the Nasi," [60] the scholars had pleaded with Akabiah. In
vain; he remained obdurate until the day of his death. He
had been ousted from the Pharisaic order, and when he died
the Sanhedrin had ordered a stone placed on his bier to
symbolize the death which they thought he should have died.

It was this penalty which the conclave revived for Eliezer
ben Hyrkanos, the most erudite of all its members.

Akiba undertook to break the terrible news to the aged

master, "lest some other, less tactful person go" and wound him unnecessarily. Akiba approached Eliezer, but stopped when he came within four cubits of him, for an observant Pharisee durst not approach too near one whose observance and purity is suspect.

Eliezer, noticing the unusual reserve, perhaps reading something sinister in Akiba's face, called out, "What is it, Akiba?" "It seems to me, my Master," Akiba replied, "that your colleagues are keeping away from you."

Eliezer, comprehending at once the full significance of these words, realized that legally he was no longer a trusted Pharisee, but a suspect *am ha-arez*. He had been divested not only of authority as a scholar, but of standing as a Jew. He was *menuddah,* "defiled," "impure," like any publican who had failed to observe the Levitical laws of cleanliness. Brokenhearted, the aged scholar sat down on the ground and removed his shoes as became a mourner; he said nothing.

Had Gamaliel been of a more imaginative nature, he would have realized that the attack against Eliezer was intended as a warning to him. His position in the academy was definitely weaker by reason of Eliezer's expulsion. For, aside from the moral defeat he had sustained, there was the loss of the man who was his main support in his patrician policies. He should have learned caution from the fate of his brother-in-law; instead, he was even more intransigeant than before, finally driving the plebeians to open rebellion.

Two occurrences hastened the break. The first might be called "The Incident of Zadok's Lamb." [61] Zadok, the old priest-scholar, had received a firstborn lamb as an offering. While the Temple existed such animals had been sacrificed; when the Temple was no more, they were given to a priest, who looked after them until they developed some blemish making them unfit for sacrificial purposes. Then they could be eaten. One day, while this particular lamb was munching its oats, it split a lip. Since no scholar may decide a question in which he has a personal interest, Zadok asked Joshua whether the lamb could still be sacrificed. The question was not easy to answer. The Law ordinarily takes no cognizance of artificial blemishes, for the owner is suspected of having produced them intentionally. But, surely, no doubt of Zadok's piety could enter Joshua's mind. The man who had fasted every day for forty years to save the Temple would not put a blot on his conscience for the sake of a little mutton. Joshua, therefore, declared the animal permitted. "We cannot apply the same standard to an *am ha-arez* and a scholar," he said.

But Zadok could not let the matter rest there. Having received Joshua's answer, he went to Gamaliel and asked his opinion. "It is prohibited," said Gamaliel; "we make no distinctions between a scholar and an *am ha-arez*."

Zadok replied, "But Joshua said it is permitted."

"Wait, then," Gamaliel said, "until the 'shield-bearers' enter the academy."

When the scholars assembled, Zadok was asked to repeat his question. Joshua, who sensed the approaching storm, tried to protect himself by prevarication. "It is prohibited," he said. "But in thy name it has been permitted," thundered Gamaliel; "stand up, Joshua, and let them testify against thee."

"If I were alive and he dead," said Joshua, "I could deny his statement; now that both of us are alive, how can one contradict the other?"

Gamaliel, not deigning to answer, began his lecture without giving Joshua permission to resume his seat. The plebeian members of the academy, seeing their leader's humiliation and the schoolboy punishment meted out to him, suddenly interrupted the lecture with the cries, "Stop! Stop!" and the meeting disbanded in disorder.

The second incident occurred about a year later. Joshua had told someone that the evening service was not obligatory, but merely optional. When Gamaliel heard of this, he again accused Joshua of rendering decisions against the vote of the conclave, which had declared this service to be as obligatory as the others. Joshua confessed his guilt and was once more ordered to remain standing while the lecture proceeded. But the members of the academy were no longer satisfied with interrupting Gamaliel. After the session broke up, they at once reassembled and voted to remove the Nasi from office.[62]

Joshua might have expected that, being associate, he would succeed to the presidency. But the members of the academy, even those of Joshua's own party, regarded this as too deep a humiliation for Gamaliel. They were willing to oust Gamaliel out of love for Joshua, but they were not sufficiently vindictive to replace the deposed leader with the man who had been the occasion of the revolt. One tradition tells us that Akiba hoped he might be appointed. But this too could not be, for one plebeian, Joshua, already held office, and the vacant place had necessarily to be filled with a patrician. A number of eminent patricians were available: Eleazar ben Zadok, Jose Ha-Kohen, Simeon ben Nethanel, Tarfon and Elisha ben Abuyah among the older group; and Johanan ben Nuri, Halafta the father of Jose, and perhaps Haninah ben Tera-dyon, who were somewhat younger. But none of these was acceptable to the plebeians, who did not wish to replace Gamaliel with another equally influential personality. Their purposes would be best suited by the appointment of a younger, well-mannered, somewhat timid teacher, who would yield the leadership of the conclave to Joshua and Akiba.

To the amazement of all the older scholars therefore, the insurgents announced the candidacy of Eleazar ben Azariah, who was hardly known as an halakist, although he had a growing reputation as an orator. Eleazar himself was surprised when the post was offered to him. "I will go home and consult my wife," he said.

"They will remove you as they removed Gamaliel," she warned him.

"It is worthwhile," he replied, "to enjoy precious glass for one day, even though the next day it may be broken."

"But you have no white hair," she said. Whereupon, the story continues, a miracle occurred, and overnight eighteen rows of white hair appeared on his head.

The real power in the reorganized conclave lay, of course, not with Eleazar ben Azariah, who was the titular president, but with Joshua and Akiba. So deep an impression did this "palace revolution" make on Jewish scholars that for centuries they referred to "that day" without further specification.[63] Soon after "that day" the conclave voted the Hillelite views binding on all Jews, setting on the Jewish religion the stamp which it has borne ever since.[64] In order to make this decision effective, the conclave began at once to collect the traditions of the opposing schools, both those of the Shammaites and those of the Hillelites.

"Why were the minority opinions recorded?" says the Mishna. "So that if some future scholar should say, 'I have this tradition, which differs from that generally accepted,' he may be answered, 'Indeed, your tradition is based on the views of the minority.'"[65]

Significantly, we are informed that on "that day" many benches were added to the academy.[66] The new seats were intended, doubtless, for the many students whom Gamaliel had refused to admit and whom the victorious plebeians now welcomed. But even more important, the membership of the conclave, which had been reduced to thirty-two, was now increased through the ordination of new members to no less than seventy-two, one more than had been permitted, traditionally, to sit in the Sanhedrin of Temple times.[67] Perhaps it was the intention of those who selected this number to distinguish the conclave from the Sanhedrin, which it superseded but could not replace. Before long, thirteen more members were added, making a total of eighty-five, equal to the traditional number of those who sat in the Great Assembly of Ezra and Nehemiah.[68]

The deposition of Gamaliel was a decisive event in his life. He seems to have realized at last that a Jewish conclave was not a Roman cohort, and that its president was not a captain. Whether in true humility or as a matter of policy, he reverted to the gentle manner of his famous ancestor, the meek, peaceful Hillel. No longer holding office, he attended all the meetings of the academy and took part in the discussions as an ordinary member. His self-conquest melted the hearts of his opponents. They forgot his tyranny and remembered only his lineage.

Before long Gamaliel considered the time propitious for his apology to Joshua, and it was probably no surprise to the assembly when the humble needle-maker announced his belief that Gamaliel should be restored to the presidency. Akiba, piqued at this change, asked Joshua, "Did we take action for any other reason than to defend your honor? Tomorrow, let both of us call on him." Ultimately it was arranged that Gamaliel should be reappointed president, but since Eleazar had held the high office, he was to lecture every third week.[69]

The leadership of the academy thus consisted of Gamaliel, who was first in rank; Joshua, the second; and Eleazar, the third. Freed from the incubus of his pride, Gamaliel became a close friend of both Joshua and Akiba, learning to appreciate their wit, their charm and their affection.

Some time later, Hananiah, Joshua's nephew and a member of the academy, was asked by a private party to settle a difficult question involving the Levitical purity of women in childbirth. He rendered a decision which contradicted a previous ruling of the academy on the same question. Hearing of the incident, the Nasi said to Joshua, "Send your nephew to me." Just as Joshua was preparing to call on Hananiah to deliver this message, Hananiah's daughter-in-law appeared before him to ask *his* advice on the very question at issue. Joshua gave her the official reply; whereupon the young woman said, "But when my mother-in-law asked you that question you gave her the opposite answer." Joshua then remembered that he had originally shared his nephew's opinions and was therefore himself responsible for the breach of discipline. He said nothing to Hananiah but wrote to Gamaliel, "My nephew decided according to what I taught him." [70] It speaks volumes for the change which had come over Gamaliel that he pursued the matter no further.

The Nasi and Joshua, who had previously visited each other only on formal occasions, were now frequently seen together. When Gamaliel went to Emmaus to buy an animal for the wedding dinner of his son, Joshua and Akiba both accompanied him, and several important halakic questions were discussed on the way. Akiba also tells how he once had occasion to provide Gamaliel and Joshua with gold coins in exchange for their silver. It is evident from such incidents that in these later years the three men were intimate associates and companions.[71]

Akiba does not appear to have held any formal office in the academy, but he was universally considered a dominant figure, the fourth member of the directing committee. Perhaps it was at this time that he was appointed overseer of the poor, a post for which he was admirably suited by character and which he filled for many years.[72] It is said that when this post was offered to him, he replied that he would have to consult his wife. As he was going home, he was overheard repeating to himself, "It will lead to error, it will lead to abuse!" [73] Nevertheless, he accepted the office.

One of his new duties, to which, apparently, he had become accustomed in the years of apprenticeship under Eliezer and Joshua, was traveling about to raise funds. His many journeys took him to all parts of Palestine, as well as to Cappadocia, Arabia and Egypt.[74]

Curious scraps of information which he brought back with him to the academy regarding the customs and languages of these countries, are preserved in the Talmud. Even more interesting are the tales which later scholars, who looked upon him as something of a Jewish Sinbad the Sailor, invented about him. They told how, when he was in Arabia, the king consulted him on the very delicate question of the Queen's fidelity. "I am black," his Majesty said, "and so is the Queen. Yet she has given birth to a white child, and I have practically determined to kill her, for she has surely been faithless to me."

"Do you have white statuary in your house?" Akiba asked.

"Indeed, I have."

"Then it is looking at them which affected the color of the child, for the Scriptures tell us that Jacob outwitted Laban by placing spotted sticks before the ewes in mating time." [75]

Another story was told to illustrate his use of the maxim,

"Whatever God does is for the best." While Akiba was on a journey with one or two companions, they came to a city without an inn or guesthouse. "It is for the best," he said and they went out to sleep in the field. They had with them an ass, a cock and a light. During the night the wind extinguished the light, a cat killed the cock, and a lion devoured the ass. When Akiba awoke and noticed the havoc, he simply remarked, "It is for the best," and went to sleep again. In the early morning hours, a band of Bedouins attacked the city and took its inhabitants captive. "Did I not say that whatever God does is for the best?" Akiba asked. "Had we found accommodation in the city, had the lights been burning in the field, had the ass brayed, or had the cock crowed, we would surely not be alive." [76]

A more trustworthy story records his conversation with the pious, wealthy, but frugal, Ben Boion.[77] While Akiba and a companion were approaching Ben Boion's house, they overheard his servant ask him, "What shall I prepare for dinner today?"

"Some vegetables," the master answered, "but get some stale ones, for they are cheaper."

When Akiba heard this, he said, "How can we ask him for a contribution?"

Nevertheless, after they had finished their collection in the town, they decided that they would not omit Ben Boion. He told them to go to his wife and say that she was to give them a measure of *dinars.*

When they brought this message to her, she asked, "Did he say an even measure or a heaped up measure?"

"Neither," they replied.

"In that case, I will give you a heaped up measure."

When they returned to thank Ben Boion, they could not

help asking him why he was so niggardly with his food, and so generous to them.

"I have a right to deny myself any superfluity," he answered, "but how can I refuse to fulfill the commands of my Maker?"

One of Akiba's oratorical devices was to illustrate the morals he was trying to inculcate by anecdotes which he told of himself. These are essentially parables in the first person, and Akiba would doubtless have been surprised to hear that future generations would gravely accept them as records of miracles.

"While I was at sea I saw a vessel founder, and I was especially distressed over a young disciple who I knew was on it. But when our ship arrived in Cappadocia, I found him sitting before the congregation, answering questions of the Law. I said to him, 'My son, how did you escape from the sea?' He answered, 'As I was about to enter the boat, a poor man came to me and begged for alms. I gave him a coin, and he said to me, "As you have given me my life, so may your life be spared to you." And when I sank to the bottom of the sea, I heard the waves calling to one another, "Come and let us save that man who has done good all his life."' " [78]

Like other effective raconteurs, Akiba had, it seems, woven this strange tale out of factual experience, which he later reported to the conclave without the embellishment of moral and miracle. He had actually seen a ship founder off the coast of Cappadocia and had been surprised to find that one of the passengers, a young Palestinian student, had escaped, as have thousands of other shipwrecked people, by seizing a plank of the ship and floating with it to the shore. [79] The incident naturally left a deep impression on Akiba. He not only used it, in fanciful elaboration, to move his hearers to deeds of mercy, but in bald literalness he urged on his colleagues the duty of instruction in swimming: "In addition to every other obligation which a father owes his child, he must teach him to swim." [80]

Akiba made one of his children the subject of another fancy which he used for exhortatory purpose. Taking his motif this time not from experience, but from the apochryphal book of Tobit, he narrated that his daughter had been warned by soothsayers that she would be bitten by a serpent on her wedding night. When the time came, she completely forgot the prediction. As she was removing her clothes after the festivities, she absent-mindedly thrust a pin into a hole in the wall. The next morning, she withdrew the pin, and discovered that she had killed a serpent with it. When Akiba asked her whether she could explain the miracle, she told him that while the wedding guests had sat at the feast, a poor man had come to the gate. Seeing that no one was paying any attention to him, she had given him one of the costly wedding gifts she had received from her father. "Does not this prove," Akiba was wont to conclude, "the truth of the verse, 'Charity delivereth from death'" (Prov. 10:2).[81]

In another tale, frankly a parable, Akiba said: "To whom may possessors of wealth be compared? To a group of people who were indebted to a king, and who had been granted an extension of time for payment. Most of them, not recognizing this favor, failed to send him any gift or show him any gratitude. But there was one in their midst who sent greetings and a gift to the king each day, saying, 'It is proper to honor the physician before the need arises.' When the final time for payment of the debts came, the king sent his officers with an execution against all the debtors. When these were arrayed before the king, he immediately singled out the courteous one and offered him his hand. The others wondered, saying, 'This man is in debt to the king, yet he is given such honor.' But the officer said to them, 'This man paid homage to the king, greeted him and sent him gifts.' "

"Now," Akiba concluded, "just as this man's gifts to the king won him honor, though he was a debtor, so shall we be singled out by the King of kings for our gifts to him. And what are the gifts we can make to God? Charity to the poor." [82]

In another address which has been preserved in part, he said, "If a man be the creditor of a petty official, he takes pride in that fact. The creditor of a ranking officer is even happier. And happiest of all is he who is creditor to the king himself. Yet God, who is the King of kings, says to us, 'Give to the poor, and ye shall become my creditors,' as it is written, 'He that is gracious unto the poor lendeth unto the Lord' " (Prov. 19: 17).[83]

He who is kind to the poor may be certain, Akiba further taught, that his prayer will be heard.[84] On the other hand, Akiba was very severe against those who asked for charity when they did not need it. "He who accepts a penny as alms when he does not need it will live to be in true want"; "he who covers his eyes or his thighs with rags and cries, 'Give to the blind!' 'Give to the crippled!' is predicting his fate"; [85] "Better a Sabbath without celebration than with alms," he said.[86]

Anxious as Akiba was to obtain all possible gifts for the charity funds which he supervised, he would not permit anyone to make contributions beyond his means. When the pious Yeshebab offered to give everything to the poor, Akiba dissuaded him. The rabbinical rule, he maintained, permits one to distribute only one-fifth of one's possessions, the rest are to be kept for one's old age and one's family.[87]

About fifteen years had passed since Akiba had come to the academy a humble shepherd, with little hope. He had risen past colleagues and masters and stood, at last, on a high pinnacle, a dominant figure in Jewish life. Later sages, in their efforts to explain his intellectual greatness to the simple, had recourse to the usual oriental device of hyperbole. One record puts the number of Akiba's disciples at twelve thouhand, another at twenty-four thousand.[88] The time of his separation from his wife, which in reality could hardly have exceeded three years, is extended over the full thirteen years from his coming to the academy until his victorious debate with Eliezer ben Hyrkanos.

Incredible as this is, the Babylonian teachers thought it insufficient, and they created a legend, according to which, when Akiba came home at the end of twelve years, he heard a neighbor berating Rachel for her self-imposed widowhood. "Were he to take my advice," Rachel is described as replying, "he would remain away another twelve years!" Hearing this, Akiba turned back without even entering his house, and thus remained separate from his wife for no less than twenty-four years. When he finally returned, Rachel could not make her way to him through the welcoming throngs. But he, recognizing her from a distance, rushed to her past everyone.

"You put us to shame," his pupils remonstrated with him. But he replied, "She suffered much while I was engaged in the study of the Law."

These apocryphal and semi-apocryphal stories are a measure of the admiration Akiba aroused in the minds of succeeding generations. His actual greatness is established by the bare record. At the age of fifty-five, still in the fullness of bodily vigor and mental alertness after an unparalleled struggle with adversity and opposition, he set out on his lifework—the reconstruction of the Law and the establishment of a permanent school.

V. ON THE HEIGHTS
AKIBA AND HIS SCHOOL

THE twenty years which followed the successful revolt against Gamaliel were probably the happiest in Akiba's life. His children were growing up, two sons and two daughters, all of them showing high promise. His wife, Rachel, was sharing with him the fruits of their common sacrifices— the friendship of their intimate co-workers and the approbation of the general public.

And yet the period began under a cloud. The Roman government, which for fifteen years had steadily pursued a policy of friendship and conciliation, suddenly reversed itself and enacted a series of restrictive regulations against the Jews. Our meager records afford no certain explanation of this change of policy, but it was probably associated with a number of notable conversions to Judaism which occured at Rome. The most distinguished of the converts to the despised, "atheistic" faith was Flavius Clemens, a kinsman of the Emperor. The intrusion of Judaism into the imperial family threw the government into a temporary hysteria. In the autumn of the year 95, news reached Palestine of new disasters pending against the Jews at Rome. No time could be lost, and a few days before the Sukkot festival the four leading scholars, Gamaliel, Joshua, Eleazar ben Azariah and Akiba set out for the capital of the Empire.[1]

Before they sailed, the scholars paid a last visit to the ruined Temple, doubtless to pray for safety and success on their perilous journey. As they approached the Temple hill, they observed a fox running out. Three of them, Gamaliel, Joshua and Eleazar, burst into tears at this sight.

"Alas," they cried, "that we have lived to see the literal fulfillment of the verse, 'The mountain of Zion which is desolate, the foxes walk upon it'" (Lam. 5:18).

But Akiba did not weep. "We should rather rejoice," he said. "For the Scriptures foretell both the utter desolation of the Temple and its reconstruction. How can we hope for the fulfillment of the good promises, until the worst has come to pass."

This commission was not the first which the Palestinian Jews had sent to Rome since the destruction of the Temple. About a decade earlier, Gamaliel, Eliezer ben Hyrkanos and Joshua had gone on a similar journey, perhaps to obtain the right to appoint a Nasi. But for Eleazar ben Azariah and Akiba the visit to the Imperial City was a new experience.[2]

The festival of Sukkot occurred while the commission was still at sea, and the members had much difficulty in the observance of its ceremonies. Gamaliel alone possessed the *Lulab,* that cluster of palm branch, myrtle, willows and the citron, which is used at the prayers of the festival. When Gamaliel had said his prayers, he handed the *Lulab,* in turn, to Joshua, Eleazar and Akiba. A more serious difficulty arose, however, with regard to the booth. Gamaliel, representing the patrician view, held that a ceremonial booth had to be a commodious, reasonably stable structure; since this was impossible on the ship, he preferred to do without it. Akiba, the plebeian, considered it quite proper to erect one on the ship. Gamaliel, softened and mellowed, permitted Akiba to have his way. But after the booth had been built, a wind blew it off the deck and into the water. "Now, where is your Sukkah?" Gamaliel asked in triumph.

While they were aboard, Gamaliel remembered that in his haste to sail he had neglected to set aside the necessary tithes of his harvest. Fortunately, it was possible to make arrangements on board ship, for Eleazar ben Azariah was a priest, Joshua was a Levite, and Akiba was overseer of the poor. So Gamaliel called them all together and said, "The tithe which I will separate from the produce of my field is hereby given to Joshua, and the place it occupies is leased to him. Another tithe, which I will separate, is given to Akiba ben Joseph, so that he may acquire it on behalf of the poor, and its place is leased to him."

Joshua then said, "One tenth of my tithe, which I will separate when we reach home, is given to Eleazar ben Azariah, and the place it occupies is leased to him." For the Levite must give one tenth of his tithe to the priest, in accordance with Numbers 18:26.

Arriving in Italy, the ship stopped first at Brundisium, the modern Brindisi. Unfortunately, it left that port on the Sabbath, putting the scholars in a serious quandary regarding a difficult question of ceremonial observance. As is well known, rabbinic tradition forbids journeys, even on foot, beyond two thousand cubits from the city limits. The plebeians considered the range of their Sabbath movement fixed by the port which they left. Since they were soon well beyond the prescribed limits, they had to remain practically motionless lest they add to the involuntary transgression. The patricians, on the other hand, held that if a person was accidentally removed from his city, he carried his Sabbath range with him, as it were, and could travel two thousand cubits from any place where he found himself. Gamaliel and Eleazar ben Azariah therefore felt free to walk about all over the ship, while Joshua and Akiba were practically fastened to their places.

"All day long," Hananiah, Joshua's nephew, reports, "they carried on the discussion with regard to the Law. In the end, Joshua was won over to Gamaliel's view so far as the ship was concerned, but he refused to extend the principle to other contingencies." [3]

On another occasion, they came into port on the Sabbath, and the question arose whether they might disembark. They all agreed to ask Gamaliel's opinion this time, and he permitted it. "I have been watching since dusk," he said, "and we have not moved a Sabbath limit." But there was another difficulty; the improvised ladder by which they had to descend had been made on the Sabbath, and a Jew must not benefit by any work done on the holy day, even if it be performed by a Gentile. Again Gamaliel set their minds at rest. "Since it was not made in our presence (and therefore was not specially intended for us), we may use it."

When the sages finally reached Puteoli—the magnificent seaport of Rome where Paul had landed half a century earlier —and heard the great bustle of the traffic, three of them burst into tears. Once more, as at the Temple ruins, Akiba stood by, dry-eyed, even smiling.

"Why are you smiling?" they said to Akiba.

"And why do you weep?" he asked in turn.

"How can we help weeping," they answered, "when Jerusalem, the footstool of God, lies in ruins and this city of idolatry flourishes so mightily?"

"And for that very reason do I laugh," said Akiba. "If this is what God gives to those who transgress his will, how great is the glory destined for those who obey him."

"Akiba," they all cried, "you have consoled us, you have

consoled us. May you be consoled by the Comforting Messiah!"

Apparently the commission remained at Rome for the whole winter, but no record has been preserved of its activities. There was a powerful and prosperous Jewish community at the capital, and doubtless some of the leaders were of great assistance to the sages, introducing them to important officials and other persons of influence. We may conjecture, too, that the sages tried to strengthen the ties between his distant community and the conclave at Yabneh.

In later times, various stories concerning the commission circulated in Palestine. There is one anecdote of an encounter between Joshua and Caesar's daughter. Admiring Joshua's wit and commiserating with his plain features, the Roman maiden is said to save asked, "How does so much wisdom happen to be put in no ungainly a body?"

"In what kind of jars does your father keep his wine?" Joshua asked in turn.

"Earthenware," she answered.

"Has he not gold or silver vessels?"

"Aye," she said, "but they would spoil the wine."

"Well, then," he said, "that answers your question." [4]

A more serious conundrum was propounded to the whole group of sages by some "philosophers." "If your God is all-powerful, as you say, and the other gods have no existence, why does he not destroy their visible images?"

The Jewish sages replied: "If the only idols worshiped were those which are unessential to the world, He might do so. But the sun, the moon, the planets and the stars are all among the gods. Shall God destroy his world because of a few fools?" [5]

More interest attaches to a curious encounter between the visiting sages and a member of the primitive Roman Church who had come to the synagogue to hear them. One of them had taken as the subject of his discourse the contrast between the wilfullness of earthly despots and God's adherence to Law. "A human ruler," he said, hinting at the notorious licentiousness of the emperors, "makes laws for others, but he himself fails to observe them; God, however, obeys the Law which he has set before men."

Hearing this, the antinomian Christian asked how the sages could justify the restrictions they placed on activity during the Sabbath. "God does not refrain from work on that day; he raises clouds, sends forth winds and makes the rain descend," he said.

The speaker, replying with calculated simplicity, said: "May not a man carry in his own house? And is not the whole universe the possession of the Holy One, blessed be He?" [6]

They were especially impressed, apparently, with the treatment they received from a Jewish philosopher who has been identified with Josephus. The life of the renegade since he had come to Rome was almost as tempestuous as it had been in Palestine. Envy and mistrust, hairbreadth escapes, startling changes of fortune and, withal, inner vacillation and hesitation, continued to be his lot. It probably did not occur to him that this curious fate, which pursued him in the new land as in the old, was largely of his own making. No one had ever been given better opportunities for self-development than he. At the age of thirty-three, in the fullness of his strength, he had come to the imperial capital, the favorite of the new rulers of the Roman world. He had good reason to believe that life was just beginning for him. To be the intimate friend of the Caesars—what an elevation for the humble priest of a distant province, what a change of fortune for the man who had had to struggle for the governorship of tiny Galilee!

Indeed, it then seemed that he had played his cards well.
He had outwitted not only his fellow officers and soldiers,
but even their God.

When Vespasian and Titus commissioned him to write a
history of the Jewish war to deter others from similar insur-
rections, he threw himself into the task with fiery zeal. He
drew up the Aramaic edition with remarkable rapidity, and
as soon as it was completed set about preparing a Greek edition for the Roman world.[7] He spared no words of praise for
the Roman conquerors or their Jewish partisans; nor of denunciation for his former comrades-in-arms, the revolutionaries. He selected only one of the rebel leaders for a panegyric:
Hanan, the Sadducean high priest, whose name was anathema
among the Pharisees.[8] He extolled the House of Herod, whom
his compatriots rightly condemned, managing to surround
even its decadence with the tragic beauty of a Greek drama.[9]
So little was he then concerned about the opinions of the
Palestinians that he made no effort to conceal his perfidy
against his fellow-soldiers. He actually boasted of the juggling
of the lots which were to decide the order of precedence in
death, and told with utter frankness how he had "counted
the numbers with cunning" [10] so as to escape the death which
they had all agreed to share. He apologized for such praise
as he had to bestow on the Jewish warriors, explaining that it
was necessary in order to show the true magnitude of their
conquerors. He could even laugh over the mourning which
the men of Jerusalem observed when they believed he had
been killed at Jotapata:

"Whereas in each household and family there was mourning
of the relatives for their own lost ones, the lamentation for the
commander was national. While some mourned for a host,
others for a relative, some for a friend, others for a brother,

all alike wept for Josephus. . . . But when time revealed the truth and all that had really happened at Jotapata, when the death of Josephus was found to be a fiction and it became known that he was alive and in Roman hands and being treated by the commanding officers with a respect beyond the common lot of a prisoner, the demonstrations of wrath at his being still alive were as loud as the former expressions of affection when he was believed to be dead." [11]

He was awakened out of this pleasant dream in the year 79 when his patron, Titus, died, and Domitian, the second son of Vespasian, became Emperor. The new ruler disliked men of letters; he drove even the greatest masters, like Juvenal, Tacitus and Pliny, into silent obscurity. There was no possibility that Josephus could win his friendship.[12] The delicate flattery and the quaint tales of Jewish life with which he had entertained the two earlier Flavians were entirely without interest for their grim successor. And alas, even the youthful charm which had helped Josephus so much in his conquest of his masters had begun to fail him now; he was in his forties.

To make matters worse, jealous enemies were busy spreading calumnies about him. He was accused of treason to the empire, and of being implicated in a riot of some Jews in Cyrene.[13] The accusations were easily refuted and quickly dismissed; yet the fact that they had been made at all deeply wounded Josephus. His sense of security was gone.

Naturally, the man who had escaped the snares of John of Gishcala and had emerged alive from the cave at Jotapata, was not one to surrender without a struggle to apparent misfortune. Throughout his life he had used difficulties as stepping stones for his ambition. He would do so again. His position at court was lost; but he would secure for himself a higher distinction, immortality in Greek letters. His account of the Jewish war had received high praise; he would produce an even greater work, of truly monumental proportions—a history of the Jews. That the Aramaic-speaking provincial should win laurels for historical and literary composition in the Hellenic world would be an even more magnificent tribute to his power than his rise to imperial favor under Vespasian. The good will of rulers might be won through accident; literary recognition could be attained only through merit.

He could not doubt that such a work would command a considerable reading public. There was widespread curiosity about this people, whose symbols had been engraved on the Arch of Titus, and who were distinguished by their faith, their courage and their peculiar customs. The most incredible stories were told about them. They were described by their friends as the greatest, and by their enemies as the meanest, of nations. They were said to worship an unseen God, more pure and exalted than any of those known to Greece and Rome; but they were also accused of having placed the head of an ass in the most sacred chamber of their Temple. They were described as most tender and merciful, avoiding any act of cruelty as a sin, and forbidding the use of blood for food; yet some writers charged them with ferocity and love of battle. All the world knew that they had dared challenge the might of imperial Rome and for four years had withstood her best legions. Even in defeat they seemed to prosper. They still continued to live according to their ancestral rites, and were winning proselytes to their faith in the highest circles. What was the truth about them?

Josephus was determined that the tone of his book should be far different from that of *The Jewish War*. It was to be more than a masterpiece, giving evidence of his own powers.

His first book had been a celebration of the triumph of Rome; his new work was to describe the greatness of the Jew. He knew at last that his connection with his people was unbreakable. He might eat forbidden food, enter into prohibited marriages, violate the Sabbath and the festivals; but he could not tear himself from the associations in which the world placed him. He may even have attributed some of his misfortunes to his Judaism; and the thought may well have occurred to him that had he striven to exalt his faith and his nation in the eyes of the world, he would not have fallen so low from his high estate. When he had written the *Jewish War,* he had felt that there was no need for a further description of the earlier Jewish history. Now he realized that it was essential. The Roman world must be taught that the Jewish people, weak in war, had an ancient lineage and a proud tradition, that it was at least as important in the development of civilization as the Greeks. A century before him, Dionysius of Halicarnassus had written a monumental *Roman Archaeology,* in twenty books; Josephus decided to write a *Jewish Archaeology* of exactly the same length. This similarity was striking enough. To emphasize it, Josephus noted a contrast. He would not, he said, include in his work any admixture of "the unseemly mythology current among others."

For fourteen years Josephus devoted himself indefatigably to his task. He paraphrased the whole of the Pentateuch, chapter by chapter, from the story of the Creation until the entrance of the Jews into Canaan. He then took up the prophetic books, using both the Scriptures and other records, and traced his people's history until his own time. He omitted the story of the Golden Calf and the Broken Tablets, which were so little to the credit of the Jews; he discussed at length the excellence of the Mosaic Law; noted the Legislator's candid acknowledgment of his indebtedness to the alien Jethro for the establishment of the Jewish judicial system; took pains to describe the Pharisees in far more favorable colors than he had used in *The Jewish War,* and now gave them, instead of the Essenes, the first place among the Jewish sects; [14] disparaged rather than praised the House of Herod; and actually denounced the high priest, Hanan, to whom he had devoted a panegyric in the earlier work. [15]

The book was thus primarily intended to be a defense of official, contemporary, Pharisaic Judaism against the attack of anti-semites. But there is evidence that the author was concerned not only with the defense of his people against their enemies, but with justification of himself before God. Anxiety for the Future Life as well as fear of persecutors was filling his heart. He was merely at the beginning of middle age, but the hand of Time was weighing heavily upon him. The shadow of death, which was to come to him in his early sixties, already tormented him. Before he completed his work he became so weary that he was compelled to hand over his notes to assistants who wrote four books, one-fifth of the whole, for him. [16] Long before he had reached that point, however, he had introduced into the book what seems to be a confession of his sin in forsaking his people. Describing King Saul's waywardness after his exaltation to the throne, he says:

"Now this king . . . gives all to understand and consider the disposition of men, that while they are private persons, and in low condition, because it is not in their power to indulge nature, nor to venture upon what they wish for, they are equitable and moderate, and pursue nothing but what is just, and bend their whole minds and labors that way; then it is that they have this belief about

God, that He is present to all actions of their lives, and that He
not only sees their actions that are done, but clearly knows their
thoughts also, whence these actions do arise. But when they are
once advanced into power and authority they put off all such
notions, and as if they were no other than actors upon a theater,
they disguise parts and manners, and take up boldness, insolence
and a contempt of both human and divine laws, and this at a time
when they stand especially in need of piety and righteousness,
because they are then most of all exposed to envy, and all they
think and all they say are in view of all men; then it is that they
become so insolent in all their actions as though God saw them no
longer, or were overawed by their power, their fear of rumors, their
willful hates, their irrational loves—these seem to them to be authentic, and firm, and true, and pleasing both to men and God;
but as to what will come hereafter, they have not the least regard
for it." [17]

What could this passionate outburst connote? Was he de-
nouncing the men of power who now ignored him, or was he
crying out against his earlier self, for his treatment of his
inferiors? Perhaps it was both. The bauble of literary fame,
like that of political advancement, was proving itself absurdly
childish and contemptible. The Future Life was rising to
mock all his vaunted achievements. The former disciple of
the sages had dared face Vespasian and Titus; but could he
appear before God? He firmly believed in the hereafter, and
in the messianic prophecies of Daniel.[18] What was he to do
when God would arise? What answer would he make for a
life of self-indulgence and hopeless apostasy? The very riches
and luxury with which he was surrounded would testify
against him in the Day of Judgment. Of what account were
his vaunted achievements? Of what use would be recognition
among the pagans? If his book were to make its way into

every library in the world, how would that avail him, if he lost his immortality? He was a Faust who dared not keep his agreement. He had rushed from the camp of rebellion to the very presence of Vespasian; but he could not come from apostasy into the presence of God. He could not claim ignorance; he could not claim misunderstanding; he could not claim undue temptation. And yet, surrounding him on all sides, was the evidence of his guilt. His wealth came from the rents of robbed estates which he had accepted from the despoiling Roman. Its rightful owners were—where? It was frightful to think. In the grave, in hopeless bondage, in houses of infamy.

Reason dictated the surrender of his affluence. But he had never been able to follow Reason, so long as an alternative presented itself. The curious hesitancy, weakness of will and doubt of his own judgment, which had made him join the rebellion when he knew it was doomed to failure, which had prevented him from surrendering to Vespasian before the siege of Jotapata and had kept him in that ill-fated fortress until it was too late to escape, was still a fundamental part of his character. He was incapable of sacrifice of present goods even for permanent happiness.

There was one thing he could do: he could indulge in passionate self-pity; he could weep. Others might envy him; they could not measure the depth of his inner unhappiness. He almost persuaded himself that he had always striven to do right, that he had acted unselfishly and that he had sought nothing but the good of his people. Rightly considered, his state was unenviable. He was spending his days in a gilded cage, in an imposing mausoleum. Better by far had it been for him to have remained with his fellow-students in Palestine. He would have dwelt in a miserable hovel, rather

than in a magnificent palace; he would have worn a scholar's
gulta rather than a Roman toga; he would have spoken correct Aramaic rather than faulty Latin. But he would have
consorted with people he loved rather than those he feared;
he would have used his unquestioned talents to build the
Divine Law rather than to fawn on a mortal prince. He had
given up more than anyone could realize; everything, in fact,
that could make life worthwhile. Not, however, to serve his
own purpose, but through the will of God.[19] Perhaps it was
to defend his people against their calumniators that he had
been sent to Rome. No one was better fitted for the task;
there were hardly three men in the world who combined in
themselves such thorough knowledge of Judaism and such
complete mastery of the Greek tongue.[20] Philo had written in
defense of the Jews, but he was ignorant of the Palestinian
traditions. Josephus had demonstrated his capability as a Jewish advocate in his *Archaeology;* he would be even more
thorough and comprehensive in other works. He projected
books on Jewish laws and customs, and on Jewish philosophy;
and he actually completed a work, usually called *Against
Apion,* in which he demolished the arguments of the anti-
semites, demonstrating both the antiquity of the Jews and
the beauty of their faith.

He had at last completed the full circle of his development.
He was no longer a Hellenist but, in spirit at least, a true
Palestinian. He was not ashamed to confess publicly his inability to master the correct pronunciation of Greek, or his
need for assistants in his literary efforts.[21] He proudly declares
that he and the other Jews have nothing but contempt for
these arts, which are "common not only to all sorts of free-
men, but to as many of the servants as please to learn
them."[22] The Jews, on the contrary, "gave him testimony

of being a wise man who is fully acquainted with our laws, and is able to interpret their meaning." The man who had fled from his people and had helped to hand them over into the hands of their conquerors, could now write, "Robbed (Gk. *Sterethomen*) though we be of wealth, of cities, of all good things, our Law at least remains immortal; and there is not a Jew so distant from his country, so much in awe of a cruel despot, but has more fear of the Law than of him." [23]

The opinions held about him by the Greeks now worried him as little as had the opinions of the Jews when he first came to Rome. Now he was deeply wounded when he was attacked by his own people. When, a few years after the visit of the rabbinical commission to Rome, some Palestinians published a history reflecting discredit on him, he felt bound to reply in his vigorous, but unfortunately far from clear or cogent, *Autobiography*. Here he tried to present himself as the persecuted lover of his people, whom self-seeking egotists tried to destroy. He could not entirely suppress his pride in the skillful maneuvers through which he had frustrated their designs; in some tactless moments he included facts which hurt his argument. He contradicted much that he had written in the *Jewish War;* and produced a literary work inferior both in style and in power. But he felt that he had vindicated himself; and that was sufficient for him.

Josephus was, doubtless, already in this final state of mind in the year 95 when the sages came to Rome. A year or two had passed since his completion of his *Jewish Archaeology,* but the Palestinian authorities could hardly have been acquainted with its contents. They could have remembered him only as the author of the Aramaic draft of *The Jewish War.* Yet members of the Roman community must have informed them of the change which had come over him since the death of Titus. Perhaps he had intimated to friends his desire to meet the sages. Joshua, at any rate, felt that they ought to call on him.

"Shall we visit our comrade, the philosopher?" he asked Gamaliel one evening.

"No," answered Gamaliel, unwilling, doubtless, to accept any kindness from his father's old enemy, the man whom the nationalists considered an arch-traitor.

It was characteristic of the changed relations between the two scholars that when the next morning Joshua repeated the request, saying, "Let us go and visit our comrade, the philosopher," Gamaliel agreed. Thereupon they all called on him, Gamaliel walking in the middle, Joshua and Eleazar ben Azariah on his right, and Akiba on his left. When they arrived at his door, they rapped thrice before any reply came. Then the door was opened. To their astonishment, he knew them. "Peace on you, sages of Israel," he said, "and to Rabban Gamaliel, above all."

For generations scholars in Palestine repeated this story, marveling at the skillful courtesy of the simple greeting. "Had he said, 'Peace on you, Rabban Gamaliel,' he would have offended the others; had he said, 'Peace on you, sages of Israel,' he would have offended Gamaliel." [24]

Perhaps it was in gratitude for this visit that Josephus, a few years later, made his laudatory mention of Gamaliel's father in the *Autobiography*. What transpired at the meeting remains unknown; the citizen of Rome could not be quoted in the academy, and so his remarks were lost to the rabbinic tradition. Yet there is one curious passage in the Sifre,[25] which seems to contain a cautiously worded allusion to Josephus's condition. As usual, the sages utilized their observation of their contemporary's experience to illumine a passage in

Scripture, the final verses in the Book of Kings, which describe the liberation of King Jehoiachin from the prison into which Nebuchadnezzar had thrown him. We are told that Nebuchadnezzar's successor, Evil-merodach, "spake kindly" to Jehoiachin and "set his throne above the thrones of the kings that were with him in Babylon. And he changed his prison garments, and did eat bread before him continually all the days of his life. And for his allowance, there was a continual allowance given him of the King, every day a portion, all the days of his life" (II Kings 25: 27). As they read this passage, the sages inevitably thought of their contemporary, Josephus, who, like the ancient king, had been elevated by the conqueror, and dwelt in an imperial palace. And from him their minds turned to his comrades, whose bodies still lay unburied on the battlefields of Palestine. They, too, had a biblical prototype, in King Jehoiakim, who died during Nebuchadnezzar's siege of Jerusalem, and could therefore not be given proper burial. Yet the prophet had declared that there was less occasion to weep for the unburied Jehoiakim than for the fortunate Jehoiachin. "We are thus taught," the Sifre remarks, "that the dead Jehoiakim, who lay exposed to the heat of the day and the cold of the night, was yet in better case than the living Jehoiachin, whose throne was above that of the other kings, and *who ate and drank in a royal palace!*"

During the Passover festival, a violent quarrel broke out between Gamaliel and Akiba, reminiscent of the struggles which had led to the overturn at Yabneh. As usual, the trouble arose from a difference regarding a trivial question of ceremonial. Gamaliel's custom forbade him to set up the candelabrum on festival nights; it had to be prepared before dark. The other sages agreed that this was the rule for the

Sabbath, but they denied that it applied to other holidays. On one of the festival nights, Akiba, finding the room dark and the candelabrum in parts, proceeded to set it up, without regard to Gamaliel's convictions on the subject. Gamaliel regarded this as a grave personal offense, for it was the first time that Akiba had *transgressed* a custom which Gamaliel considered sacred. On the earlier occasions when Akiba had defied Gamaliel, he had taken the severer view, and was to that extent justified. But in this instance, his view was the more lenient. Moreover, the prohibition against setting up the candelabrum had not originated with Gamaliel; he had received it from his father. It seemed incredible that this upstart from the Judean countryside should dare to violate such a custom in the presence of the Nasi.

"Why do you always put your head into quarrels?" Gamaliel cried.

"You have taught us," Akiba answered, as on a former occasion, "that the decision of the majority is binding, and the majority agrees with me in this." [26]

The sages would probably have returned empty-handed, had not Domitian died during their stay in Rome. He was succeeded in September, 96, by Nerva, the first of the five good Emperors, who ruled only sixteen months, yet in this short time managed to bring new hope to the Jews, both at Rome and in distant Palestine. A medal was struck in honor of the occasion bearing the likeness of the Emperor on one side, and on the other, the words: *Fisci Judaici Calumnia Sublata.*

The visit to Rome marks a turning point in Akiba's life. The talmudic sages indicate this when they remark, with that special delight which they find in the discovery of any similarity between Akiba and Moses, that both men were in recognized positions of authority for the same duration of time, forty years.[27] To arrive at this calculation, Akiba's activity must be computed from the year 97, when he returned from Rome. Had Akiba died before he undertook this diplomatic task, he would be remembered as the most brilliant member of the illustrious academy at Yabneh. But from that point on, his achievement as a leader competes with, and eventually overshadows, his reputation as a scholar. To what extent the commission owed its success to his adroitness and personal charm we are not told. Probably as one of the younger members he was kept in the background during the conversations with the more distinguished officials. But in such missions the formal meeting with the final authority is frequently of less permanent importance than the preliminary work done in conference with secretaries and other subordinates. The story of his encounter with the Roman general, and the friendship which later developed between him and Rufus, as well as the significant fact that from the time of his return he was held in increasing reverence by both his colleagues and the masses, all point to distinguished services by him during this difficult time.

For the thirteen years after his return, from 97 to 110, while the Jewish community enjoyed unusual prosperity and peace, Akiba devoted himself to the formulation of his juristic principles, the clarification of his theological ideas and the establishment of his school.

"To what may Akiba be compared?" asked one of his pupils, describing the activities in which he engaged at this time. "To a peddler who goes about from farm to farm. Here he obtains wheat, there barley, and in a third place, spelt. When he comes home he arranges them all in their respective bins. So Akiba went about from scholar to scholar, getting all the traditions he could; and then he proceeded to arrange them in an orderly granary." [28] It is probable that the division of the Mishna into six orders, and even the subdivision into treatises, go back to him.

Except for a few treatises describing the ancient Temple and its service, the earlier compilations were not arranged by subject-matter at all. They were strings of legal norms put together according to the similarity of their literary formulation.[29] There was, for instance, one collection which began: "The First Adar and the Second Adar are alike except that the reading of the scroll of Esther and the gifts to the poor are observed only in the Second Adar; festivals and the Sabbath are alike, except that on the festivals food may be prepared; the Day of Atonement and the Sabbath are alike, except that one who willfully violates the Sabbath may be punished by a human court, while the violation of the Day of Atonement is punishable only by God." A number of other statements of the same kind are given, having no inner connection whatever, put together merely because their similarity of formulation made a kind of mnemonic. Akiba realized that while such a method was satisfactory for fragments of the Law, it was altogether inadequate for a complete code. A code of Jewish Law required logical division and subdivision, and must sacrifice rhythm to reason.

Having decided on the method which he would follow in the arrangement of his material, Akiba even more boldly replaced ancient norms with others which represented his own opinions. Such, however, was the authority he came to enjoy that within a generation the rejected material was almost unknown.[30] Indeed, much of it has been irrevocably lost, but a few fragments were preserved and handed down by antiquarians like Akiba's disciple, Jose ben Halafta.[31] In many other instances, the views of the Hillelites, while known and recognized, had not yet been reduced to standard norms. Akiba supplied this need.[32]

The trenchant, epigrammatic style which he had developed for his apothegms and decisions proved invaluable to him in his new activity. The effective combination of brevity and precision was a boon to the student, who had to memorize the text, and it set a good example for all future codifiers. His Mishna became so popular in his own lifetime that even those parts which he rejected in his older years continued to be studied.[33] Being oral texts, they could not be issued in new editions; once memorized, they could not be withdrawn from circulation, as it were.[34] The original statements were repeated in the academies, with the qualifying remark that Akiba had changed his mind about them, in part.

The later talmudists rated these achievements so high that they declared Akiba had saved the Torah from oblivion. They ranked his work with the discovery of the Law in the days of Josiah and Ezra. "Had not Shaphan arisen in his time, and Ezra in his time, and Akiba in his time," a homilist of the next century remarks, "would not the Law have been forgotten in Israel?" [35] Some of the more imaginative sages saw in Akiba a second Moses. In fact, one of them describes Moses as praying that God might choose Akiba to give the Law to Israel.

When Moses ascended into the heavens, he found God binding small coronets about the letters of the Law.

"Why these coronets?" Moses asked.

"Because," God replied, "at the end of many generations there will arise a scholar by the name of Akiba ben Joseph, who will interpret each one of these letters."

"Show him to me," asked Moses. But when Akiba arose in the

vision of the future, and Moses heard him discussing the Law, the great prophet called out, "Master of the Universe, dost Thou have such a man before Thee and yet givest the Torah to Thy people through me?"

"Be silent," God replied, "such is My thought." [36]

Indeed, one of the greatest scholars of the following century, Simeon ben Lakish, insists that God *revealed Akiba's activity to Adam.* The ancestor of the human race was permitted to see each generation with its leaders, its sages and its teachers. But apparently Adam remained unmoved with the achievements and distinction of his posterity until Akiba appeared. "He rejoiced in Akiba's learning and was saddened by his death," says Simeon ben Lakish.[37]

For centuries the Mishna of Akiba was recalled as an outstanding achievement of rabbinic learning. Not only Jewish scholars but Christian Church Fathers referred to it.[38] One of the best-informed authorities of the third century tells us that it became the core of the Mishna of Meir, which in turn was incorporated into the final redaction of Judah the Patriarch—still the basic codification of rabbinic Law.[39]

"The truths which were not revealed to Moses," says a later teacher in his enthusiasm, "were uncovered to Akiba"! [40] When he left Palestine on his various journeys, "there remained not his equal in all the land," asserted his younger contemporaries.[41] When he died, "the arms of the Law were broken, and the fountains of wisdom were stopped up." [42] No wonder that legend describes him as being buried by none other than Elijah.[43]

Akiba's influence in the academy gradually became paramount. The principle, accepted by later talmudists and codifiers, that Akiba's opinion must be given preference to that

of any of his colleagues doubtless originated in the attitude
taken toward him in his own lifetime.[44] Sometimes his opponents, losing patience with his mode of inference, would cry
out bitterly against him. His insistence that words which were
not essential to the meaning of a passage must have some
special significance. His new rules of hermeneutics, and his
utter independence of tradition were freely attacked. "Akiba,"
Eleazar ben Azariah once shouted at him, "even if you continue to repeat for a whole day that the superfluous word
proves your point, we will not listen to you!" [45] In his arguments Akiba drew on every source of experience. Sometimes
he would even fall back upon his knowledge of animal
anatomy, acquired during his shepherd days. Thus in a
controversy with Johanan ben Nuri regarding the ritual status
of an animal, Akiba maintained that it was "fit," and that
when it was slaughtered its organs would demonstrate this.
Although his prediction was only partly fulfilled, Akiba
would not yield. "How long will you continue to feed our
people forbidden food?" Johanan, exasperated at this intransigeancy, cried to Akiba.

"And how long will you continue to waste our people's
money?" retorted Akiba.[46]

Johanan was more successful in his protest against Akiba's
rigorous rule recommending the divorce of a wife who is the
subject of evil gossip, though there be no proof of her in-
fidelity. "If we accept your opinion," Johanan ben Nuri said,
"not a single daughter of Abraham will be safe with her
husband. Yet the Torah says that a woman shall be divorced
only if the husband find some unseemly thing in her (Deut.
24:1). And again we read, 'At the mouth of two witnesses,
or at the mouth of three witnesses, shall a matter be established'" (Deut. 19:15).[47]

Another scholar, Yeshebab, also objected vehemently to Akiba's stringency in regard to questions of chastity and marriage. "Come and let us cry out against Akiba ben Joseph," he said, "for his rule unduly extends the taint of illegitimacy in Israel." [48]

It was only occasionally that Akiba was outvoted in the academy. Johanan ben Nuri sorrowfully admitted this to his fellow-Galilean, Halafta, whom he visited. Twice in the course of their discussions of various legal matters, he remarked, "I agree with you on this point, but what can be done, since Akiba opposes us?" [49]

Akiba's dialectic genius could not of itself have given him this complete control; he had, in addition, the devotion of a group of younger colleagues. The most important of these was Ben Azzai, a remarkable sage, whose character and history are hardly inferior in interest to those of Akiba himself. He was apparently a provincial from Galilee, and he retained throughout his life some of the intellectual and emotional prejudices of that district. It was perhaps to his origin in the semi-pagan North that he owed his knowledge of Greek. Even more important, he inherited from the country a deep respect for the memory of Akabiah ben Mahalalel, that famous patrician sage, the contemporary of Gamaliel I, who had been expelled from the Pharisaic order for intransigeancy. Most of the scholars at Yabneh paid no attention to the traditions which were preserved from Akabiah, but Ben Azzai went so far as to quote verbatim—with slight additions and interpolations—a heterodox maxim he had composed: "He who considers four things will never commit a transgression: Whence he comes, whither he goes, what he is destined to become, and who is his Judge. Whence does he come? Out of darkness. Whither does he go? To the deepest darkness.

What is he destined to become? Dust and worms. Who is his Judge? The King of Kings." [50] This unequivocal denial of personal immortality was doubtless partly responsible for the severe punishment meted out to Akabiah; and only a bold man would repeat it in the academy after half a century. True, Ben Azzai embellished the statement with additions which demonstrated his own orthodoxy, yet the citation proved him an adherent and admirer of the ousted scholar. [51]

With such a background we should naturally have expected Ben Azzai to join the patricians. But his poverty during the early days in Yabneh drove him into the ranks of the plebeians. He did not earn enough to supply his personal wants and, of course, could not even think of marriage. When he was urged to marry a wife who would support him, or to find one who would be content with his modest income, he said: "There are three people whose life cannot be called life at all: he who must rely on the table of another, he who lives in another man's garret, and he who is ruled by his wife." [52] Pride and independence were characteristic of Galilee. Akiba had acknowledged his poverty and borne its consequences cheerfully; Ben Azzai did neither. It was inevitable that such a person should suffer much at the hands of his colleagues. When he once remarked, innocently, that "a person who has no children limits, as it were, the image of God," Eleazar ben Azariah turned upon him with the ruthless retort, "There are those who are fair in precept, and fair in deed. Ben Azzai is fair in precept, but not in deed."

Deeply humiliated, poor Ben Azzai could only stammer, "What shall I do? My spirit desires the Law. The world must be preserved by others." [53]

Ultimately he married one of Akiba's daughters who, emulating her mother's romantic example, undertook to provide for him.[54] Perhaps Ben Azzai was ready to accept from Akiba's child the support which he would have spurned at the hands of another, because he knew that the family tradition would enable him to retain his self-respect and sense of independence in spite of the arrangement.

This new tie, naturally, brought Ben Azzai even closer to Akiba, of whom he spoke with unsurpassed admiration. "Compared with this baldhead," he once said of his father-in-law, "all the sages of Israel are as inconsequential as the dried skin of garlic." [55] When compelled to disagree with Akiba, he would begin with an apology. "I speak not as one who disagrees with his master, but rather as one who supplements his words." [56] And indeed, his disagreement arose most frequently from an excess of plebeian zeal, natural to a recent convert.

Having studied under Joshua ben Hananya longer than Akiba, Ben Azzai was frequently able to correct his master's traditions. "So did Joshua teach," Ben Azzai would remark.[57] On a few rare occasions, Ben Azzai opposed Akiba's views without the support of an older tradition. One such controversy arose from the difference in the early training of the two men, for Akiba believed in the dignity of labor, while Ben Azzai could not free himself from the Galilean prejudice against it. This disagreement led to a controversy regarding the right of the Temple to pay artisans out of gifts which it received.

"If a man give his estate to the Temple, and include in it animals which may be offered as sacrifice, they may be given as wages to workers," Akiba said.

"This is improper," said Ben Azzai. "Temple property can be exchanged only for money, not for labor." [58]

Closely associated with Akiba and Ben Azzai, was Simeon

ben Zoma, who, too, remained unmarried because of his poverty. He was more famous as a homilist than as a scholar, and even in his own field, he achieved glory rather for emphatic assertion than for artistic and skillful presentation. The foundation of his preachment was the ethical principle of contentment, which had been traditional with the plebeians for more than half a millennium. Indeed it was inevitable that it should arise and be sponsored by men who met frustration at every turn. Unless they could convince themselves that "everything which occurred was for the best," they could hardly have continued to live. When Ben Zoma, who earned little more than was essential to keep body and soul together, saw a crowd assembled anywhere, he would say, without any attempt at sarcasm or concealed bitterness, "Blessed be God, who created all these people to wait upon me. How much work did Adam perform before he could taste a bit of food? He had to plough and sow and reap and gather and thresh and winnow and select and grind and sift and knead and bake, and only then could he eat his bread, while I awake in the morning and find everything prepared for me. How many diligent workers must arise at dawn so that my needs may be satisfied when I awake!"

"A generous guest," he remarked, explaining the attitude which man should take to God, "says, 'Blessed may my host be. What good meat he put before me, what good bread he brought to me.' A bad guest says, rather, 'What did I enjoy of his viands? I ate one piece of meat and drank one cup of wine. The preparations he made were only for his wife and children.' " [59]

Among his most famous maxims are: "Who is a true sage? He who learns from every man. Who is truly strong? He who controls his passions. Who is truly wealthy? He who is content with his portion. Who is truly honored? He who honors his fellow-creatures." [60]

It is in these teachings of Ben Zoma that we must seek the interpretation of Akiba's principle, "It is forbidden to partake of any enjoyment in the world without pronouncing a benediction." [61]

Even Elisha ben Abuyah, Akiba's old opponent, now became reconciled to him, and joined him, Ben Azzai, and Ben Zoma in the organization of what we should call a philosophical society. [62] Akiba was the recognized leader of the group, and it was doubtless considered no mean achievement that he had made the patrician, who had formerly expressed such contempt for him, one of his followers.

Later legend tells how the four scholars, during one of their mystical reveries, entered Paradise. Before they undertook the perilous journey, Akiba said to them, "When you come to the pillars of pure marble, do not say, 'Water, water,' for it is written, 'He that speaketh falsehood shall not be established before mine eyes.'" (Ps. 101: 7). [63] What this peculiar cipher can mean, and from what context it was transferred to its present mythological setting, is a problem which modern scholarship has tried in vain to solve. The one fact which emerges out of the obscurity is the close association of the four scholars with mystical speculation.

How Akiba overcame Elisha's deep seated antagonism is not recorded; presumably the younger man finally fell victim, as had so many others before him, to the irresistible charm of that mighty personality. If so, this must be recorded as one of the most significant triumphs of Akiba's whole life. But from the beginning a tragic dénouement might have been foreseen. For Akiba alone among the four members of the society had a sufficiently powerful intellect to cope with the abstruse prob-

lems in the solution of which they were engaged. His phenomenal mind, which had discovered such an easy path
through the intricate labyrinth of the Law, and had, in addition, so successfully mastered the various arts of aggadic
oratory, diplomatic statesmanship and institutional adminis-
tration, could also adjust itself to the abstractions of theology
and metaphysics. Ben Azzai, though far inferior to Akiba, was
yet gifted with unusual assiduity, if not with extraordinary intellect.[64] Ben Zoma was eloquent but not profound. Elisha
ben Abuyah lacked even these endowments. He was intended
by nature for neither study nor abstract thought. He was, in
fact, a dilettante. His father, a wealthy landowner, had dedicated him to Jewish learning because he realized that, after
the destruction of the Temple, this course was the only road to
honor and influence.[65] But, though he had come to the academy at approximately the same time as Akiba, he had attained
to nothing like the proficiency of the former shepherd. He
had, it appears, a reasonably retentive memory, but the
few maxims which have been preserved from him indicate
neither originality nor depth. While his legal sayings and
decisions have disappeared, we can hardly believe that they
were either many or important, since the only later scholar
who is described as having studied under him at all was Meir.
Akiba's attempt to re-orientate the minds of these men after
they had reached maturity, could end only in disaster. Elisha
lost his faith, Ben Zoma his reason and Ben Azzai his life.[66]

But this tragic sequel was still far off in the unknown
future. For at least a decade Akiba continued to associate with
his three younger colleagues. Strong in his convictions, supported by numerous friends and disciples, he formulated his
doctrine and perfected his method.

Perhaps, however, the most distinguished person Akiba

drew into his circle was the famous proselyte, Aquila of Pontus. This Roman citizen, possessed of great wealth and considerable learning, had first become converted to Christianity, but had ultimately become a Jew and a faithful disciple of the rabbinical sages. In his love for the new faith and its literature, he decided to undertake a translation of the Scripture which would represent it more accurately than did the Septuagint. His work, of which only a few fragments survive, is a monument of industry, cleverness and deep-seated devotion. Akiba's influence is obvious throughout. Every Hebrew particle is rendered by a characteristic Greek word whether that makes sense or not. This naturally interferes with the flow of the Greek sentences and makes the translation almost unreadable. Yet the author was a gifted stylist. Where he drops these self-imposed bonds, his writing is far more fluent and beautiful than that of the Septuagint. It was certainly a happy day for Akiba and his colleagues when they discovered Aquila in their midst.

To offset these gains, Akiba had to deal with two opponents, who had entered the academy after him, but had now reached maturity and were providing leadership for the declining patrician cause—Jose the Galilean and Ishmael ben Elisha.

Jose's appearance in the conclave, years before the overthrow of Gamaliel, was almost as dramatic as Akiba's had been. The young man, who had come down from the north to complete his studies, sat quietly by, day after day, until on one occasion he suddenly joined forces with Tarfon in opposition to Ben Nannos and Akiba. "Ben Nannos had refuted Tarfon, when Jose the Galilean came to Tarfon's assistance and refuted Ben Nannos. Akiba then refuted Jose the Galilean. After some time, Jose the Galilean thought of an answer to Akiba, and he moved to reopen the discussion. 'Will you permit me to reply now?' Jose asked Akiba." Akiba agreed, and Jose presented an argument to which Akiba could offer no adequate answer. Thereupon the thirty-two sages who composed the conclave voted to support the views of Tarfon and Jose! [67]

Jose fulfilled the early promise to which the story testifies and became one of the leading teachers of the conclave's patrician wing. He revived the defense of the ancient Shammatic doctrines and proposed new rules in their spirit.[68] His brilliant mind would probably have brought him greater achievements had he not been burdened with a shrewish wife, who wondered, doubtless, that he should waste time with scholars when he could be working for his family.[69]

Ishmael ben Elisha was a younger and far more forceful man. Descended from a patrician, priestly family, he had all the virtues, and also all the failings, of his class. He was morose, narrow, chauvinistic and reactionary, but also generous, tender, candid, direct and determined. Joshua ben Hananya, who had been his main teacher, had struggled in vain to transform him into a Hillelite; he accepted the plebeian teachings so far as they had been formulated, but he refused to apply their underlying conceptions to changing conditions. One of his foremost principles from the beginning of his studies had been that the Torah must be interpreted like any other literary document, and he had therefore opposed the new and ingenious rules of hermeneutics introduced by Nahum of Gimzo and Akiba. When Eliezer ben Hyrkanos, who in general agreed with him in this, used these weapons in defense of a patrician teaching, Ishmael, although much younger, and hardly more than a pupil, protested. "You say to the verse, 'Be silent, until I interpret you!'" he remonstrated. To which Eliezer retorted with his usual brusqueness, "You are as unproductive as a highland palm!" [70] In time, however, this particular palm did bear fruit, and of a kind which would have appealed to Eliezer's palate. But that was long after the latter had been expelled from the conclave and after Ishmael had already become Akiba's foremost antagonist, the leader of the reconstructed patrician opposition.

The issues between Ishmael and Akiba were in principle identical with those which had divided the Shammaites and the Hillelites and had led to the ousting of Eliezer ben Hyrkanos and the temporary removal of Gamaliel II. Ishmael defended the rights and traditions of the patricians, the farmers and the priests, while Akiba opposed them. So obviously did Ishmael represent ecclesiastical opinion in his decisions that his colleagues coined the saying: "Ishmael, the priest, favors the priests." [71]

The fact is, however, Ishmael was not merely pro-priestly; he was also pro-agrarian, pro-patrician, and pro-property. He upheld the views of his class not out of conscious bias, but because he could not free himself from its point of view.

For more than twenty years, he and Akiba were engaged in an almost continual debate regarding every conceivable aspect of Jewish life: law, ceremonial, history, future, and policy toward Rome. Each of the two teachers gathered about him a school of followers who in turn became the teachers of the subsequent generation and thus exercised a determining influence on the development of talmudic thought. The later sages grouped them together as the "fathers of the rabbinic world." [72]

The seat of the private academy, which Akiba founded while still attending the sessions of the conclave, was the little village of Bene Berak, a short distance from Yabneh.[73] The conclave at Yabneh had assembled in a vineyard; Eliezer ben Hyrkanos had given his decision from a rock; Akiba preferred to lecture in the shade of a broad-leaved fig tree. Students flocked to him from all parts of the country and were drawn from the most diversified groups. There were among them Simeon, the son of that wealthy Galilean, Yohai, who remained on terms of intimate friendship with the Roman governors even during the Bar Kokba rebellion and the Hadrianic persecution;[74] Meir, the enigmatic scholar, who earned a livelihood as a scribe, but, married to the daughter of the aristocratic Haninah ben Teradyon, disdained the companionship of the ordinary proletariat and continually tried to identify himself with the patricians, both in thought and in action;[75] Jose ben Halafta, the humble tanner, whose asceticism and self-control are described in terms which would be incredible were they not so well authenticated;[76] Judah ben Ilai, whose poverty was such that at one time he and his wife possessed but a single over-garment which they used in turn, and who was, nevertheless, one of the happiest men in the whole rabbinic tradition;[77] Eleazar ben Shammua, the priest; Nehemiah, the potter; Johanan, the cobbler; Benjamin, the Egyptian proselyte; Hanina ben Hakinai, the mystic;[78] and others of whom we know nothing more than their names. The disciples of Ishmael, who also had a private academy, were naturally drawn from a narrower circle. Most of them were rich men; for example, Josiah, Isaac, and Nathan the Babylonian, who was related to the exilarch. Jonathan, who alone among Ishmael's pupils upheld plebeian views, was a priest, and it was perhaps for that reason that he was admitted into the aristocratic academy.[79]

In his relations with his students, Akiba displayed the same charm and courtesy which had won him the affection of his masters and his colleagues. When any of the young men fell ill the Master was sure to visit him. He did not consider it beneath his dignity on such a visit to arrange his pupil's room, to sweep the floor or perform any other service. "Whosoever neglects the duty of visiting the sick," he taught, "is guilty of shedding blood." [80]

If any especially sensitive student felt aggrieved by some untoward incident, such as frequently occurs in academic life, Akiba was quick to appease him. Perhaps he had the greatest difficulty with Simeon ben Yohai, a provincial who had not the wit or impulse to conceal his vanity, bordering on megalomania. "I have looked about for those destined to Paradise," Simeon once said, "and they are few indeed. If there be three, my son Eleazar and I are of them; if there be two, they are my son and I; if there be one, it is I." [81] "My merit is sufficient to free the world from punishment for sin from the day of my birth until now; and if my son Eleazar should join me, we might free it from all the sins which have accumulated from the day of Creation." [82] "My master, Akiba, gave four interpretations with which I disagree, and my opinion appears to be the more correct," [83] he said, in an age when even Ben Azzai apologized for being compelled to differ with the great sage. But even more amazingly—almost blasphemously—Simeon remarks, "There are four things which the Holy One, blessed be He, hates, and I too dislike." [84] What the four things were is perhaps of less interest than the naïve temerity of the remark. No wonder this extraordinary young man was hurt when Akiba showed a preference for Meir.

But the master, understanding something of the suppressions which sought such fantastic compensation, said to him, "My child, it is enough for thee that thy Creator and I recog-

nize thy powers!" [85] So much did Simeon appreciate this
kindness that he became more deeply attached to Akiba than
to any other person, and he had his moments of humility too.
"My children," he said many years later to his disciples, "study
my principles, for I have gleaned them carefully from those
handed to me by my master, Akiba." [86]

Akiba's power over his disciples arose not merely from his
tenderness to them, but from his pedagogic ability. If, as
Fenelon says, *"L'ordre est ce qu'il y a de plus rare dans les
opérations de l'esprit,"* Akiba's contribution to the spirit of
rabbinic Judaism cannot be overestimated.

His part in the making of the Mishna has already been
described. But the codification of the law was only part of his
contribution. He also arranged the laws and traditions as
comments on the biblical verses from which they were derived. Two of his pupils, Judah and Simeon, preferred this
method, which they developed even further, while two others,
Meir and Jose, made Akiba's codes the foundation of their
compilations.[87]

Ishmael did not, so far as we know, undertake the formulation of any codes, but he did compile commentaries on the
Pentateuch, which, like those of Akiba, became a framework
for the additions of his disciples and their successors.

These works were not put into writing, for it was a cardinal
principle of Pharisaism at the time that rabbinic traditions
must be preserved orally.[88] They were handed down from
generation to generation by a special class of professional
memorizers. Only in the fifth century, perhaps even later,
when it became obvious that any further attempt to retain the
old tradition would result in the disappearance of the whole
Law, was permission granted to intrust this material to parchment. During the three centuries in which the books had

remained an oral tradition, they had naturally changed considerably in form. Yet even now the stamp of the opposing schools is still clear, and permits us to reconstruct with reasonable accuracy the methods of teaching and inference which were current in the days of Akiba and Ishmael, seventeen centuries ago.[89]

Akiba's mode of interpretation of Scripture is, as we would expect, a development of that which he derived from his master, Nahum of Gimzo. Superfluous letters, words and verses are the meat whereon he thrives. By the use of them he is able to read his whole juristic program into the Scriptures. But what he calls superfluous words would hardly seem such to us. Thus he maintains that wherever the Scriptures insert the word *lemor* (which in biblical Hebrew always introduces direct discourse) special significance attaches to that fact.[90] The juxtaposition of the various chapters has a meaning which must be discovered.[91] He rejected the old Hillelite principle of inference by generalization from particulars, and replaced it with a curious and complicated rule of his own invention which he called "Inclusion and Limitation." Neither rhetoric nor grammar offered a bar to his imaginative argument. Indeed, were we to accept at their face value the technical reasons he gives for his decisions, we should be forced to the conclusion that, far from being the greatest of the talmudists, he was simply a brilliant example of extraordinary—but wasted—ingenuity.[92] But the rules which he derives through his curious and intricate logic are so reasonable that when we examine them we are even more impressed with his judgment as jurist, than with his skill as debater. It is obvious that he considered the interpretation of the written law merely a form which had to be followed in the derivation of desirable rules from the scriptural text.

Ishmael opposed this whole system of interpretation. "The Scriptures speak in human language," he maintained.[93] Hebrew has its grammar and its rhetoric with rules which bind even divine utterance. The only arguments Ishmael recognized were those based on the traditional rules of Hillel which, however they might have been extended in actual academic and juristic usage, had roots at least in ordinary logic. These included such modes of argument as *a fortiori,* analogy and simple generalization; and such further rules as, "When two verses seem to contradict each other, you cannot solve the difficulty by a compromise until you discover a third verse substantiating your opinion." [94]

The difference between Akiba and Ishmael in the technique of demonstration was quite distinct from their equally comprehensive and vastly more significant opposition with regard to the content of the rules which were established. The argumentative use of superfluous letters which, since Akiba, had become identified with the plebeian faction, was already known to Eliezer, Akiba's patrician teacher. Indeed, he had been rebuked for this by Ishmael himself. On the other hand, the rules of interpretation to which the patrician-provincial, Ishmael, adhered were derived from the system established by Hillel, the founder of the plebeian school. These seeming contradictions have confused and misled the historians of the period, who have struggled hard to interpret Ishmael as a Hillelite, and have been altogether at a loss regarding Akiba. It was a purely fortuitous circumstance, quite unconnected with their respective philosophies, which made Ishmael, the future spokesman of the patrician faction, a disciple of Joshua, the foremost plebeian of his age. Inevitably, when Ishmael became a recognized scholar, he reverted to the teachings which were suited to his class and his temperament. With equal inevitability, he continued throughout his life to use the intellectual tools which he had received in his master's schoolhouse. Hence, the patrician came to be the protagonist of Hillel's technique of interpretation. To use a talmudic metaphor, he accepted the husk of his master's teachings but rejected the kernel.

Akiba's situation was different from Ishmael's. He was driven to seek a new method of interpretation by the necessity of basing his revolutionary doctrines on a recognized foundation. He was trying to change the complexion of the inherited Law. To accomplish this he had to find an authority superior to that of his predecessors and accepted by everyone. Only one instrument could fulfil these requirements—Scripture itself. Had Joshua ben Hananya and the older plebeians opposed Akiba in his rejection of the technique of interpretation which had become traditional among them, it might have gone hard with the young man. But these teachers were far more concerned with the substance of the Law than with the mode of its demonstration, and gladly accepted Akiba's proffer of assistance, whatever the weapons he chose. When Joshua praised Akiba for having discovered proof of a plebeian rule which Johanan ben Zakkai had declared undemonstrable, plebeian opposition to Akiba's technique of exegesis vanished.[95] Thereafter Akiba's arguments were heard in the conclave with the same respect as was accorded to those of his opponents; his methods had supplemented, if they had not supplanted, those of Hillel.

One of Akiba's rules was destined to become especially famous; indeed it has, with slightly changed significance, passed into a proverb. He used to say "Between a wide and a limited interpretation, choose the limited." [96] It would be easy to show that he himself violated this rule frequently; but its formulation brings a breath of wholesome logic into the stuffy atmosphere of academic technicalities. It shows that Akiba's mind was logical; when he departed from scientific ratiocination it was not because he had become confused in the web of his own words but because he was seeking to serve a higher cause than literal exegesis—the cause of human happiness.

When his colleagues mocked his arbitrary interpretations, Akiba simply replied by citing the verse, "For it is no empty thing for you" (Deut. 32:47). "And," he continued, "if you think it empty, it is because of your inability to interpret it!" [97] No part of the Torah is devoid of meaning for the scholar.

Brilliant as Akiba's mind was, he valued erudition above acumen. Diligence he considered the most important part of a scholar's equipment. Having in mind the oriental habit of chanting one's studies, he would exhort his pupils: "Sing continuously, sing!" [98] The duty of the teacher was to repeat his instruction until the student understood it completely and clearly, and mastered it entirely. He must literally put the Torah "into his pupils' mouths" [99] as Moses was commanded to do (Deut. 31:19).

He had little respect for scholars who in their desire to be original made sure that they were not burdened with too much information. The preparation of the ideal teacher is described, he said, in the verse of Proverbs (5:15): "Drink water from thy cistern, and running water from thy fountain." The metaphor of the cistern, which only collects water, applied to one's student days, which should be spent in the mastery of old traditions. The disciple who has obeyed this rule, he assures us, will find that in his maturity fresh, living waters of original thought will come to him, and that disciples will gather about him to drink from them.[100]

While he considered erudition of primary importance, he endeavored in his discussions to sharpen his pupils' dialectic. The lecture generally began with a call for information. "Anyone having any information on the question before us today is requested to give it," he would say. If a student volunteered a tradition he had heard from some other master, Akiba would ask him to defend it. "Not he who answers quickly is worthy of praise, but he who can support his views," was his maxim.[101]

Never, either as student or as master, did he call for the adjournment of a lecture, except, characteristically, on the eves of the Passover and of the Day of Atonement.[102] On both occasions he would hurry home for the sake of the children. On the eve of the Passover, he wanted to begin the picturesque ceremony before they went to bed; on the eve of the Day of Atonement, he wanted to be sure that they got their meals before the Fast Day set in. Even when his son Simeon lay ill with a fatal disease, Akiba would not disrupt his class. One messenger came from home, saying "He has taken a turn for the worse." But Akiba did not stir. Another messenger came, and yet Akiba continued. Finally, word came that the young man had died. Thereupon Akiba arose, removed his phylacteries and tore his clothes, saying, "Until this moment, it was our duty to study; now we must pay honor to the dead"![103]

Yet Akiba was always mindful of the duty of his disciples to their families. Two of the young men who sat before him, Simeon ben Yohai and Hanina ben Hakinai, had left their homes to devote themselves entirely to their studies. One day Akiba said to Hanina, "Your daughter must be of marriageable age; go home and get her married." Hanina, who had not even written home during the years he had been at the academy, so frightened his wife by his sudden appearance that she fell in a swoon. "Never enter your house suddenly," Akiba remarked, with obvious reference to this accident.[104]

The duty of teaching seemed to him paramount. "Though you have given instruction to some disciples in your youth, you must continue to teach in old age," he said. "This is the meaning of Ecclesiastes 11:6, which reads, 'In the morning sow thy seed, and in the evening withhold not thy hand; for thou knowest not which shall prosper, this or that, or whether both shall be alike good.'" Ishmael, on the contrary, laid less stress on instruction and more on learning. "The verse means that even though you have studied much in your youth, you must continue to study in old age," he said.[105]

Akiba describes the value of a teacher to his pupils in three beautiful similes. The occasion of his remarks is itself interesting. According to a report, Eliezer ben Hyrkanos had boasted that "If all the seas were ink, and all the reeds pens, and the heavens and earth rolls of parchment and all men scribes, they would not suffice for the writing of the Torah which I have studied; yet have I not achieved more of the totality of the Torah than can be drawn up by inserting a finger into the sea; nor have my pupils taken from me more than a brush dipped into a bottle"!

When Akiba heard this he said, "I cannot even say that I have taken from my teacher even so much as he admits. What I received amounts to the fragrance given off by the citron, and the light taken from one candle to another, and the water drawn from a brook. The beneficiary enjoys the odor, increases the light, and is refreshed by the water; but the giver has lost nothing!"[106]

VI. ON THE HEIGHTS
AKIBA'S JURISTIC PHILOSOPHY

AKIBA'S various utterances regarding ethics, law, religion, theology and politics, form a complete, coherent and unified system, which we may rightly call a philosophy. His various decisions and apothegms were applications of general principles which were clear in his own mind, although he did not organize them for posterity in the form of abstract propositions. This was due first, to the nature of his judicial office, which required decisions in concrete cases rather than philosophic statements of general policy; and secondly to the Semitic tradition which, unlike the Hellenic, has never given up the primitive preference for the concrete and the individual. Perhaps we may summarize in the following principles his fundamental approach to the juristic problems he faced.

1. Whatever be the inequalities which we find in the world, we must not permit them to intrude on the worship of God. Hence, ceremonial law must be interpreted so as not to exclude the weaker social groups from participation, or to demand too heavy sacrifices from them. This implies that no opportunity may be given to the more fortunate to invent ceremonies or refinements of ritual which the poorer cannot imitate. Nor, on the other hand, may expensive devices be utilized as evasions of burdensome laws.

2. So far as the civil law is still fluid and open to interpretation, it is just to use this as a means for the rectification of social inequalities. Hence the rules of law should favor the

oppressed groups: the plebeian, the artisan-merchant, the shepherd, the slave, the women and children.

3. It is especially important that the prerogatives of the priests be limited, and that the gross inequality between them and the Levites be minimized.

4. The possibility that the emancipation of women may lead to the disruption of family life should be met by the imposition of severe penalties for faithlessness.

5. In the attempt to ameliorate the conditions of slaves, care must be taken to protect the status and rights of free labor.

6. Pious merchants must be protected from the handicaps resulting from their observance of the Law.

7. There is no room for superstition in Judaism.

8. The ideals of peace and human equality are fundamental principles of religion.

Akiba was convinced that his decisions introduced nothing new into Judaism. He was merely the mouthpiece of the Torah, applying its principles to new cases as they arose. "Know before whom ye are standing," he said to the litigants at the opening of each trial. "Not before Akiba ben Joseph, but before the Holy One, blessed be He." [1]

The manner in which Akiba applied these principles to specific cases is discussed in the appendix to this volume. Some aspects of his juristic ideas can, however, be presented here. They cover (a) his attack on provincial superstition, (b) his respect for urbanity, (c) his leniency in punishment, (d) his attitude toward women, (e) his attitude toward slaves and his principle of human equality.

ATTACK ON PROVINCIAL SUPERSTITION

Akiba recoiled with especial disgust from the superstitions which filled the contemporary rural mind. He held, rightly, that the biblical law forbidding contact with the dead had as one of its purposes the suppression of the use of bones as charms, a custom which was still prevalent among the provincials of his day. In fact, one of his disciples who was inclined to tolerate rustic aberrations declares that the use of animal bones for this purpose is not "an Amoritic habit" and is therefore not forbidden.[2] A century after Akiba, Johanan ben Napaha, one of the foremost teachers of his day, used to carry about with him a bone from his son's skeleton![3] To evade the law which declared such relics defiling, the provincials would collect small pieces of bone from various bodies, each piece being too small in itself to contaminate the holder. Akiba denounced the subterfuge, but Dosa ben Arkenas, the great Shammaitic scholar, defended it.[4]

He had scant respect even for superstitions which had an aura of religious sanctity. The most important of these concerned the high priest's ritual on the Day of Atonement. Among the various ceremonies in which the high priest participated, one of the most picturesque was the casting of lots between two he-goats, one of which was offered as sacrifice, the other sent to Azazel. Current belief considered it a good omen if the he-goat which stood on the right was chosen as sacrifice to God. When the matter was discussed in the academy, someone suggested that when the left one was chosen it might be brought to the right, to weaken the power of the evil spell. "Do not give the heretics an opportunity to control," Akiba said when he heard this.[5]

He even found it difficult to pray for those who were hopelessly ill. "When the words of prayer come easily to me," he said, "I know that the patient will recover; but when I stumble over my words, I know that the hope is gone."[6]

In Akiba's opinion, anyone who believed in days of good

or bad omen transgressed the biblical law against witchcraft; [7]
and those who used magical formulas to cure disease were
unfit for immortal life.[8] The tales of miracles which various
sectaries told of their founders he considered pure fiction.
When Jose the Galilean, in whose native province such stories
were especially current, tried to show that they were not inconsistent with Judaism, Akiba cut him short with the words:
"Heaven forbid that God should stop the sun, the moon and
the stars in their course for the sake of those who disobey His
will!" [9]

His opponents were astonished to discover, by accident, that
there was one reason for which he would relax his purist
opposition to pagan customs—good form. At the wedding of
his son, he opened jar after jar with the toast, inherited doubtless from early wine producers, "Wine for the life of scholars
and for the life of their disciples!" [10] The provincial and patrician scholars, like Gamaliel and Eleazar ben Zadok, who
would not say "Good health," when someone sneezed, because they considered that superstitious,[11] must have found
Akiba's tolerance strange. But his respect for good manners
overcame even his objection to the expression.

HIS RESPECT FOR URBANITY

Perhaps it was because Akiba had become acquainted with
urban amenities only late in life that he attached to them
greater significance than did any other of the sages. Ishmael,
his antagonist, who could trace his ancestry back through
generations of priests and patricians, had so identified himself
with the provincial attitude of mind that he elevated uncouth-
ness into a philosophy. "The Scriptures command us," he said,
"merely to do what is right in the eyes of God."

Akiba, replying, pointed to the verse: "And thou shalt do

what is good and what is upright in the eyes of the Lord, thy God" (Deut. 6:18). And, applying his theory of economy of divine expression, he asserted that the parallel phrases "good" and "upright" must each have its special meaning, that is, "what is good in the eyes of God, and what is upright in the eyes of man." [12] He elaborated the thought further in his famous maxim: "He who gives delight to his fellow-creatures, also gives delight to God; but whosoever gives no delight to his fellow-creatures, gives no delight to God." [13]

So anxious was Akiba, in his early days, to master what must then have seemed to him the recondite rules of proper behavior that he followed every action of his teachers with the closest scrutiny and recorded their slightest habits in his tenacious memory. On one occasion he actually followed Joshua into a privy, "and I learned from him three good habits," he said many years afterward.[14]

"How could you be so disrespectful to your teacher?" asked the astonished Ben Azzai.

"I considered everything part of the Torah, and I needed to learn," Akiba replied.

In later years he was wont to record even the most trivial customs which he met in the lands he visited. "I like the Eastern peoples for three of their habits," he said; "they put meat on the table to be cut; they kiss one another only on the hand; and they discuss private affairs only in the field" (where others cannot be offended at the secrecy).[15]

He took advantage of every opportunity to inculcate good manners, among strangers as well as among his disciples. Some vegetable having been served up ill-cooked, one of the students, unable to bite it through, took it in both hands to tear it apart. "Not so, my child," Akiba said, "put your heel on it, to hold it down while you tear it!" [16]

Once he noticed that a provincial, whose guest he was, used a piece of bread to support the plate from which he was eating. Such use of food was especially painful to Akiba, who, therefore, took that particular slice of bread and ate it.

"Is there no other bread on the table?" inquired the simple host, who had altogether failed to take the hint.

"I was afraid," said Akiba, quoting a current proverb, "that lukewarm water [i.e., a hint] would pain you; but you insist on being scalded." [17]

Akiba disliked the unsanitary habit of passing the wine-cup from mouth to mouth. When a man whom he and Ben Azzai were visiting, offered him a cup of wine after he had taken a sip, Akiba said, "You had better drink it all." The host did so, and then filled another cup for Akiba, but again followed his own conception of good manners by taking a little for himself.

Akiba was in a dilemma, wishing neither to offend his host nor to break his custom; but Ben Azzai saved him by saying, "How long will you continue to give Akiba cups which have been tasted!" [18]

The intemperate outbursts of anger to which provincials of the day were given seemed to him as wicked as idolatry. "A person who tears his clothes or breaks dishes in anger will end by worshiping idols," he said. "For such is the nature of temptation; today it demands expression of anger; tomorrow it bids one serve foreign gods." [19] "One who throws bread on the ground or scatters money when one is angry," Akiba taught on another occasion, "will live to be in need of charity." [20]

He held it to be part of good breeding to eat only food which agreed with one. "A person who eats food which is unsuitable for his constitution violates three commandments," he taught. "He disgraces himself, he disgraces his food and he recites a blessing without reason." [21]

In his respect for the proprieties, Akiba was prepared to waive the biblical rule requiring a widow to expectorate as part of the ceremony of *Halizah*. Eliezer ben Hyrkanos and Ishmael insisted that if the expectoration was omitted the ceremony was without validity; but Akiba said, "If she removed the shoe and recited the prescribed verses, she is free." [22]

He could not brook ostentation, even—perhaps especially— in prayer. When he prayed in private, his disciple, Judah ben Ilai, tells us, "one would leave him in one corner and find him in another, to which he had wandered through the multitude of his kneelings and prostrations." But when he prayed in public, he "would finish quickly, lest he keep others waiting for him." [23]

Yet urban as Akiba had become in his habits and outlook, he was sensible of the fine, simple virtues of village life: its cordial friendship, its sense of mutual obligation, its community of interests. A burial in a small settlement brings out the entire population; in a large city, where relations between people are more impersonal, the catastrophe of death attracts little attention. Hence Akiba's warning: "Help others that you may be helped; bury the dead, that you, too, may find proper burial." [24]

There was one occasion when he considered civility forbidden—as a recognition of a monetary favor. "A person must not offer greetings to another just because he borrowed money from him. To do so is almost equivalent to the payment of usury," [25] he said. Defender of trade as he was, he would not even in this light matter tolerate any deviation from the ancient agricultural standard which forbade the acceptance of benefits from loans of money.

While Akiba was thus concerned with good manners, we must not suppose that the humility which was one of his most distinguishing characteristics was affected or even deliberate. When he had appeased Eliezer's wrath at the success which greeted his prayer for rain, he had not been acting with calculated tact, but had expressed the deep convictions of his own soul, in which there was no trace of pride or vanity. "He who glories in his knowledge of the Law," Akiba would say, "is like to the carcass of an animal which lies in the road." It attracts the attention of all, it is true, "but whosoever passes by puts his hand on his nose and turns away from it"! [26]

LENIENCY IN PUNISHMENT

The influence of the city goes deeper, however, than conventional politeness; it affects the whole mentality. Habits of kindness, designed originally to attract custom, gradually soften the soul of the trader. Penal leniency was characteristic of the urban groups from the very beginning. The Hasideans, the Pharisees and the Hillelites were all known for their tenderness even to transgressors.[27] Akiba, following the precedent set by earlier teachers of his class, tended to become extreme in his aversion to penal severity, maintaining, for example, that the false witness could not be punished in either civil or criminal procedure if he confessed his guilt.[28]

When the Sanhedrin had to judge a capital case, its members were forbidden to taste food or drink during the whole day, he says.[29] If the members of a court are witnesses to a crime, they cannot be judges; they can appear only as witnesses and prosecutors before another court.[30]

He declined, however, to accept the ruling of Simeon the Temanite, which would have reduced the whole of Jewish criminal procedure to a mockery. Simeon insisted that when a man was on trial for murder the weapon used must be produced in court. Suppose, Akiba argued, the murdered person was not struck with a weapon at all, but was thrown from a building, must the building be brought into court? [31]

Only in one instance do we find Akiba inflicting a punishment which seems unduly severe; he fined a man four hundred *zuz* (twice the normal dower of a virgin), because he insulted a woman by uncovering her head in the market place. The man brought witnesses to prove that the woman had herself gone about with uncovered head on other occasions. "That is no defense," said Akiba. "The fact that a man injures himself cannot be cited to justify injuries inflicted on him by another person." [32]

Akiba's tenderness to the sinful and the criminal was not limited to the duration of life; it extended beyond the grave. Ishmael maintained, for instance, that a suicide should be buried with the words, "Alas for the fool, alas for the fool."

"Let him rather remain undescribed," said Akiba. "Do not praise him and do not blame him." [33]

He could not bear to ascribe to God a hardness which he found objectionable in man. Hence he denies that the wicked are subject to endless torment in hell. "The punishment of the sinful in Gehenna is limited to twelve months," he says. He proves this by recalling that the Deluge, which came as a retribution on the most sinful of generations, lasted only a year.[34] Those whose sins cannot be overcome through the prescribed time simply lose their share in the Future Life. They are annihilated at death.[35] Though this reduction to nothingness seemed to him the worst evil which can befall man, its negative and painless nature made it less objectionable to him than any other form of punishment. In fact, taking a position somewhat akin to that developed a millennium later by Maimonides, he seemed to hold that the future life is a privilege to be gained through positive upright living rather than an inherent right which can only be forfeited as a penalty. Sometimes he asserted God's mercy to be such that a single meritorious act will win a man admission to the future world. He found support for this view in a fanciful interpretation of Isaiah 5:14, which he rendered, "Therefore hath the netherworld enlarged her desire and opened her mouth—*for the lack of an observance*." "It does not say for the lack of *observances*," he remarked, "but of an *observance*; only those who possess no good deeds at all will descend into the netherworld." [36]

He repeated this doctrine to Gamaliel when they were discussing the beautiful Psalm 15 which describes the qualities of him "who will sojourn in Thy tabernacle, who will dwell upon Thy holy mountain." The holy mountain and tabernacle meant for the sages, of course, immortal life in Paradise. Gamaliel wept when he considered the prerequisites for admission to the company of the blessed. "He that walketh uprightly, and worketh righteousness, and speaketh truth in his heart; that hath no slander upon his tongue, nor doeth evil to his fellow, nor taketh up reproach against his neighbor; in whose eyes a vile person is despised, but he honoreth them that fear the Lord; he that putteth not out his money on interest nor taketh a bribe against the innocent. *He that doeth these things shall never be moved*." "Who can fulfill all these commandments?" the Nasi cried. "Are we then all doomed?"

Akiba replied, "Will you not admit that good is more powerful than evil? With regard to evil, we read in Scripture, 'Defile not yourselves in any of these things' (Lev. 18:24), meaning that any source of impurity can contaminate a person. May we not therefore rightly infer that any single source of merit will save him? The Psalm must not be interpreted to mean 'he who does all these things will not be moved,' but, 'he who does *any one* of them.' " [37]

The anti-Manichaean argument regarding the relative power of good and evil appears frequently in Akiba's homilies. On another occasion he said, "He who eats forbidden fat must bring a sin offering in the value of a silver piece. If he is not certain whether or not he ate it, he must bring a guilt offering in the value of two silver pieces. If that is the penalty which Scripture exacts from one who puts himself into the possibility of sin, how great will be the reward for those who observe the commandments!" [38]

Nevertheless, at other times, he insisted that certain sins would lead to the loss of the Future Life. Among those whom he assigns to this perdition are they who read uncanonical books at the public service; they who treat the Song of Solomon with levity; and they who fail to associate with scholars.[39]

HIS ATTITUDE TOWARD WOMAN

His attitude toward woman and marriage was, naturally, deeply influenced by his own romantic experience. When the usual question, "What is true wealth?" was raised among the sages, Tarfon, the great landowner, replied readily, "The possession of a hundred vineyards and a hundred slaves to work them."

Young Meir, Akiba's disciple, said more modestly, "Contentment and satisfaction with one's riches."

But Akiba said, "A wife who is comely in her deeds." [40]

He objected to the ancient tradition which forbade women to adorn themselves during their menstrual periods. "Such a rule," he said, "can only lead to loss of marital love, and

divorce." [41] It is hard for a modern to realize the full significance of the revolution implied in these words. The permission to use cosmetics and fine clothes when marital intercourse
was forbidden implied a new conception of the whole relation between husband and wife. The wife was no longer a
convenient instrument for the gratification of desire; her
beauty and companionship could be appreciated without
thought of sexual congress. We may observe that Akiba had
no authority whatever for this change in what was, at the
time, a fundamental principle of ceremonial law.

Not satisfied with having removed this taboo against
attractiveness during "impurity," Akiba sought to limit the
period itself. Earlier sages, in their fierce zeal for the Law,
had declared that any fleck which might possibly be caused by
menstrual fluids makes a woman defiled and forbidden to
her husband. To Akiba this rule seemed unnecessarily harsh,
and in his efforts to change it he amazed both colleagues and
disciples. [42]

The emphasis on marital love had, however, also other,
perhaps more debatable, implications: it meant that the disappearance of mutual affection justified the disruption of the
marriage. [43] This doctrine seemed outrageous to the patricians
and the provincials. In their eyes, divorce remained a punishment to be meted out to faithless wives. This had necessarily
been so in the earlier rural economy of Palestine where a
woman could hardly live without relation to a family and a
homestead. To send one's wife away meant to expose her to
the utmost rigors of degradation and destitution. No husband
would resort to such penalties except for the most flagrant
abuse of his confidence. If he had ceased to care for his wife,
he could get himself another; but he would not deny the
rejected one basic needs of food, clothing and shelter. In the

city, however, a woman could support herself respectably, and divorce was not the tragedy it was in the country.

On the other hand, a plebeian husband who had taken a dislike to his wife could not afford the luxury of a second marriage unless the first was dissolved. Hence we find that long before Akiba, the Hillelites had protested against the Shammaitic rule which forbade divorce except for adultery. "A wife may be divorced by her husband if he have nothing else against her than that she spoiled his dinner," the plebeians said. Akiba, accepting the Hillelite principle, rejected their evasiveness; he said, "A husband may divorce his wife for the sole reason that he has found someone more comely than she." But the view of the Shammaites was upheld by Eliezer ben Hyrkanos and Eleazar of Modin; even Ishmael added only that conversion to idolatry also justifies divorce.[44]

Akiba's whole conception of marriage was summed up in his saying, "When a husband and wife have merit, God's presence may be found in their midst; when they lack merit, a fire consumes them." [45] From this proposition, he naturally inferred that man could commit no more heinous sin than to marry a woman whom he did not love. "He who marries a wife who is unsuited to him inevitably transgresses five commandments," he said, "namely: (a) Thou shalt not take vengeance; (b) Nor bear any grudge against the children of thy people (Lev. 19:18); (c) Thou shalt not hate thy brother in they heart (*ibid*. 19:17); (d) Thou shalt love thy neighbor as thyself; and (e) That thy brother may live with thee (*ibid*. 25:36)—for since he hates her, he comes to wish her dead." [46]

Another saying attributed to him in this connection is: "Whosoever hopes for the death of his wife, that he may marry her sister, and whosoever hopes for the death of his brother, that he may marry the widow, will surely be survived by them, as it is written, 'He who diggeth a pit shall fall therein.' " (Eccles. 9:8).[47]

Suitability in marriage meant for him, however, not merely mutual compatibility and love; it also implied the absence of any legal or moral hindrance to the union. Hence, he was more severe than any of the other sages with regard to incestuous or forbidden unions, declaring them all void, and maintaining that the children born of them were illegitimate. In this, he differed not only from the patricians, who allowed the validity of at least some of these prohibited marriages, but even more sharply from Joshua ben Hananya who, representing the dominant plebeian view, limited the taint of illegitimacy to the offspring of the most heinous incests.[48]

His conception of marriage as based on love made him object to the Levirate system, according to which a childless widow was bound to marry her brother-in-law. Like other plebeian scholars he felt that the ceremony of *halizah* which released the woman from this obligation was preferable to the marriage.[49]

His defense of the rights of women brought him into continual conflict with the patrician-provincial scholars, who objected to his violent reversal of the tradition of feminine inferiority. He conceded that a married working woman should turn over her wages to her husband. But he ruled that if she earned more than he spent on her maintenance, the difference belonged to her. To this revolutionary opinion, Johanan ben Nuri took strenuous exception.[50]

Akiba rejected the traditional rule which, for purposes of legal evidence, recognized relationship only on the father's side. According to this conception no one could testify for or against one who was a possible heir, as for example, a brother by the same father, or a paternal uncle. Akiba established the rule that no relative, on either the maternal or the paternal line, can testify.[51]

He recognized that the emancipation of woman might place new strains on the family relationship. These, however, he thought might be met by the education of women to their responsibilities. Hence he was very severe in his insistence that women should keep themselves free from all suspicion of unfaithfulness, and was ready to impose rigorous disadvantages on women who married a second time without being certain that the first marriage was dissolved.[52]

The spiritual significance which he attached to romantic love led him to appreciate the Song of Solomon more than any of his colleagues or predecessors. He could not bear to hear its beautiful verses sung in a spirit of ribaldry.[53] The poem, he said, was nothing less than an allegory describing the love between Israel and God, in which the love between wife and husband is raised to infinite beauty. "Eternity is not worth more than the day on which this great poem was given to Israel," he said. "For all the books in Scripture are holy, but the Song of Solomon is the holy of holies." [54]

His abhorrence of vulgarity in the interpretation of the Song of Solomon arose not merely out of respect for the book, but out of his hatred of any levity in connection with sex life. Although he loved humor and was himself a ready wit, he could not brook obscenity. "Laughter and levity accustom men to immorality," he taught.[55]

THE LAW OF SLAVES AND AKIBA'S PRINCIPLE OF HUMAN EQUALITY

Akiba's attitude toward slavery was a resultant of two incongruous forces. There was, first, the traditional plebeian antipathy to human bondage in any form. Hebrew slavery had been abolished by the Levitical Code (Lev. 25:42); but this was not enough. The plebeians demanded the recognition of the human rights of the "Canaanite slave." The writer of Job puts this thought in a passage, unexcelled for beauty or force in the whole of the Scripture:

> "If I did despise the cause of my man-servant,
> Or of my maid-servant, when they contended with me—
> What then shall I do when God riseth up?
> And when He remembereth what shall I answer Him?
> Did not He that made me in the womb make him?
> And did not One fashion us in the womb?" (31:13-15)

The Pharisees had incorporated the spirit of this and similar passages in their legal and theological programs.[56] The Hillelites had further emphasized it.[57]

But the destruction of the Temple and the consequent distribution of the former artisans and traders among the peasants had created new problems. The landless plebeian, deprived of his shop in the market of Jerusalem, sought his livelihood as the competitor of the slave in the farmland of the Shefelah and the coastal plain. This could not be helped. But while Akiba saw no possibility of the emancipation of the slaves, he recognized that there was grave danger of degrading the formerly independent plebeians to a status not far removed from serfdom. The only way in which this could be effectively prevented was to retain a clear distinction between bondsman and freeman. It is interesting to see how Akiba met this problem without adding any real burdens to the slave.

He first of all carried the Levitical law regarding Hebrew slaves to its logical conclusion. A Hebrew, he held, could not sell himself into slavery for more than six years, the time prescribed in the twenty-first chapter of Exodus. This the patricians denied, holding that the biblical term applied only to those sold into bondage by the court in punishment for crime.[58] He then abolished the whole institution of the female Hebrew slave who was both bondswoman and concubine. A girl sold as a slave became her master's wife in the full sense of the word.[59] If a captive Jew was redeemed by anyone other than his relatives he could not be enslaved. His relatives might, indeed, hold him to labor, since they probably went to extraordinary sacrifices to free him, and in any event would doubtless treat him as one of their family. Jose the Galilean objected to both parts of Akiba's ruling. Among the patricians and provincials where family ties were strong, the redemption of a relative was taken as a matter of course. On the other hand, if the community at large had redeemed a man from among the idolaters, Jose believed that they were entitled to keep him as slave. They were obligated to make the outlay, but not to lose it.[60]

With regard to the Canaanite slave, Akiba insisted that a woman half slave and half free might marry a free man.[61] This revolutionary doctrine was intended to break down the social stigma attaching to bondage. But Akiba hesitated to extend this same principle of social equality to male slaves. He insisted that it was illegal to set slaves free.[62] He also maintained that the slaves whom Scripture declares free because their owner has infringed on their rights require a writ of manumission. The owner is compelled to give this to them; but the requirement makes their liberation a ceremonial act, separating bondage from freedom.[63]

No such reservations interfered with Akiba's determination to grant equality to all the free people. When the patricians proposed a rule varying the sum to be assessed for personal injuries according to the social status of the plaintiff, Akiba said, "The poorest man in Israel must be considered as a

patrician who has lost his property; for they are all descendants of Abraham, Isaac and Jacob." [64] "Only two classes of
Israelites can properly be considered poor," he said on another
occasion: "swindlers, and those who fail to marry off their
daughters." [65] He objected especially to laws bestowing special
privileges on royalty. An ancient rule permitted the removal
of graves when the public convenience demanded it, "except
the graves of a king or a prophet." "Even those graves may
be removed," said Akiba.[66] When Jose the Galilean declared
that a king was not obligated to bring the usual sin offerings
under certain conditions, Akiba protested.[67] "All Israel are
the children of kings," he insisted.[68]

But his doctrine of equality was not limited to the Israelites;
it included the proselytes, the Samaritans and even, in some
respects, the idolaters. This aspect of his teaching is, however,
associated with his theology and his political ideals, both of
which must be discussed in the next chapter.

VII. ON THE HEIGHTS
AKIBA'S THEOLOGICAL AND POLITICAL IDEALS

WITH the passing of the years Akiba's theology underwent an interesting metamorphosis. In his student days he retained the simple anthropomorphic conception of God which as a shepherd he had shared with the other untutored peasants. When the curious verse of Daniel (7:9), "I beheld till *thrones* were placed and one that was ancient of days did sit," was discussed in the academy, Akiba explained that the thrones were intended for God and David.

Hearing this almost blasphemous remark, Jose Ha-Kohen cried out, "Akiba, how long wilt thou describe God profanely? The thrones are intended one for Justice, and the other for Mercy." [1] Akiba, in his youthful innocence, accepted this interpretation as authoritative, and one day repeated it in the presence of Eleazar ben Azariah, who in his turn scolded him.

"Akiba, what have you to do with homilies?" Eleazar said, "Your field is rather the difficult law of Plagues and Tents. The two thrones are intended, one as a chair, the other as a footstool."

To this early period we must ascribe such remarks as, "God bent down the highest heavens to Mount Sinai so that he might speak to Israel from heaven"; [2] and "Three laws were unintelligible to Moses until God pointed out the objects involved with his finger: the first was the new moon, the second, the candelabrum of the Temple; the third was the list of prohibited animals." [3]

But in his later years, Akiba not only abandoned, but opposed, such interpretations. Dosa ben Arkenas, who adhered to the simple provincial belief in an anthropomorphistic God, said that the verse, "For a man cannot see Me and live," (Exod. 33:20) implies that "men do not see God during their life, but they see him at the moment of death."

To this Akiba responded: "The passage must be explained thus: 'Neither man nor any other living creature can see Me.' This means that even the Holy Beings who bear the Throne of Glory do not see the Glory itself."

Ben Azzai said, "I am not challenging the words of my master, but rather paraphrasing them. Even the angels, who live forever, do not see the Glory." [4]

This new conception of God led Akiba into a series of conflicts with the provincial scholar, Pappias, whose ideas were as naïve and primitive as Dosa's. For instance, the verse: "I have compared thee, O my love, to a steed in Pharaoh's chariot" (Song of Sol. 1:9), seemed to Pappias a suitable text for the following fancy: "When Pharaoh rode a male horse, God appeared against him on a male horse; when Pharaoh exchanged the horse for a mare, God too appeared on a mare." Again, Pappias explained that the words, "Behold, man is become as one of us," (Gen. 3:22) meant that Adam had become like an angel. Akiba decried both of these interpretations. The first passage has nothing to do, according to Akiba, with any appearance of God as horseman; the second merely implies that man had obtained free will: "God put before him two ways, the way of death and the way of life, and he chose the way of death." [5]

The very fact that the provincials—and the patricians who

were psychologically so much akin to them—could not fully
comprehend the plebeian idea of a spiritual God who had
neither form nor human appearance, prevented them from
accepting the belief in angels. Their God was so little more
than man that to surround Him with angels would have been
a perilous approximation of polytheism. This apprehension,
no doubt, accounts for the omission of any reference to angels
in most of the prophets. Isaiah speaks of *"seraphim,"* and
Ezekiel of "Beasts" and "Men," who perform in functions of
angels, but from the time of Hosea until that of Zechariah—
a matter of two centuries—the word *Malak,* "angel," does not
occur in literary prophecy. Even afterward a definite group
of biblical writers apparently opposed the doctrine. The contrast is dramatized in the Book of Job, where the pious friends
frequently mention angels while the sufferer himself never
does. The earliest sections of Enoch [6] enumerate the denial of
angels as one of the gross sins of Sodom; and according to the
Acts of the Apostles,[7] the negation of angels was a fundamental principle of the Sadducees. It is obvious that while
the plebeians, with their highly spiritual conception of God,
felt free to re-introduce angels, the provincials retained the
older prejudice against them.

The issue had become vague in Akiba's time, for the doctrine of angels had too long been an integral part of Pharisaic
belief to be rejected by the patrician sages. Yet we notice that
some of them speak of these semi-divine beings with reserve
and hesitancy. Perhaps the difficulty arose out of the special
anxiety of the plebeians to impute human characteristics to
the angels, so as to make them quite different in nature from
God. Thus Akiba interpreted the verse, "Beside them dwell
the fowl of heaven," (Ps. 104:12) to refer to the ministering
angels.[8] He also held, more plausibly, that the expression,

"Man did eat the bread of the mighty" (Ps. 78:25), means, "They ate bread which the ministering angels eat." When these comments were reported to Ishmael, he said: "Go and tell Akiba that he is mistaken. Does he really think that angels eat bread?" [9]

These controversies only touched the periphery of Akiba's theological speculations; the inner substance has been irrevocably lost. We know, however, that like Johanan ben Zakkai and Joshua ben Hananya before him, Akiba brooded much over the elemental problems of the world.[10] With no training in Greek metaphysics, and with little knowledge of the philosophies of other peoples, these Palestinian sages attempted to project the logic which was so helpful in their own talmudic world to that of the wider universe. Perhaps it is just as well that we do not know too much about the results at which they arrived. The Gnostic literature which has come down to us from similar, though perhaps less gifted and less well trained, thinkers is singularly unedifying; and not much more can be said of scraps of metaphysics which the *midrashim* have preserved from the discussions of Eliezer and Joshua.[11] When the sages discuss ethics and law, which are their primary concern, they speak with profundity and clarity; when they turn the same powerful minds to questions of ultimate reality, their observations are barren and confused.

Yet their interest in these speculations betokens a breadth of imagination and intellect which, regardless of achievement, is itself noteworthy. Perhaps the speculations would have led to more permanent results had not Akiba's first attempt at organized metaphysical research ended in the tragedy which has been mentioned. It was perhaps the recollection of what had happened to Elisha ben Abuyah and Ben Zoma which impelled Akiba to suppress public lectures on theology and other special problems. "It is forbidden," he taught, "to discuss the laws of forbidden marriages with so many as three disciples, or the Creation with so many as two, or the Heavenly Chariot even with one, unless he be particularly gifted so that he will follow without too much interpretation." [12] Such a rule was especially necessary in the plebeian schools whose doors were always open to any pupil; the patricians, who selected their students with great care, had no need to limit the curriculum. The result of this difference between the second century teachers is still noticeable in the talmudic works which have come down to us. The Mishna, which is derived primarily from the School of Akiba, has no treatise devoted to forbidden marriages, although some of them are discussed in connection with other matters. The *midrash* on Leviticus, from the same school, omits all comment on the eighteenth and twenty-first chapters, which deal with incest and adultery. The more restricted School of Ishmael provided a *midrash* for these chapters, which later copyists and printers used to fill the lacuna in the parallel work.

Illuminating as are Akiba's controversies with Ishmael regarding law, custom, ethics, manners, theology and pedagogics, and important as they were in their time, they yield in dramatic interest to the long conflict between the sages regarding the policy of the Jews toward Imperial Rome.

For almost a millennium the plebeians of Jerusalem had been advocating a policy of peace and internationalism. They were opposed to aggressive wars against weaker neighbors, and favored submission to the powerful imperialist states which from time to time arose about Judea. But the farmer-landowners were continually fomenting strife; and when the nobility of the capital, largely drawn from these landowning groups, sided with them, they brought Judea into armed con-

flict with surrounding states. The history of this tripartite
struggle between the pacifist plebeians, the warlike provincials and the opportunist patricians, has not yet been written, but it forms one of the most interesting and revealing
sociological studies in all Jewish history.

The militarist policy, advocated by the opponents of the
prophets during the First Commonwealth, by the Sadducees
under John Hyrkan, and by the Shammaites during the last
century of the Second Commonwealth, had repeatedly led to
disaster. The catastrophes, however, while they exacerbated
the conditions which led to rebellion, had not crushed the
spirit of the rebels. The provincials could not forget that once
in their history the militaristic policy had proved successful,
when the handful of Maccabees had won independence from
the Syrian Empire. They refused to remember that Syria had
had to face two hostile powers of the first magnitude at the
time—Egypt in the West and Parthia in the East, whereas,
in spite of the survival of the Parthians, Rome was the un-
disputed master of the world.

Ishmael became the leader of these patriots. His attachment
to his people was violent and demonstrative. "The people of
Israel, may I be accepted as an atoning sacrifice for them!" [13]
was his usual manner of referring to the Jews. Disagreeing
with Akiba's contention that God's favor depends on loyalty
to the Torah, he used to teach: "Beloved is Israel, for God has
made the nations his ransom!" [14] He would have forbidden
commercial transactions with pagans for the three days preceding, and for the three days following, an idolatrous
festival.[15] He shocked the plebeian judges by saying that if a
pagan and an Israelite were to come before him for trial,
he would give the Israelite the benefit of both Roman and
Jewish law.

Akiba remonstrated against this perversion of justice with especial anger: "If they ask for Jewish law, you must decide according to Jewish law; if they ask for Roman law, you must decide according to Roman law." [16]

But his legal partiality was not enough for Ishmael; with the help of like-minded colleagues he preached discontent, and organized rebellion against Rome. In the universal chauvinist fashion, Ishmael claimed that the Romans had attained their recent victories only through treachery in the camp of the Jews. "When the people of Israel obey their judges," he said, "God gives them victory over their enemies; but when [as in the late war against the Romans] they disregard their judges, God gives them no victory over their enemies." [17]

Ishmael remembered vividly the civil war which had raged in Jerusalem while the Roman army was at its gates, and in the usual homiletic-historical manner of the sages, he projected it back into the wilderness. The catastrophe of the spies whom Moses had sent into Palestine was due, he said, to the disorder and lack of discipline in the ranks of the people. When the people had approached Moses with the request that he appoint judges over them, they had come in proper form, the young respecting the old, the old respecting the officials; but when they came to discuss the spies, "the young pressed on the old, and the old pressed on the officials." [18] No one who is at all familiar with the history of Jerusalem during the last years of its existence, before 70, can fail to see in this word picture the clear reference to the mob-violence which distracted the Jewish capital during that period.

Alone among the sages of his day, Ishmael never mentioned the Messiah. He did not expect the salvation of Israel to come from heaven; he hoped that he and his friends would, like the Maccabees of earlier times, bring it about in a purely natural manner.

In Ishmael's early days he was kept in some restraint by his master, Joshua ben Hananya, the famous plebeian pacifist.[19] Later, his main opponent was Akiba, whose views on the subject of nationalism and pacifism were far more mature than those of either the earlier plebeians or the contemporary patricians and provincials.

The basis of Akiba's policy was the conviction that the individual has little say concerning the course either of his own life or that of his people. Neither piety *nor* prudence can really change man's destiny on earth as it is foreordained by Providence, working through the immutable forces of heredity and the laws of reward and punishment. This applies first and foremost to the individual. "The merit of a father determines," Akiba taught, "the beauty, the strength, the wealth, the wisdom, and the life-span of the son; and it also fixes the number of generations which will arise from him, which implies the End." [20]

The theological mold in which the thought is cast must not conceal from us its inherently human character. Akiba himself indicated this, in a discussion with his colleagues.

They said to him, "The father determines the son's affairs only while he is a minor; after that his life depends on his own merit."

Akiba replied, "Have you ever seen anyone who was lame, or deaf, or blind, until the time of puberty, become normal thereafter?" [21] Obviously, then, the forces which are determining in childhood continue to operate afterward.

Akiba's statement that a son's wealth depends on his father's merit, must not be interpreted cynically. He was not referring merely to the fact that children inherit their ancestral estates.

He meant, primarily, that the son's prosperity will depend on his father's piety. He made this clear when he said: "Whosoever does not engage in the study of the Law brings poverty on his children." [22]

He admitted that a person's derelictions might shorten the life-span to which his father's merit entitled him; but nothing could lengthen it. His colleagues, however, held that the duration of individual life was not fixed at all. They cited in support of their view the case of King Hezekiah, who had been warned by the prophet Isaiah of imminent death, and yet, after he had prayed, was granted a respite of fifteen years. "But," Akiba replied, "the years were his own"; that is to say, his well-timed repentance had only gained him restoration of the years which were his through his ancestors' grace.

It was by this principle that Akiba explained to a friend, Zonen, the undeniable therapeutic efficacy of idolatrous shrines. "You and I know," Zonen said to Akiba, "that idols are nothing. Yet we see people going into their houses of worship halt and returning well."

Akiba replied: "I will explain this with a parable. There was in a certain city a man whom everybody trusted so completely that they would leave their valuables with him for safe-keeping, without taking the precaution of having witnesses present. Only one especially suspicious individual insisted on witnesses when he brought his property. One day, when this man neglected his usual precautions, the wife of the pious depositary said to her husband, 'Let us repay him in kind, and keep his packet.' 'What,' replied her honest husband, 'shall I destroy my character because he played the fool!'

"So, also," continued Akiba, "pains are sent to a person under strict orders, as it were, fixing their duration, the physician and the means of their cure. When their time is over, the man sometimes happens to be in an idolatrous temple and the pains are naturally tempted to refuse to leave. But they consider, 'Shall we transgress our orders because he acts the fool?' " [23]

In this parable, as in others, Akiba implied far more than is apparent on the surface. Zonen may have been satisfied with the superficial aspects of the answer; he probably did not take the trouble to analyze the metaphysics and the theology implied in the parable. Akiba, obviously, held that the events of human life are irrevocably determined in all their phases and details. A sick person does well to call a physician, he indicates, for the instrument of healing is itself fixed by God. But actually the cure is automatic.

Akiba's belief was challenged, as we have observed, by anonymous "colleagues." Who these opponents were becomes clear from a study of the *midrashim* which have come down to us from the rival schools of Ishmael and Akiba. These works show that Ishmael and his pupils denied the doctrine of *Zekut Abot,* "the merit of the fathers," and held that the course of a man's life is fixed by his own acts; while the School of Akiba adhered to the deterministic teachings of its founder.[24] But, as we know from Josephus,[25] the issue was new only in formulation; fundamentally, it was identical with that which had been debated decades before between the Pharisees and the Sadducees. The former, with their plebeian outlook on life, had held that "everything is determined"; while, the latter, representing patrician opinion, believed that much depends on the individual.

Akiba summarized his views on this subject in his famous four-word apothegm, "All (is) foreseen, (and) choice (is) granted." [26] Man is free to do what he will, but his decisions,

and the results which must flow from them, are predeter-
mined. The paradox, basic to the theology of the Pharisees
and of all religions which derive from them—not to mention
many systems of materialist philosophy—cannot be resolved;
but it has never been stated more tersely and emphatically
than by Akiba.

It is interesting to remark that just as the Essenes—who
were simply the extremist Pharisees of their days—denied
Free Will altogether, so Ben Azzai took issue with the second
half of Akiba's statement. He was a thorough-going deter-
minist, allowing of no compromises and paradoxes. "By thy
name shalt thou be called; in thy place shalt thou be seated;
and thine own shall be given thee. No man can touch what
is prepared for his comrade, and no kingdom can take a
hairsbreadth of what is destined for its neighbor," Ben Azzai
taught.[27] "Freedom is granted," he says, "only in the sense
of the verse, 'So far as concerneth the scorners, He addeth
to their scorn; but unto the righteous, He giveth grace' (Prov.
3:34). From this we may infer that if a man desires to study
the Torah a little, he will be given the opportunity to study
it much; if he desires to forget even a little of it, he will be
made to forget much more." [28] In other words, man may take
the initiative either in self-improvement or self-debasement.
Putting the same thought more succinctly, he said: "The reward of observance is that it leads to further observance; the
punishment of sin, that it leads to further transgression." [29]

Akiba admitted the force of habit. He too held that "the
attraction of sin is at first as feeble as a spider's thread, but
ultimately it becomes as strong as a ship's cable." [30] Yet he
derided those who inferred from this statement a philosophy
of determinism in the moral sphere.[31] He saw no contradic-

tion between his views and the general doctrine of reward and punishment. "The verse, 'Wherefore doth the wicked contemn God, and say in his heart, Thou wilt not require,' (Ps. 10:13) must be paraphrased," Akiba holds: "The wicked maintains that there is no Judge and there is no judgment; but he is in error, there is both Judge and judgment." [32] When Pappias interpreted one of Job's outcries to mean, "He alone judgeth all creatures; and none can object to His decisions," Akiba protested. "The verse means rather, 'No complaint may be raised against the decisions rendered by Him, but all is done in accordance with truth and justice.' " [33]

But the Divine Judgment differs from man's in this, that it is Mercy.[34] In his usual manner, Akiba seized on a trivial incident as text for a beautiful homily on this doctrine. He noticed that when the figs ripened on the tree which served as his academy, the owner arose at dawn to pluck them. It occurred to him that this agility might be due to a suspicion that the disciples were stealing the fruit; and he moved to another tree.

When the owner of the tree observed this, he came to him in tears: "I have had this one good deed to my credit, that my tree gave shelter to learning, and now you rob me of it!"

"Why then did you rise so early to pick your figs?" Akiba asked.

"Because the figs are spoiled if they remain on the tree after they ripen," the peasant said.

"Ah!" cried Akiba, when he heard these words. "Just as the owner of this fig tree watches each of his many fruits, and whenever one becomes ripe, he removes it lest it decay, so also, the Holy One, blessed be He, knows his righteous children and watches them; and when they are ripe enough for His treasury, he garners them." [35]

"How manifold are Thy works, O Lord," he once said, quoting Psalm 104, verse 24; and then he continued: "Thou hast creatures which flourish in the sea, and others which flourish on land. If the sea-animals were compelled to live on land, they would perish; if the land-animals were compelled to live in the water, they would perish. What is life for one beast is death for the other. Yet thou hast chosen for each the place which suits it most admirably. 'In wisdom hast thou made them all, the earth is full of thy creatures.' " [36]

His sympathy for all who suffered led him to believe that "the world is judged with mercy"; yet "everything depends on the majority of one's actions." In a fine image drawn from the market place he describes his conception of man's relations to God. "The shop is open; the hand writes. Whosoever desires may come and borrow, but the collectors make their daily rounds, and the payments cannot be evaded. The warrant is there, the judgment is correct and everything is prepared for the feast." [37]

Seen from this point of view, human suffering is a gift from God to man. When it occurs as a retribution for sin, it averts greater evils after the final judgment. "God inflicts slight pain on the righteous in this world to save them from severer punishment in the future world." [38] If the suffering is unmerited, there are special divine reasons which transcend human understanding. Since in any event it is a good, it must be accepted with gratitude. Sullen resignation is not sufficient; submission to the inevitable must be cheerful. Complaint is unjustified even as protest is futile.

The idea was not altogether new; in fact, it had been put into imperishable verses by the author of the third chapter of Lamentations (vv. 26-30):

"It is good that a man should quietly wait
For the salvation of the Lord.
It is good for a man that he bear
The yoke in his youth.
Let him sit alone and keep silence,
Because He hath laid it upon him.
Let him put his mouth in the dust,
If so there may be hope.
Let him give his cheek to him that smiteth him,
Let him be filled full with reproach."

Akiba merely carried the ancient Pharisaic philosophy to its logical conclusions, expressing it in terms of talmudic norms. "The verse, 'Thou shalt love the Lord, thy God, with all thy heart, and with all thy soul, and *with all thy might'* (Deut. 6:5) means that thou must love him whatever be the measure which he mete out to thee." "Do not act toward me," Akiba pictures God as saying to Israel, "as the pagans act toward their gods, thanking them when good comes, and cursing them when evil comes. Israel is unlike them; when I bring good on them, they give thanks; and when I bring evil, they give thanks." [39]

"Suffering is good," Akiba once said to his master, Eliezer, when he found him sick. "We may infer this from the story of Manasseh. Though his father, King Hezekiah, had carefully instructed him in the Torah, and given him all possible protection, that did not avail to make him pious. Yet suffering led him to repentance, for it is recorded in Chronicles that when he was in distress he turned to the Lord" (II Chron. 32:12). [40]

From these premises Akiba inferred that poverty is better than riches. "Poverty is as becoming to the daughter of Israel as a red strap on the neck of a white horse." [41] He believed that all the evils into which Israel had been led were the result of wealth. "All the prophets complained of the silver and gold which Israel brought out of Egypt. Isaiah (1:22) says, 'Thy silver has become dross'; Hosea (2.10), 'The silver which I multiplied for her and the gold have they used for the Baal.' " [42]

Except for the somewhat ambiguous expression used in one of the passages already cited, "the number of generations before him, which is the End," Akiba never applied the principle of determinism to the life of the nation. Yet both his predecessor, Joshua ben Hananya, and his disciple, Jose ben Halafta, are particularly insistent that Israel's fate is unalterably fixed. [43] Whether Akiba accepted this teaching is uncertain, but there can be no doubt that he did adhere to the pacifist and universalist policy which the other plebeians based upon it. For, contrary to the general impression, Akiba was not at all a militarist. This will become evident from our study of his activities during the last twenty years of his life; it is implied, also, in some of his utterances during the period now under discussion. He opposed the Shammaitic contention that pagans may not send sacrifices to the altar; it was, in fact, the open refusal to offer Temple sacrifice for the Roman Emperor, which, as both the Talmud and Josephus record, precipitated the Rebellion of the year 66. [44] The ultranationalist view was still held by many; indeed it was defended in the following generation by Simeon ben Yohai. Jose the Galilean, Akiba's contemporary, who agreed that pagans might send animal sacrifices, denied that they could contribute money offerings for the Temple. [45] Akiba, however, insisted that so far as the gifts to the sanctuary are concerned, the pagan has the same status as the Jew. [46]

He ruled that documents drawn up by the Roman courts,

and witnessed by pagans, were valid; [47] and he applied this principle even to such instruments as writs of divorce and manumission which have ceremonial as well as civil significance. Elihu, the young sage who arose to refute the heresies of Job, was none other than the pagan Balaam, he said; Eleazar ben Azariah, unable to impute such eloquence and piety to the heathen prophet, identifies Elihu with Isaac.[48] The Samaritans, he insisted, were righteous proselytes; and their bread may be eaten by Jews.[49] He extended the principle laid down by Joshua ben Hananya that the various limitations prescribed in Scripture against proselytes from Ammon, Moab, Egypt and Edom no longer applied. "Sennacherib," he said, "came up and confused all the races. None of these peoples are any longer in their own land." [50]

Summarizing his whole doctrine of the relation of Jew to Gentile, he said: "The fundamental principle of the Torah is the commandment, 'Love thy neighbor as thyself' " (Lev. 14:18).

Ben Azzai, hearing this, went further, and reminded Akiba that the expression *thy neighbor* is open to nationalist interpretation, as meaning only a fellow-Israelite. He preferred a more generous text. "The verse, 'This is the book of the generations of Adam,' implies a greater principle," he insisted, "for it concludes with the words, 'In the day that God created man, in the likeness of God he made him; male and female created he them' " (Gen. 6:1).[51]

Akiba apparently accepted his colleague's correction, for on another occasion he said: "Whosoever sheds human blood may be described as having diminished the image of God." [52] Again he remarks: "Beloved is man that he has been created in the image of God. A special love was shown him when he was told that he had been created in the image of God." [53]

This does not prevent him from adding however, "Beloved are Israel that they are called children of God and that they have been given the precious instrument with which the world was created."

This opinion necessarily led to the doctrine that the greatest day in Jewish history was not the Exodus; but rather the anniversary of the Revelation.[54] The birth of Israel as a people was secondary to its rebirth as the people of God and the Torah.

Like Johanan ben Zakkai, before him, and peace-lovers, generally, he opposed conscription in time of war. The verse which demands that the "fearful and faint-hearted" be excused from military service was taken by him in its full literalness. Jose the Galilean said it referred only to the crippled.[55]

Impatience with the long delayed redemption of Israel seemed to Akiba a grave sin. "God became angry at Moses," he remarked, "only when he said, 'Neither hast Thou delivered Thy people at all' " (Exod. 5:23).[56]

When the redemption would come, it would be limited in its scope. Disagreeing with nationalists like Eliezer ben Hyrkanos, he said that the Ten Tribes would never be restored. "Just as the day goes, never to return, so they have gone, never to return."

But Eliezer said, "On the contrary, just as the day becomes dark and then light, so they also having been reduced to darkness, will come back into light." [57]

The Kingdom of God was for him of international significance. He disagreed altogether with the conception developed by some nationalist Galileans that it implied a political kingdom in which Israel would again become dominant. He maintained that his conception of the kingdom was emphasized in each of the psalms which the Levites intoned at the daily services of the Temple.[58] But he believed that Rosh Ha-Shanah, being the anniversary of the Creation, was an especially appropriate season for celebrating the Kingship of God.

Akiba denied further, the nationalist significance which tradition attached to the ceremony of sounding the *Shofar* or ram's horn, on Rosh Ha-Shanah. For centuries the *Shofar* had been used to call the tribes together for war, and in the popular mind this martial origin overbore the religious purpose. But Akiba reminded the patriots who supported this view that the same notes had been used when the people had suffered natural catastrophes: drought, locust and bad harvests, "for every trouble which comes upon you."[59]

In what sense, then, could God be described as being in a singularly intimate relation with Israel? Only in so far as He has chosen to give them "the precious Instrument by which the world was created." "Happy are you, people of Israel," He says, "when you consider before Whom you are being cleansed, and Who it is that cleanses you; your Father Who is in heaven."[60] Israel must expect neither power, nor riches, nor prestige, as the select of God; it has been given nothing but the opportunity to serve Him. It is Israel's mission to glorify Him before the nations, but even in the end when all will accept God, Israel will continue to understand Him more completely than the others.

This seemed to Akiba the profounder significance of the poetical dialogue in the Song of Solomon (5:9 ff). "The peoples of the world say to Israel, *'What is thy Beloved more than another beloved?* Why do ye permit yourselves to be slain for Him? Ye are comely, ye are strong, come and mingle with us.' But Israel replies: 'Do ye know Him? We shall sing for you some of His praises. *My Beloved is white and ruddy, the chiefest among ten thousand. His head is the most fine gold, His locks are curled, and black as a raven. His eyes are like doves beside the water-brooks, washed with milk, and fitly set.'* When the nations hear this praise of God, they say, *'Whither is thy Beloved gone, thou fairest among women? Whither is thy Beloved turned aside that we may seek Him with thee?'* But Israel answers, *'Ye have no share in Him, I am my Beloved's and my Beloved is mine.' "* [61]

The peculiar dependence of God on Israel for the spread of his doctrine through the world justified for Akiba the bold words which he put in the mouth of Israel, "When Thou didst redeem us from Egypt, Thou didst redeem Thyself, as it is written, 'Thy people which Thou didst redeem out of Egypt, the people and its God' " (II Sam. 23:7). [62]

The conception was even more fully and daringly expressed by Akiba's disciple, Simeon ben Yohai, who said, "The Scriptures declare, 'Ye are My witnesses, and I am God.' This means, 'So long as ye testify to Me, I am God; but if ye cease to testify to Me, I am no longer God.' " [63]

The divine revelation came to the prophets, therefore, not as a reward for their individual piety, but "for the sake of Israel." "Go out and say to them," God commands Moses in Akiba's interpretation of the Scripture, "that for their sake am I speaking to thee." [64] Indeed, Israel's leaders have no significance except as instruments for their people's safety. "Just as the bird cannot fly without wings, so Israel cannot continue without its sages," he says. [65]

His love for the land of Israel had the same religious overtones. "Do not leave the Holy Land, lest you come to worship idols," he warned his disciples, "for does not David say, 'For they have driven me out this day that I should not cleave to

the inheritance of the Lord, saying, Go, serve other gods'
(I Sam. 26:19)?" [66] And again: "Whoever is buried in Pales-
tine is as though he were buried underneath the altar, for all
Palestine is fit for the altar."

The conflict between Ishmael and Akiba thus covered every
aspect of Judaism, from the simplest questions of ceremonial
to the most recondite problems of theology and the most
perplexing issues of diplomacy. The following chapters will
show with what ultimate success Akiba applied his principles in political life during one of the most turbulent and
calamitous eras in Jewish history, and how, in his second
metamorphosis, the scholar who had once been a shepherd
became one of the supreme statesmen of his people.

VIII. A PERILOUS SUMMIT

THE years 110-12 were epochal both in the life of Akiba and in the history of his people.[1] In his seventieth year the great sage was still at the flood tide of his strength. His health was perfect, he had retained all the physical and mental vigor of his youth, and his native genius was now supplemented by the skill born of thirteen years of intellectual leadership. If the discovery and development of unsuspected faculties within one's self, the conquest of adverse circumstances and the achievement of universal applause can give happiness to man, Akiba must certainly have been happy.

In addition to the other blessings which had come to him, Akiba at last attained economic independence. He was not wealthy; he could not afford any slaves, like Tarfon, Eliezer and Gamaliel; nor did he possess the golden tables and the beds with golden ladders which some imaginative aggadists ascribed to him.[2] When his son, Joshua, married, it was still necessary to stipulate that the bride support the husband while he pursued his studies.[3] But Akiba no longer had to engage in gainful occupation, and had sufficient income to supply all of Rachel's modest needs and, at least on one occasion, to give her a costly present.[4]

Various accounts are given concerning the manner in which he obtained this competence. According to the most reliable record, he received a considerable bequest from a Roman proselyte with whom he became acquainted during his mission at the capital in the year 95.[5] The later scholars who described Rachel as the daughter of Ben Kalba Sabua, explained that Akiba's father-in-law ultimately became reconciled to him and left him half of his enormous estates. According to another fable, Akiba obtained his money through a miracle. Needing funds for his disciples, and unable to obtain them from friends, he asked a pagan lady for a loan. She agreed to make it, but stipulated that God and the Sea be guarantors. How the agreement of these guarantors was obtained, the story does not take the trouble to tell. It continues that when the time for payment came, Akiba happened to be ill, and could not meet the obligation. Whereupon the generous lady went to the shore of the sea, and said: "Master of the Universe, Thou knowest that Akiba cannot repay his debt. I look to Thee to fulfill Thy pledge." Hardly had she uttered these words, when a box of jewels which an insane princess had cast into the sea, was washed up at her feet. When Akiba recovered and came to pay his debt, she said to him, "Thy guarantor has more than reimbursed me; here is the surplus."

The situation of the community was equally happy. Never since the destruction of Jerusalem had Judea been economically more prosperous, or politically more tranquil. The aftermath of the war had passed; the ruined population had once more settled to normal habits of work and trade; the city of Ludd in the lowland had partly replaced Jerusalem as the metropolis of Judea and absorbed some of the destitute artisans and merchants. A new generation had grown up accustomed to the Roman yoke and apparently willing to bear it. In distant Rome, the affairs of the Empire had for a dozen years been in the capable hands of Nerva and Trajan, the first and second of the "five good emperors." It was natural that the thought of the people should turn to the possibility of the restoration of the Temple. During the years which had elapsed since the burning of the sanctuary, the Jews had continually prayed for its reëstablishment. They had never ceased to study the intricate sacrificial system, and many of them were more expert in it than had been the priests of Temple times. The daily synagogue services, which had originated quite independently of the Temple, probably without the consent of the priesthood, had been transformed into substitutes for the abolished sacrifices. Nor had the people forgotten Jerusalem, the Crown of Beauty. Much of Akiba's jurisprudence and philosophy, as we have observed, centered about the problems of Jerusalem's market place. The habits of the patricians of Jerusalem, too, had been carefully recorded and were being handed down from master to disciple. Above all the scholars had continued to maintain the rigid discipline of Levitical purity, though it had no significance except in connection with the Temple and Jerusalem. During the confusion of the last days of Jerusalem, someone had had the presence of mind to escape from the city with the ashes of the last red heifer and the water of purification, which, in accordance with the nineteenth chapter of Numbers, were required to purify anyone who had become defiled. The precious relics were kept in the "Treasury of Yabneh," throughout the troublesome days of the reconstruction, and were still to be found in Galilee a century after the events which we are now recounting.[6]

These measures indicate how deep and how obstinate was the desire for the Temple and a restored Jerusalem. The relaxed severity of Roman rule led many Jews first to hope, and then to believe, that the Temple was about to be restored. They were encouraged, perhaps, by a popular legend which held that the Temple would be in ruins for a jubilee. Since the destruction had taken place in 70, the restoration was due in 119. This belief, like others in human history, set in motion the forces needed for its own fulfillment. A certain degree of provincial autonomy was not considered incompatible with complete imperial authority, and it was the general policy of the Romans to grant their subject people every concession which cost nothing and involved no danger. It was therefore a reasonable expectation that the government would reward the tractability of the Jews with permission to return to Jerusalem.

The political situation made the moment especially auspicious for action. Trajan, the last emperor who extended the Roman domains, was about to undertake his expedition against the Parthians, that stubborn people which more than once resisted the might of imperial arms. On the eve of this campaign Trajan needed the full support and devotion of the various provinces, but especially of those near the scene of activities. In addition, there was a considerable settlement of Jews living under the Parthians in Babylonia, and their good will was not without importance.

The meager records of the time give us only a tantalizing glimpse of the course of events, and tell us nothing of the negotiations which accompanied them. The Jewish community in Rome may have exerted some influence favorable to their Palestinian brethren, but it seems more likely that the imperial officials relied in most of their subsequent decisions on the local administrators. Hence, we hear of no commission to Rome asking for the reconstruction of the Temple. It is a fair presumption, however, that there were conversations on this subject between the leaders of the Jews and the Roman governor, and we cannot be wrong in the assumption that among the chief representatives of the Jews were their peace-loving teachers Joshua and Akiba. The result was that one day

the Jewish world was startled by an imperial pronouncement
permitting the restoration of the sacrificial service in Jerusalem and placing the proselyte Aquila, the friend and disciple
of Akiba, in charge of the reconstruction of the Temple.[7]

As usual in such pronouncements, the terms were intentionally made ambiguous; but it was obvious from the outset
that what was planned was not a replica of the Herodian
structure, which was really a fortress, but a more modest
edifice, sufficient only for the purposes of sacrifice.

It can hardly be a mere accident that the announcement
was made on the twelfth of Adar,[8] immediately before the
festivals celebrating the great victory of the Maccabees over
the Syrian general, Nicanor, and the miraculous deliverance
of the Jews from the hands of Haman. The selection of the
date betrays the hand of the scholars who carried on the
negotiations with the Romans, and who obviously intended
that the anniversary be joined to Nicanor's Day and Purim
in a perpetual three-day festival. And this was indeed effected
when the conclave voted to make the twelfth of Adar a permanent half-holiday, to be known as Trajan's Day.

The willingness of the Romans to restore the Temple led
Akiba to believe that more energetic representations on its
behalf might have saved it in the first place. He blamed
Johanan ben Zakkai for not exerting his influence to this
end. "The verse, 'He turneth wise men backward and maketh
their knowledge foolish' (Isa. 44:25) applies," he said, "to
Johanan ben Zakkai, as he stood before the Roman general
begging for the academy at Yabneh, when he might have
saved the Temple at Jerusalem." [9] Such depreciation of the
savior of the Torah would be incredible in the mouth of anyone who had not himself conducted successful negotiations

with the conquerors, and thus felt that he might justly voice an opinion regarding their pliability.

To Akiba and many others it seemed that the Messianic era was at hand, but it was taking a form different from what had been expected. There was no miraculous appearance of the son of David or of Elijah the Prophet, there was no resurrection of the dead or day of divine judgment. The obvious explanation was that the Messianic era had been wrongly confused with the Future World, the *Olam Habba,* which was in reality quite distinct from it. The two were to be carefully distinguished hereafter; the Messiah would usher in the freedom of Jerusalem and the Jews, the world cataclysm would be brought about by no human agency, but by God Himself. Estimates regarding the probable length of the Messianic era now became a popular preoccupation. Eliezer ben Hyrkanos, in his retirement, gave his opinion that it would last three generations.[10] Akiba, however, would not give up the hope that his own generation would see the revelation of the Divine glory. "The Messianic age will last," he said, "forty years, as it is written in the Prayer of Moses, 'Make us glad according to the years wherein Thou hast afflicted us, according to the years wherein we have seen evil'" (Ps. 90:15).[11] The statement as it stands is a childish fancy, of a type foreign to Akiba's mind. Seen in the context of the times it assumes serious meaning. It was a cryptic reference to a hope which Akiba, now a responsible statesman, dared not voice openly. Forty years had in fact passed since the destruction of the Temple. The next forty years were to be a happy Messianic prelude to the Future World.

The general reception accorded to the Trajan Declaration was one of extravagant enthusiasm. A new prayer was added to the Grace after Meat, thanking God "Who is good and does good," for this favor of the Romans.[12] At the Passover service, Akiba, with the acquiescence of most of his colleagues, added to the benediction thanking God for having "redeemed us and our ancestors from Egypt," the following prayer: "So may the Lord, our God, cause us to reach new festivals and pilgrimages, rejoicing in the building of our city, and happy in His worship; and may we eat there of the offerings and paschal sacrifices, the blood of which will be poured out on the wall of His altar for His acceptance." And then he ended with the doubly significant benediction, "Blessed art Thou, O Lord, Who hast redeemed Israel." [13] The same conclusion was added to a benediction inserted after the reading of the *Shema.*[14]

While the majority unaffectedly rejoiced in the happy turn of events, two groups among the Jews were dissatisfied: the nationalists and the primitive Christians. The former received the Roman promise with derision; the latter with apprehension. What cause was there for this wild acclaim, the nationalists asked. The promise was small, its fulfillment doubtful. At best the proposed Temple was to be less imposing than that which had been destroyed; nothing had been said about Jewish autonomy; the question of reëstablishing the walls of Jerusalem had not even been raised. When Tarfon heard of the extended benediction which Akiba proposed to insert in the Passover service, he opposed it. We could only thank God for the exodus from Egypt, he held; there had as yet been no other equally important redemption. Jose the Galilean objected to the use in a house of mourning of the benediction which had been added to the Grace.[15] He could not, of course, generally oppose a supplementary blessing of gratitude to God as the one who is good and does good; he indicated his opposition to the whole innovation by the limitations he put on the use of the new benediction. He went further and declared that it was illegal to accept the gift of a Temple structure from pagans.

"But," Akiba urged, "you admit that we may accept sacrifices from them; why not other offerings?"

"Even if you argue all day," retorted the intrasigeant Jose, "I insist that only whole burnt offerings and peace offerings can be accepted from them." [16]

When some human bones were discovered in the course of excavations in the Temple grounds, the nationalists moved that the holy site be declared impure, so as to make the restoration quite impossible except through the intervention of a miracle. Joshua, the peace-maker, who was struggling to obtain the full consent of Rome to the reëstablishment of the Temple, cried out bitterly against this excess of patriotism. "It is a shame and a disgrace for us that we should condemn our Temple as defiled. Where are the dead of the Deluge? Where are the dead of Nebuchadnezzar? Where are all those who were slain in the last war, and until the present? The principle laid down by the sages is that only a known impurity is defiling; an unknown impurity is not defiling!" [17]

At first, Ishmael, who was primarily the priest, joined Akiba in his joy over the prospect of a restored Temple service. The fourth benediction of the Grace, which had just been composed, was, according to him, adumbrated in Scripture itself.[18] Having accidentally mended the wick while reading on the Sabbath eve, he later entered the transgression in his note book: "I, Ishmael ben Elisha, have through error mended the wick on the Sabbath; when the Temple is rebuilt, I will bring a fat sin offering." [19]

The members of the infant Judeo-Christian Church were dismayed by the Trajan Declaration. They had considered the destruction of Jerusalem and its Temple an inevitable and appropriate punishment visited on the Jews for their rejection of Jesus. But now the Roman government was apparently taking steps to restore the metropolis and the sanctuary to the sinful and still recalcitrant people! One of the writers of the period is at great pains to reassure the members of the Church that the reconstruction of the Temple does not imply the restoration of the Jews to divine favor. God has no need for any Temple, he says, pointing for corroboration to the prophecy of Isaiah, chapter 66, "Thus saith the Lord, the heaven is my throne and the earth is my footstool. Where is the house that ye may build unto me? And where is the place that may be my resting place?" What was happening before their eyes was the fulfillment of another verse of Isaiah, "Behold they that destroyed this Temple shall themselves build it." "So it cometh to pass," he says, "for because they went to war was it destroyed by their enemies. Now also the subjects of their enemies shall build it up." But the reconstruction will be only temporary: "For the Scripture saith, 'And it shall be in the last days that the Lord shall deliver up the sheep of the pasture and the fold and the tower thereof to destruction.' " [20]

This open and vociferous opposition to the imperial policy suddenly forced on the Roman governors a realization of the fact which had long escaped them—that Judaism and Christianity were distinct religions. For many years Christianity had been tolerated under Roman dominion as a variety of Judaism, which was a recognized and permitted form of worship. Individual emperors like Nero and Domitian had undertaken to persecute the Church for personal and transient reasons, just as Tiberius had expelled the Jews from Rome at one time. But no edict had been issued outlawing Christianity or authorizing its persecution. When Flavius Clemens became converted to monotheistic religion, the doctrines which he accepted were so vague that both the Jews and the Christians could claim him as their own. Probably he made no effort to comprehend the nice distinctions between the two religions, which, though they loomed so large in the eyes of the Palestinians, were really insignificant to the outsider. The Trajan Declaration was the wedge which finally cleaved the two groups asunder. Its enthusiastic reception by the Jews, and its equally enthusiastic rejection by the Christians, ended all possibility of reconciliation between the Jews and the Judeo-Christians.

In the persecution which ensued, Symeon, a near relative of Jesus, who had attained advanced age, and was the recognized head of the Church of Jerusalem, was crucified by the Romans; and Ignatius, the Bishop of Antioch, was sentenced to die in the Roman arena.[21]

So little, however, did the Romans yet understand the new sect or its tenets, that they arrested Eliezer ben Hyrkanos on the charge of belonging to it. Driven from the Sanhedrin, the old sage had apparently sought the companionship of sectarian teachers. This fact, and his failure to attend the sessions of the conclave, was sufficient for the Roman gendarmes. Eliezer was seized and brought to trial on the charge of being a Christian.[22]

As he was being led to prison, a woman, taking advantage of his helplessness, bespattered him, it is said, with the household refuse. The changed and chastened Eliezer, who had been driven into a rage when someone ventured to contradict him, now merely remarked, "I think that my colleagues will take me back into their midst today, for it is written, 'He lifteth up the needy out of the dunghill' " (Ps. 113:7).[23]

This prophecy was not to be fulfilled; but there can be no

doubt that Eliezer's former colleagues, Gamaliel, his brother-in-law, as well as Joshua and Akiba, rallied to his defense. The failure of the Talmud to mention them in its brief resumé of the trial must be because it records only public proceedings, while the sages interceded for Eliezer in private interviews with the judges and officials. When the matter came before the court, we are told, the judge asked Eliezer how so respected and venerable a sage could waste his time on "vanity" such as that of which he stood accused. "May the Judge be accepted as my witness," Eliezer replied, meaning that God could testify to the purity of his faith. But the Roman interpreted the words to mean that Eliezer was calling on *him* as witness to the absurdity of the charge. Deeply flattered, he immediately dismissed the complaint.

The form in which the question was put to Eliezer, as well as the quick decision in his favor, amply support the conjecture that his colleagues had prepared the way for his acquittal. What happened in court was a mere formality; the judge was convinced of Eliezer's innocence before the trial began.

As soon as Eliezer was free, Akiba rushed to see him and comfort him. The old man was still disconsolate; he could not understand why God had chosen to place him in such peril. "Perhaps," Akiba suggested, "it is because you enjoyed what one of the sectarians taught you."

"Indeed, it must be so," Eliezer replied, and he told Akiba of an interpretation which a certain Jacob, of the new Church, had given him.

The opposition of the Christians to the Trajan Declaration led to difficulties not only in the Holy Land, but throughout the Empire. A few years later, Pliny the Younger, the Governor of Bithynia, inquired of Trajan concerning the status of the new faith, and was told that its members were subject to punishment. Pliny was indeed not to "seek them out," but when they were brought before him for trial, they were to be treated severely.[24] In the light of the more severe persecutions of later times, this famous rescript of Trajan seemed to the Church historians extraordinarily lenient; but in its own time it was a definite step toward the legal degradation of the Christians.

While the opposition of the Christians to the Trajan Declaration could bring harm only to themselves, there was another group, the Samaritans, whose antagonism finally frustrated the whole plan. Those ancient enemies of the Jews, who had almost prevented the construction of the Second Temple in the sixth century B.C.E., had heard the announcement of Trajan's offer with a consternation which was exactly proportionate to the joy of the Jews. They resorted to the tactics used by their ancestors under Darius and Xerxes, and appealed to the capital of the empire. The government, embarrassed by the unexpected development, sought a graceful retreat, first in delay, and then in a process of attrition, reducing the grant to the smallest possible proportions.[25]

The Roman governor, apparently acting under orders from his superiors, proposed various interpretations of the plighted imperial word. He seems to have suggested that the reconstruction of the Temple be delayed until Trajan would himself arrive in the East, and that in the meantime sacrifices be resumed in the vacant Temple area. Joshua, who trusted the Romans completely, and saw clearly the governmental difficulty with which they were faced, was in favor of this procedure. "I have a tradition," he said, "that sacrifices may be offered though there be no gates separating the Temple courts; they may be eaten though there be no Temple walls;

and the tithes and lighter sacrifices may be eaten in Jerusalem though it be unwalled." [26]

In their anxiety to win over the nationalists, Joshua and his colleagues turned to Eliezer ben Hyrkanos, whom they had ousted from the conclave decades earlier, and asked him to intercede. The old nationalist remembered enough from the last war against the Romans to desire peace above everything; and perhaps he was flattered by the anxiety of his former opponents to be reconciled. He offered a compromise suggestion, that curtains be set up in the sanctuary to divide the various courts from one another. That must have been done, he said, when the Second Temple was being constructed, and sacrifices were being offered on the altar.[27]

But neither of these suggestions were acceptable to the nationalists. Having first sought to prevent the rebuilding of the Temple, they now opposed any offerings until the Temple building was restored.

The division among the Jews soon reached such proportions that it could not be concealed from the Romans, who, already taken aback by the Samaritan outcry, were surprised by the enthusiasm of the pacifists and alarmed by the opposition of the nationalists. Akiba's interpretation of their gesture as the first step to Jewish national independence seemed to corroborate all the charges of the Samaritans, and was almost as seditious from the Roman point of view as Ishmael's contemptuous rejection.

Five years passed in these futile negotiations. The Romans became continually more convinced that they had committed an error; the Jews remained determined to obtain their Temple. In the meantime Trajan arrived in the East to reduce Armenia and vanquish the Parthians. Faced with these difficult tasks, he had little time for the Jewish question; and when the noisy demands of this little people were placed before him, he settled them hastily—on paper. The Jews might have Jerusalem as their city, but the reëstablishment of the Temple was indefinitely postponed. The offhand decision of the Emperor, for it could hardly have been given after due deliberation and consultation, was catastrophic. The hopes of the Jews were shattered; the Samaritans were victorious. On that day the bloody war which was to end in the complete annihilation of Judaea became inevitable.

Akiba was thunderstruck. The worst predictions of the nationalists had come true; the Roman word had proved altogether unreliable. Ishmael did not for a moment hesitate; the new offer was to be rejected summarily. Arguing with cold legal formality, he said: "We might suppose that a Jew is permitted to take his second tithe to Jerusalem and eat it there, now that the Temple is destroyed, but this cannot be. The Law requires two kinds of offerings to be consumed in Jerusalem, the firstlings of animals and the second tithe. Like the first, the second can be brought to Jerusalem only while the Temple is in existence." To Akiba's amazement, Ben Zoma, his close friend and colleague, seconded Ishmael's view, and demonstrated the legal point by an argument based on Akiba's own dialectical rules.

But it was the nationalists' turn to be jubilant. There could be no doubt, they maintained, that the Temple would soon be rebuilt. They expected this to be achieved, however, not through the Romans, but through the Parthians. Encouraged rather than mollified by Trajan's offers and attempts at conciliation, they felt certain that they could achieve a victory as memorable as that of the Hasmoneans, provided they avoided the errors which, they believed, had brought defeat in 66-70.

The leaders of the nationalist movement were Ishmael, who

had completely broken with Joshua and Akiba and a certain Simeon, probably Simeon ben Nethanel, brother-in-law of the Nasi, Gamaliel.[28]

In vain did such patriots as Gamaliel and Eliezer, and such pacifists as Joshua and Samuel the Little, warn leaders and followers of the folly of the enterprise. The days of the Messiah, even were they at hand, would be among the most difficult in all history, Gamaliel told them. The redemption of Israel could come about only through widespread war and suffering, such as no generation would of its own accord seek. "In the generation when the son of David will come," he said, "the House of Assembly will be turned into a brothel, Galilee will be devastated, the men of Galilee will wander about from city to city and will receive no kindness, the wisdom of the scribes will decay, the pious will be despised, and the face of the whole generation will be like the face of a dog. Truth will be lacking, and he who withdraws from evil will be considered a madman!" [29]

Apparently Gamaliel expected the new rebellion, like that of the year 66, to break out in Galilee, and he was therefore led to think that this district would suffer the brunt of the war and bear the heaviest burdens of defeat. Little did even he realize the full consequences of the insane struggle which was about to be precipitated.

Samuel the Little, that gentle pacifist who could not brook to pray for the downfall of Rome, also exhorted his colleagues to desist from the dangerous venture. About to die, he sent for them, and uttered the prediction which was soon to be fulfilled: "Simeon and Ishmael will die by the sword; the rest of the people will be pillaged; and great suffering will come on the land." [30]

Eliezer ben Hyrkanos, the old nationalist, was equally pessimistic. The leadership of the people was, in his opinion, beneath contempt. There was no hope anywhere in the visible world. "Since the day when the Temple was destroyed," he said, "the sages have become mere scribes, the scribes mere teachers, the teachers have become like the peasantry, and the peasantry is daily becoming poorer and humbler. On whom then shall we rely? Only on our Father who is in heaven!" [31] This was the burden of his teaching. Direct action, which he might have urged in earlier times, was useless. The Jews could be redeemed, but only "through repentance and good deeds." [32] If only they would observe the Sabbath properly, he said, they might escape the three evils which awaited them: the tribulations of the Messianic age, the eschatological wars of Gog and Magog, and the Day of the Final Judgment.[33] But Eliezer had little hope that his advice would prevail. When the scholars visited him during his illness, he predicted the dark days which were soon to come upon them. "I see fierce anger in the world." [34]

"I should be surprised," he said, looking at them, "if you die a natural death."

Akiba, the peace-lover, could not help asking, "What will my end be?"

"Worse than theirs!" cried the master, brusque as ever.

In his efforts to calm the nationalists, Joshua paid Ishmael a visit in the little village of Azziz, on the Edomite border, whither the latter had retired.[35] The influence of the aged scholar was still great; apparently Ishmael agreed to hold the nationalists in check. But the efforts of the experienced leaders to keep the peace were frustrated by the ill-timed daring of the more intransigeant leaders abroad. As frequently happens, these expatriates were more extreme in their objectives and unreflecting in their methods than the most ardent patriots in the homeland. Seeing that the Roman garrisons in Africa had been weakened to supply soldiers for the Parthian campaign, the Egyptian Jews raised the banner of revolt against the Empire. Perhaps they were stimulated to this by what they regarded as a heaven-sent portent—a great earthquake which destroyed Antioch while Trajan and his army lay encamped there. Many delegations which had come with petitions for the Emperor perished in the upheaval. Trajan himself escaped through a window from the room in which he lay trapped. "As the shocks continued for several days," Dio Cassius reports, "he lived out of doors in the hippodrome." [36]

It had always been predicted that natural catastrophes, and especially earthquakes, would herald the advent of the Messiah; and it was altogether natural that so widespread a disaster, happening in the particular city where the Emperor was wintering, should have been interpreted by the excited Jews as a signal from heaven. The riots which ensued covered the provinces of Egypt, Libya and Cyrene and the Island of Cyprus. Two leaders of the insurrection, Julianus and Pappus, appeared in Syria and threatened the Roman power in Palestine at closer range. The unrest spread to Palestine itself, where the nationalist leaders tried to coöperate with the rebel leaders of the Diaspora. An interesting discussion between Tarfon, who seems to have taken an active part in this movement, and some younger scholars, has been preserved.[37]

Tarfon said to them, "By what merit did the tribe of Judah attain to royalty in Israel?"

"Because," they answered in orthodox fashion, "its ancestor, Judah, confessed his sin with Tamar."

"But does not this interpretation put a premium on wrongdoing?" Tarfon objected.

"Because, then," another said, "he saved Joseph from death."

"That reply, too, is inadequate," Tarfon countered. "The merit of saving Joseph from death merely offset the sin of selling him as a slave." When they confessed their inability to reply, he said: "Because Judah was the tribe which sanctified the name of God at the sea. For when the various tribes of Israel came to the Red Sea, at the Exodus, each said, 'I will descend first.' The tribe of Judah, however, sprang into the sea. Hence it is written, 'When Israel came forth out of Egypt, the house of Jacob from a people of strange language, Judah became sanctified to Him, obtaining dominion over Israel' " (Ps. 114:1).

The Roman historian, Dio Cassius, followed by some later writers, has circulated incredible stories of the number and ferocity of the rebels. There was never any reasonable possibility of their success. But they did alarm Trajan, whose affairs were not prospering in the East and who was facing a real revolt in Mesopotamia. Even the contemporary writer, Appian, speaks of war between Trajan and the Egyptian Jews; and this may be taken to indicate that the disturbances were more than mere riots. Trajan acted with characteristic speed and decisiveness. He dispatched Marcius Turbo to suppress the insurrection in Africa, and appointed as governor of Palestine Lusius Quietus, an able Moorish general who might be relied upon to deal mercilessly with any resistance. And, indeed, within a short time peace was restored everywhere. The Jews of Egypt and Cyrene paid heavily for the irresponsibility of their leaders. The Cypriotes, in their vengeful fury, massacred the whole Jewish population and enacted a law—which survived for centuries—against Jewish immigration. The Palestinians, who had hardly had an opportunity to help the insurrectionists, were suppressed with an iron hand. The "war of Quietus"—a battle of armed legions against a disarmed, though restless, community—was long remembered with terror. It is even said that the lascivious Moor introduced into Judea the fearful *Ius primae noctis,* permitting his soldiers to seize newly married brides and carry them off before they were taken to their bridal chamber. The terrified Jews tried to escape the decree by celebrating their marriages in secret, or changing the customary wedding night from Wednesday to Tuesday. In some places, it even became customary for betrothed couples to live together without a marriage celebration, so as to evade the danger.[38]

Julianus and Pappus, who had been captured in Laodicea, were given a public trial, intended, doubtless, to impress the people with the futility of resistance.

"If your God can perform the miracles which you expected," the general taunted them, "why does He not save you from our hands, as He saved Hananiah, Mishael, and Azariah from Nebuchadnezzar?"

"Because," they answered staunchly, "Nebuchadnezzar had merit enough to be the occasion for a miracle, but you are not worthy of such an honor." [39]

The trial and execution of Julianus and Pappus had, however, the very opposite effect of what the Romans intended; it did not terrorize the nationalists, it infuriated them, and their fury infected even the saner elements among the people. Trajan's Day was abolished,[40] as if to serve warning on the Romans that the Jews no longer wished the restoration of the Temple at their hands. The two heroes were declared martyrs whose place in heaven was above that of all the saints.[41]

A generation later, when the rebellion initiated by Julianus and Pappus could be seen clearly as the beginning of the incredible disaster which had befallen Judea, Meir, the fiery patriot, still said, "The verse, 'and I shall break down the pride of your strength' (Lev. 26:19), applied best to Julianus and Pappus, the men of might and courage." [42]

But Joshua, and Eliezer who now fully coöperated with him, were far from converted to the cause of rebellion. When the people of Ludd declared a fast on Hanukkah to bespeak God's mercy for the seditious leaders, both Eliezer and Joshua publicly showed their disapproval of the action. "Go out and fast to obtain forgiveness for having fasted on the holy day," they said to the people.[43]

The Romans, whether unaware of the views expressed by the authoritative leaders, or indifferent to them, were as bitter as the nationalists themselves. Kindness having failed, they reverted to repression. They accepted the gauntlet thrown down by the Jews in the abolition of Trajan's Day and discarded the plans for the restoration of the Temple.[44]

For a time, Gamaliel, although he had been opposed to the rebellion, was sought for imprisonment, but a friendly Roman had warned him of the government's intention and he was in hiding.[45] The conclave, however, which the Romans mistakenly considered the center of the seditious propaganda, was suppressed.

Just at this time Trajan suddenly fell ill and decided to return to Italy, leaving the army under the command of Publius Aelius Hadrian, who had married his niece. When Trajan died en route, the army at Antioch declared Hadrian his successor, and the latter immediately demanded that the Senate confirm the choice. Established as the ruler of the world, Hadrian, who in spite of his literary tastes and general humanitarianism was sometimes petty and revengeful, at once removed Lusius Quietus (who had opposed his accession) from the governorship of Palestine and ordered him executed.

IX. APPROACHING THE PRECIPICE

THE sudden death of Trajan and the consequent fall and execution of Quietus, following so quickly on the death of Julianus and Pappus, made a deep and lasting impression on the minds of the people. They could not but see in these events the finger of God, avenging the suffering of his beloved ones on their persecutors. The later sages who repeated the tales apparently considered it incredible that both the Emperor and his general should have met such deaths, and merged the two miracles into one. They told how Trajan, after executing the two heroes, was visited by a pair of officials from Rome who killed him. For once, legend was compelled to minimize, rather than to exaggerate, reality.

Hadrian was, of course, hailed as a deliverer. An Egyptian-Jewish writer, posing as the Sibyl, speaks of him in most glowing terms: "A silver-helmed man, he shall have the name of a sea; he shall be a most excellent man and shall understand everything. And in thy time, most excellent, most noble dark-haired prince, and in the time of thy scions, all these days shall come" (Sibylline Oracles, Book V, verses 46-48).

The new governor of Palestine permitted the conclave to reassemble, but fearing that Yabneh might become a second Jerusalem and center of nationalist ferment, he changed the seat of the legislature to Ludd. The question immediately arose whether the conclave, in its new home, could claim all the authority which had been vested in that of Yabneh. Most of the scholars felt that it might; but Eliezer ben Hyrkanos, still in retirement, denied this. He admitted that Johanan ben Zakkai, his teacher, had claimed for the gathering at Yabneh practically the full authority of a Sanhedrin.

"But," Eliezer maintained, "Johanan made his ordinance only regarding Yabneh, not for any other place."

His colleagues, however, retorted: "The ordinance applied both to Yabneh and to any other locality where a conclave is established." [1]

While the scholars thus endowed the gathering at Ludd with full rabbinic authority, its prerogatives were definitely limited by the government. It was especially forbidden to exercise the one function which had made the conclave a legislature for all Jewry, namely the regulation of the calendar.

The confusion which this interdict threatened in Jewish religious life is obvious. The Jewish calendar, as we have already noted, had not yet been reduced to an automatic system. The beginnings of the months and the years were still announced by the court, whose duty it was to add an intercalary month about once in three years, so as to harmonize the Jewish year, based on the revolutions of the moon, with the solar year which is about eleven days longer. This essential arrangement might be omitted for a little time without grave confusion, but neglect for more than five or six years would bring Passover, the spring festival, into early February, the middle of the rainy season, and Sukkot, the festival of ingathering, into the beginning of August, midsummer.

The scholars were at a loss. It might be supposed that a few of them could have gathered in secret and arranged the calendar. But such a secret gathering would have involved the omission of ceremonies held sacred by all Jewry which were impressive symbols of Jewish unity. The alternative was to send someone beyond the Roman borders where, under the shelter of another government, the traditional ritual could be carried out. To this, however, grave objection was raised. Even when it was suggested that application be made to Rufus for permission to perform the ceremonies in Galilee, or to attempt to carry them out in the northern province without the knowledge of the Romans, Haninah of Ono protested. The calendar had been fixed in Judea from time immemorial; the scholars could not transfer the ceremony elsewhere. Haninah admitted, at last, that a decision on the subject of the intercalary month reached by scholars meeting in Galilee would be valid; but as for going to any country outside of Palestine, that was not to be considered.[2] Finally, unable to get permission to add the intercalary month anywhere in Palestine, and pressed by the impending dislocation of the festivals from their proper seasons, the scholars dispatched Akiba to Nahardea, which was under the Parthian dominion, with authority to perform the necessary ceremonies there. That Akiba, then almost seventy, should have undertaken such a long and hazardous journey may seem strange. But the ceremony was considered one of the most important in Judaism, and it was doubtless felt that it ought to be performed by a distinguished scholar. Perhaps Akiba's known pacifism and his friendship with Rufus were expected to protect him from the imputation of any treasonable motive in making the trip across the border.

While he was in Nahardea, Akiba had the opportunity of speaking to some of the Jewish emigrés who, as young men, had fled thither after the fateful war of 66-70.[3] From them he received several important traditions which he transmitted to Gamaliel. The most important was the rule, which had been established by Gamaliel I but apparently forgotten in the Palestinian academïes, accepting the testimony of a single witness as sufficient evidence to the death of a man, so as to permit his wife to remarry. In the unrest which filled the country—with the consequent disappearance of husbands, both by murder and in battle—this was an important reform. It was destined to become even more important in the later centuries when the Jews, scattered through the various countries of Europe, were perpetually on the move, and it was frequently impossible to find two eye-witnesses to a death by violence.

It is characteristic of the manner in which traditions were handed down in those troubled days that when Akiba reported this conversation in the academy, Gamaliel suddenly recalled that he had, himself, in his boyhood, heard such a decision rendered. Thus defended by both Gamaliel and Akiba and supported by a few others, the new principle was accepted. This was probably Gamaliel's last important public act. Exhausted by a lifetime of public service, worn out by the continual necessity of appeasing both the Roman masters and the Jewish subjects, sickened by the new anxieties arising out of the rebellion, he broke down before his time. He was younger than either Joshua or Eliezer, and the fact that they survived him, as well as the manner of his death, made a deep impression on the people, who supposed that he had suffered for the sin of agreeing to Eliezer's expulsion from the academy! It was said that Eliezer's wife, Imma Shalom, who was Gamaliel's sister, had never permitted her husband to recite the special individual petitions, customary after daily prayer, fearing that such an appeal to God might bring dire punishment on her brother. She had neglected that caution once, and while Eliezer was at his prayers, Gamaliel died.[4]

The presidency, which was left vacant with Gamaliel's death, could not be filled. The Romans, who did not permit the announcement of the calendar, would certainly forbid any effort to appoint a new president. Joshua naturally became the leader of the people, retaining his former office as Ab Bet Din. But when he tried to obtain the consent of the conclave to set aside some of Gamaliel's rulings, he was effectively opposed. Johanan ben Nuri, Gamaliel's friend, cried, "I see that the body follows the head. As long as Rabban Gamaliel lived, we accepted his views; and now that he is dead do you wish to set his words aside? Joshua, we will not listen to you!" And strangely, the conclave which had once voted to depose the living Gamaliel because he had offended Joshua, agreed with Johanan ben Nuri in defense of the dead Nasi.[5] This reversal of sentiment cannot be explained simply in terms of reverence for the departed; Johanan's intemperate defiance of Joshua, who was by far the older man, and indeed had been instrumental many years earlier in obtaining the post of overseer for him, is evidence that the quarrel was not personal but partisan. What had happened becomes clear in the light of the historical situation which has been described.

Between 90 and 95, when the struggle between the plebeians, Joshua and Akiba, and the patricians, Gamaliel and Eliezer, was being fought out for the first time, the plebeians had been in the majority. They had retained their power in the conclave for almost two decades. But, as had happened before, the wave of nationalism which was sweeping over the country toward the end of Trajan's rule made itself felt in the acceptance not merely of patrician-provincial politics, but also of the corresponding juristic point of view.[6] This explains the curious statement of Johanan ben Nuri that in late years the law had always been decided in accordance with the

views of Gamaliel, the patrician Nasi. It also explains Joshua's
hope that the death of Gamaliel would enable him and his
fellow plebeians to reassert their views. He discovered, when
Johanan ben Nuri, the Galilean, opposed him, that the increasing loyalty which had been shown Gamaliel of late had
been more than personal; it arose out of the strength with
which nationalism had endowed the patrician wing.

Hardly any of Akiba's partisans remained loyal to him; his
most intimate friends became adherents of the rising, militant, nationalist group. Ben Zoma, who had been the first to
show signs of disagreement with the Master, namely when he
seconded Ishmael's opposition to Trajan's last offer, openly
joined the nationalists. Together with other partisans, he
insisted that the prayers be reëdited so as to emphasize their
patriotic aspirations more clearly. In particular, he demanded
that a biblical passage recalling to the people the miracles
which had once been performed on their behalf during the
Exodus from Egypt, be recited in the evening, as well as at
the morning services. This had long been advocated by the
nationalists. "I am almost seventy years old," Eleazar ben
Azariah said, "and I could never persuade my colleagues to
have the Exodus mentioned in the evening service until Ben
Zoma proved from Scripture that it ought to be done." [7]

But it was too late for Ben Zoma to seek new laurels among
the nationalists. In the effort to adjust itself to the new conceptions, his mind, already wearied with the years of concen-
trated speculation about theology and philosophy to which he
had been subjected, at last gave way. The first one to notice
his derangement was Joshua ben Hananya. Joshua had been
walking along a road with some disciples when Ben Zoma
passed them and failed to greet them. Not at all offended by

this, Joshua called after him, "Ben Zoma, whence and whither?"

"I was considering the Creation," the poor scholar replied, "and the distance between the Upper Waters and the Lower Waters is no more than a handbreadth."

Perhaps it was the manner in which these strange words were spoken, as well as their content, which convinced Joshua that his colleague was no longer sane. "I am afraid," he said to his disciples, as they went on, "that Ben Zoma is without"; and so indeed the event proved.[8]

Ben Zoma's estrangement and his illness must have been heavy blows to Akiba; but worse was to follow. Elisha ben Abuyah, foreseeing the growing tension between the Jews and their governors, decided to throw in his lot with the Romans. He had become convinced that he could never attain distinction in Jewish scholarship and, indeed, the time had come when this no longer disturbed him. So far as he could see, Judaism, having set itself against Rome, was doomed to extinction; within a generation the pedantic preoccupations of the scholars would all be forgotten. The present and the future belonged to the pagans. The desire for social preferment, as well as anxiety about his huge estates, pointed to one policy—friendship with the powerful. His wealth won him easy admission to their palaces and thither he turned, beginning as apostate and ending as traitor.[9]

Ben Azzai, contrasting these two men, remarked: "He who loses his wits through learning is still in happier case than he who forsakes his learning because of his wits."[10]

But Ben Azzai, himself, was no longer faithful to Akiba's teachings. He could not help admiring Ishmael's boldness and activity, which contrasted so sharply with his father-in-law's resignation. The crisis destroyed the thin plebeian-pacifist veneer which Ben Azzai had put on to please Akiba. He was once more the hot-tempered Galilean enthusiast. If the scholars were not ready to fight for Judaism, at least they should be ready to die for it, he thought. The ease with which they yielded to Rome, the sending of Akiba to Babylonia to fix the calendar, the supine surrender of their religious rites, seemed to him worse than cowardice. "God must be loved," he insisted, "with all one's soul";[11] and this he interpreted, "even if He demands one's soul." So deeply was Akiba impressed with this, that in his last moments he recalled Ben Azzai's remarks and quoted them.[12]

Simeon ben Nannos, the third plebeian who had stood by Akiba in his many struggles, and who was especially remembered for his valiant defense of the master in his first controversy with Jose the Galilean, also went with the stream.[13] Simeon ben Yohai, whose father was almost as Romanophile as Elisha ben Abuyah, was a secret revolutionary.[14] Meir, who had studied under Ishmael before he came to Akiba, asserted his adherence to Shammaitic teachings in several important controversies, and defended the cause of the priests, whom Akiba had opposed.[15] To the astonishment of colleagues, teachers and the general public, this favorite pupil of Akiba publicly renounced his allegiance to the master and declared himself the disciple of Ishmael, under whom he had studied for a short time early in his career.[16] So impressed were the hearers with the gravity of this statement, that the place where it was made was pointed out with wonder for more than a century.

Even Jose and Judah, who were destined to lead the pacifist plebeian groups in the next generation, after the confusion had subsided, were for the moment carried away by the general excitement. They refused to accept Akiba's correct interpretation of Deuteronomy, exempting from military service those who were faint-hearted. "The verse must be taken literally," the Master said. But Jose answered, "The weak and the faint-hearted are those who have entered into an illegitimate marriage"; while Judah, without taking issue on the specific question, denied that the Law applied to the war which they were anticipating. "In a war of duty, a bridegroom must leave his room, and a bride her bridal canopy," and give their services to their people. The extreme nationalists said that this was true even in a war to reconquer the ideal boundaries of Palestine; but Judah hesitated to go as far as that.[17]

To these young and ardent scholars, who felt certain that the Messiah was awaiting their call, Akiba's patience seemed strangely weak and pusillanimous. The prudence which was born of experience and the pacifism which had its roots in the historical plebeian outlook on life could not, in their perspective, be distinguished from the cynicism of the coward. Akiba regarded the principle that "there is no distress save that which affects individuals,"[18] as a truism; they denounced it as selfishness. He asked how a people could be described as suffering when its members were prospering; to them the Nation had a reality of its own, which transcended the lives and needs of its members. With all their respect and reverence for Akiba's genius and his years, they considered him, as he himself had in his earlier years considered Joshua, a flaccid compromiser.

Just about this time occurred an event which must have seemed to Akiba pregnant with mighty possibilities for the people. Tineius Rufus was appointed governor of the province, and from the first he showed himself friendly and generous to the people. He apparently came under the spell of Akiba and opened the doors of the governorate wide for him.

Of course, he must have recognized in the Jewish sage a man who could be of the greatest use to him in his new charge. Yet it would be uncharitable to assume that his friendship was nothing more than hypocrisy and that the bluff Roman was entirely without genuine appreciation of the Jewish scholar's genius.

The friendship which developed between the two men led to various discussions on religion and politics, some of which have been preserved.

"If your God loves the poor," Rufus once asked Akiba, "why does He not supply their needs?"

"So that we may supply them ourselves, and thus be saved from the punishment of Gehenna," was Akiba's strange reply.[19]

The unphilosophical Roman did not think of asking why a large part of the world should suffer merely that another part might use it as an instrument of salvation. But he knew enough of court life to make another response. "On the contrary, it seems to me," he said, "that your charity will bring severe penalties on you. Suppose a king ordered a servant imprisoned and kept without food or drink, and someone fed him, would not that person incur the sovereign's anger?"

"We are the children of God, not His slaves," Akiba countered. "Will not even a human king who ordered his child arrested and starved, be grateful to the minister who disobeys him?"[20]

"Why should your God, if He is as great as you say, be envious of non-existent rivals?" Rufus asked Akiba on another occasion.

Instead of replying to the question, Akiba said, "I dreamed last night of two dogs; the name of one was Rufus, the name of the other, Rufina."

"What," cried the enraged Roman, "could you not call the dogs by any other names than mine and my wife's?"

"What difference is there between us and the dumb beasts?" Akiba said. "We eat and they eat; we multiply and they multiply; we die and they die. And yet, because I called two nonexistent animals, which I happened to see in a dream, by the names you and your wife bear, you are offended. How then shall the Holy One, blessed be He, not be offended when a piece of inert wood is called by His name?" [21]

It was perhaps in later years, when the government undertook to suppress Jewish ceremonial, that the debates concerning the Sabbath and circumcision occurred between the two men.

"Why should one day be honored more than another?" asked Rufus.

"And why should one person be honored more than another?" Akiba replied, with obvious reference to Rufus's own exalted position.

"I hold my office," Rufus replied, "because my master appointed me."

"So the Sabbath, too, was appointed by the Master of the Universe," Akiba said.

"What do you consider superior, divine creation or human art?" asked Rufus.

Akiba, realizing immediately what the general had in mind, replied, "Human art."

"How can you say that?" Rufus continued. "Can man bring into being anything which approaches the beauty and dignity of heaven and earth?"

"I am not speaking of the creations which man cannot imitate, but only of those things where his art is effective," Akiba said.

"Why, then," asked Rufus, "do you, Jews, insist on attempting to improve God's creation through circumcision?"

"I knew that it was the circumcision which you had in mind," Akiba stated candidly, "and that is why I gave you my reply before. But to answer your question, consider ears of grain and loaves of bread. The ears of grain are the creation of God, the loaves of bread are manufactured by men. Which are more useful?" [22]

In the course of Akiba's visits to Rufus at the governorate in Caesarea, he doubtless became acquainted with the general's wife. It is probable that she was as much attracted as was her husband to the interesting and witty old sage. An incredible legend tells that she was attracted a great deal more, for, it continues, she became converted to Judaism out of love for Akiba and ultimately married him! [23]

Rufus's friendship may have flattered Akiba, but it could not make him happy. The more he saw of the governor, the more he must have realized the futility of the hope for any real amelioration of the conditions of the Jews. There was no possibility at all of the reconstruction of Jerusalem, and the temper of the ruling people was such that repressive edicts might be expected at any time. The burden of these public anxieties and disappointments was made heavier for Akiba by private sorrows. His son, Simeon, who had achieved distinction as a scholar, and his son-in-law, Ben Azzai, who in spite of their late differences had continued to be his closest associate, both died.

The words which Akiba spoke at his son's funeral are characteristic of his deep humility. "My brethren of the house of Israel, hear me! It cannot be that you have assembled because I am a sage, for there are among you many who are far wiser; nor because I am wealthy, for there are among you many far wealthier. The men of the South know Akiba, but how do the men of Galilee know me? The men may know me, but whence come the women and the children? But I am certain that your reward will be great because you have come for the honor of the Torah and to fulfill the commandments. I should be comforted though I had seven children and had buried them all when my son died." [24]

The aged Eliezer ben Hyrkanos, too, whom Akiba had loved throughout his life in spite of their violent differences, died about this time. During the past few years he had become reconciled to his former colleagues and had heartily coöperated with Joshua in preventing—or at least postponing—the disastrous war. Akiba was at Caesarea, doubtless importuning Rufus for some leniency to the Jews, when the aged patrician breathed his last. The sage, who had stoically continued his lectures while his son lay sick and dying, broke down with grief when the news of this blow to the cause of peace reached him. "My father, my father!" he wailed again and again, in the words which Elisha used of Elijah, "the chariots of Israel and its horsemen!" And then, as he thought of the grave problems which rested on the shoulders of the sages and the mighty assistance which Eliezer's prestige had given to the peace party, he cried, "I have many coins, but where shall I now go to have them exchanged?" [25]

Joshua, too, was deeply moved. He and some colleagues had sat by Eliezer's bedside during the last hours of his illness, when the end was obviously approaching. The sage's mind had been lucid until the last. They discussed various questions of ritual, and the sick man responded to each question, saying, "This is pure," "This is impure." Those who were standing by regarded it as a good omen that his last spoken word was "pure."

"His body was pure," cried one of them, "and his soul left him as he said 'pure.'"

"The vow is released," said Joshua, referring to the pronouncement of excommunication which the conclave had issued against Eliezer decades earlier.[26]

Within the house he could control his grief, but when he passed the stone from which Eliezer had for so many years taught, and which had stood unused these decades, Joshua's heart melted at the thought of the needless sorrow they had caused the great teacher. He forgot Eliezer's earlier antagonism and remembered only the coöperation of the later years. He had come to understand his old opponent, and he also perceived—what had eluded him throughout the years—that in spite of their small differences, he and Eliezer were essentially at one in their outlook on life. The real enemies of his ideals were more numerous, more powerful, and less subject to attack. Suddenly he bent down over the rock and began to kiss it, crying, "This stone is like unto Mount Sinai, and he who sat here may be compared to the Ark of the Covenant." [27]

This was not a mere outburst of passion or an expression of formal grief. When, some time after Eliezer's death, the sages gathered to review his decisions, and criticized some of them harshly, Joshua said, "The Lion cannot be refuted when he is dead!" [28] In fact, Joshua persuaded the conclave to accept several of Eliezer's opinions which had previously been rejected in favor of his own. "So long as Eliezer lived," we are told, "Joshua's decision was followed; but when Eliezer died, Joshua insisted that his opponent's views be accepted." [29]

Joshua was left alone of the older scholars. He continued to exert some restraint on Ishmael. Akiba's relations with Ishmael remained what they had always been, friendly but formal. Akiba always spoke of Ishmael with respect; and only once or twice did Ishmael allow himself such an expression as, "Go and tell Akiba that he is mistaken." [30] Sometimes the two scholars would walk together, but then they avoided any questions which might lead to sharp controversy. Once they discussed different demonstrations of the rule which all accepted, that the preservation of life sets aside the Sabbath. In another conversation Akiba explained to Ishmael how he interpreted the first verse in Genesis.[31]

When Ishmael's sons died—how is not recorded—Akiba and the other sages, Tarfon, Jose the Galilean and Eleazar ben Azariah, visited him in accordance with the usual custom.

"You know," said Tarfon, "that he is a great scholar, and an expert aggadist; do not let any of us interrupt the other when we console him."

Akiba thereupon remarked, "I will speak last." But Akiba's muse forsook him, for his remarks can hardly be described as either moving or comforting. "If Ahab, King of Israel, who had only one good deed to his credit was mourned so widely," he said, "how great must be the public grief for the sons of Rabbi Ishmael." [32]

While the general community was bewailing its losses in leadership, the nationalists were solidifying their forces. They announced that none of them would eat meat or drink wine until the Temple was restored. The peace party sent Joshua to reason with them.

"My children," cried the aged pacifist, "why do you abstain from meat and wine?"

"Because they were offered on the altar, which is now destroyed," Ishmael and his colleagues answered.

"Then how can you eat bread, for that was used in the meal offerings? How can you drink water, which was poured out in the Sukkot libations?" [33] "You remind me," he said to them on another occasion, "of the fable of the crane and the lion. The lion had swallowed a bone, and in his fear of imminent death offered the most tantalizing gifts to anyone who would save him. The crane, thrusting its long beak into the lion's throat, drew out the bone. But when the bird demanded its reward, the King of Beasts replied: 'It is quite sufficient for you to have had your head in the lion's mouth and to have escaped unscathed.' So, too," said Joshua, "let us be grateful that no harm has come upon us, rather than insist on the literal fulfillment of the promises which were made to us." [34]

The tension continued through the reign of Hadrian. Terrorism could not smother the popular movement; indeed the nationalists gained strength from the harshness of the oppressive measures enacted by the government. In vain did Akiba continue to resort to Rufus; the time for personal intercession had passed. The suppression of the Jews had become a definite Roman policy.

Just at this time, Ishmael removed from Azziz, in southern Judea, where he had resided for many years, to Usha, in Galilee. The reasons for this transfer are obscure. It is possible that he considered Galilee a better field for revolutionary activity, but it is equally possible that the Roman government banished him from Judea. The Ishmael of these days resembled in few respects the young man who had carried on the series of legalistic controversies with Akiba. In his thirst for rebellion, and in his expectation of victory, his enthusiasm for everything else had become dampened. A curious story illustrates both his ignorance of Galilean geography and of his new attitude toward ceremonial. A man had brought before him a bill of divorcement which had been written in the village of Sasai, in the district of Acre. Now, according to rabbinic law, such a bill, drawn up outside of Palestine, may be validated by the court if the person bringing it testifies that it was written and signed in his presence. Documents originating in Palestine require two witnesses for validation. Ishmael, hearing that the village from which the writ came was in the district of Acre, assumed that it was outside the borders of Palestine, and said to the man, "Testify that it was drawn up in your presence, so that we will not need witnesses to validate it."

After the man had made his statement and left, Ilai, a native Galilean scholar who was present, said to Ishmael, "My master, the village of Sasai belongs to Palestine, and is nearer to Sepphoris than to Acre."

Whereupon Ishmael replied, with the utmost coolness, "Be silent, my son. Since the permission has been granted, let it stand." [35]

About the year 125, the relations between the Jews and the Romans took a definite turn for the worse. Whether the increasing rigor was due to the suspicion of nationalist activity on the part of Ishmael and Simeon is unknown. It is certain, however, that edicts were promulgated forbidding the practice of circumcision, the pretext being the Roman law against mutilation of the body, and it is probable that the recitation of the *Shema* at public services, the reading of the Book of Esther on Purim, and the sounding of the *Shofar* on New Year's Day, were also prohibited, as being ceremonies with specifically nationalist implications. In addition, Jewish courts were enjoined from issuing divorces or performing the ceremony of *halizah,* through which the widow of a man who died without issue is released. [36]

The Jews resorted to various devices to observe the interdicted ceremonies. Meir, a disciple of Akiba, records, for instance, that they would recite the *Shema* under their breath as they sat in the academy, so that the soldier who stood guard at the door might not overhear them. In some communities, it became customary to utter the response to *Shema* (Blessed be the name of His glorious kingdom forever and aye) which was especially nationalistic, in an undertone. Other groups included the *Shema* in the midst of the prayers, where the Roman spies would not recognize it.[37] The blasts of the *Shofar,* which had punctuated the regular prayers of the New Year's Day, were postponed to the end of the service, where it was less offensive to the rulers. Johanan ben Nuri, and doubtless others, read the Scroll of Esther on the evening of Purim, instead of in the morning. Courts became accustomed to tear the writ of divorce as soon as it was handed by the husband to the wife in accordance with the prescribed ceremonial, thus destroying any evidence of the violation of the Roman interdict.

A whole generation was to pass before these various edicts were rescinded. In the meantime, the practices adopted out of cruel necessity, became integral parts of Jewish tradition, so that even to this day Jewish ritual bears the marks of the ancient persecution. The response to the *Shema* is still recited in a whisper, except, significantly, on the Day of Atonement.[38] Apparently, even in those darkest days, the Jews, who had made this compromise with their consciences during the year, could not bear to suppress the affirmation of their faith on their holiest day, and shouted the interdicted words, no matter how dangerous that might be. The new generation which grew up under the Marrano conditions, knowing nothing of the origin of this difference, adopted it and handed it down as a permanent custom. Throughout the Jewish world the Scroll of Esther is still read at night as well as in the morning; the trumpet is sounded on Rosh Ha-Shanah both during the prayers and aside from them; and every writ of divorcement is cut as soon as the man hands it to the woman.

Ishmael and his party offered no more resistance to these decrees than did Akiba. This is the more remarkable because when Ishmael was younger he had held that the least commandment of the Law justifies martyrdom. He had let his nephew Ben Dama die rather than permit a heretical physician to heal him.

"Call him," poor Ben Dama had cried in his agony, "and when I am well I will prove to you from Scripture that it is permitted."

But Ishmael had not yielded, and when Ben Dama died, he said, "Happy art thou, Ben Dama, that thou didst not transgress the words of thy colleagues!" [39]

The fanatical pietist had, however, become a revolutionary general, and we have already observed that his ardor for the ceremonial had cooled as his hopes for victory grew. To violate the Roman law was to court death, at a time when Judaism, in his opinion, needed not martyrs but soldiers. He therefore announced the amazing principle that "faced with the threat of death a Jew may violate any commandment, even that against idol-worship." [40] In accordance with this policy, he permitted the *halizah* ceremony, which traditionally had to be performed publicly, by day, and in the presence of at least five judges, to be carried out secretly, at night, and with no other witness than himself present. [41]

The first and most disastrous effect of the restrictions was the further division of the Jewish community into bitterly hostile factions, reminiscent of the last century of the Second Commonwealth. The nationalists now fast becoming a majority, corresponded, of course, to the Zealots of former times. Opposed to them were the Romanophiles, who may be compared to the earlier Herodians, for they not only opposed the war with the Romans, but coöperated with the latter in every way. This party adopted the stand taken by Elisha ben Abuyah when he left the academy. It numbered in its midst those of the patricians who felt that in a measure of strength with Rome Judea was certain to be crushed. In addition, many of the common people wanted peace.

The natural leader of the Romanophiles was, of course, Elisha ben Abuyah. He used his knowledge of the Law to discover to the oppressors any stratagems which the Jews employed to evade the hateful decrees. Some Jewish laborers who were compelled to work on the Sabbath, arranged, for instance, to carry their burdens in pairs, since technically that involves a lesser violation of the Law. Elisha, noticing this, immediately informed the appropriate officer of this "dereliction." He entered the elementary schools where the children were studying their scriptural lessons, and with the help of soldiers dispersed them. "Let this child be apprenticed to a tailor; that one to a cobbler," he would say, and his orders were carried out.[42]

Some of the less affluent apostates became Roman soldiers. At a later time, when the persecution of students was intensified, one of these, himself a former student, is said to have encountered two disciples of Joshua who had exchanged their scholars' tunics for workers' clothes, to escape molestation. Recognizing them in spite of this disguise, the renegade said, "If you are the children of the Torah, why do you disguise yourselves? And if you are not her children, why do you continue to be loyal to her?"

"We are her children," they answered, "and are ready to die for her."

Stricken, perhaps, with momentary remorse, the soldier said to them, "If you explain three difficulties in Scripture to me, I will save your lives," and he asked them for the interpretation of one verse each from the Pentateuch, the Prophets, and the Hagiographa. When they had given their replies, the soldiers said: "I prefer the exegesis of your master, Joshua," and he told them how the difficulties had been explained in his time.[43]

In their desire to dissociate themselves from Judaism, some of the assimilationists adopted the methods which had been used by the Hellenists three centuries earlier. They did not hesitate to undergo the painful and even dangerous operation necessary to conceal the evidence of circumcision.[44] Naturally, there were many who sympathized with the general purposes of this group but would not go to such extremes. Among these moderate Romanophiles we may count Jose ben Kisma, who tried to persuade Haninah ben Teradyon against martyrdom, and Pappias ben Judah who performed the same office for Akiba.[45]

Perhaps it should be recorded here that these efforts to escape the common fate failed completely. Some time after Akiba was imprisoned, he was surprised to see Pappias ben Judah brought in by the soldiers. "Happy are you, Akiba," Pappias said to him, "that you are suffering for the Law; I, too, am suffering, but for things of vanity."

Jose ben Kisma, who died in the midst of the confusion incident to the collapse of the Bar Kokba rebellion, showed in his last remarks that the persecution had destroyed the last vestige of his affection and respect for the Empire. In the privacy of the room where he lay dying, he predicted the victory of the Parthians over the Romans. "Bury me deep in the ground," he said to his family, "for there will be no coffin in all Palestine which will not be used by the Parthians as a trough for their horses." "When will the Messiah come?" his disciples asked. Expecting a long conflict between the empires, with varying fortunes, Jose replied, "When that gate will have been destroyed and rebuilt twice, it will fall for the third time, and then the Messiah will soon be at hand." [46]

Elisha ben Abuyah, too, obviously repented before his death. The Romans, having made full use of him, ignored him, while the Jews treated him with undisguised hatred and contempt. The only one of the scholars who continued to associate with him was Meir, who suffered much at the hands of his colleagues on that account.

"Repent," Meir said to him one day.

"It is too late," Elisha replied, "I have heard from 'behind the partition' that everyone will be admitted to repentance, except Elisha ben Abuyah."

His services to the government apparently did not even save his property for his family, for his daughter came begging to the door of Judah the Patriarch. "Think of my father's learning," she pleaded, "forget his wicked deeds." [47]

Corresponding to the milder Romanophiles were the non-violent nationalists who were ready to die, but not to kill, for the Torah. The precursor of this group had been Simeon ben Azzai, but in later times it numbered among its adherents such men as Tarfon, Jose the Galilean, Judah the Baker, Yeshebab the Scribe, Huzpit the Announcer, and many others who were martyrs for Judaism. There are some points of resemblance between the otherworldiness which the members of this group developed in the crisis, and the doctrines of the Essenes of Josephus's day. They did not adopt the rules of the famous order; they were not celibates and did not live in communes. But their devotion to the Law, their extreme piety and their willingness to endure martyrdom for an iota of the Law, marks them as heirs to those great ascetics.

Some of the moderate nationalists were tempted to seek in exile both safety and the opportunity to observe the Law. But their consciences would not let them find so easy an escape. To dwell in Palestine was itself a commandment and, in the eyes of many, one which outweighed all others.

Pathetic incidents are recorded to illustrate the inner struggles of many of these scholars. Two scholars, Eleazar ben Shammua and Johanan the Cobbler, had actually reached Zidon when, "remembering Palestine, they burst into tears, and returned to their native places." Another group, including Judah ben Bathyra, Matthew ben Harash, Hananiah the nephew of Joshua, and Jonathan, had a similar experience. As they left the Palestinian border behind them, "they tore their clothes" in grief; but they continued on their journey.[48] Judah ben Bathyra settled in Nesibis, on the borders of Mesopotamia; Hananiah and Jonathan went to Babylonia; and Matthew sought safety from persecution in the imperial capital, Rome.

Finally, there were the rationalist-pacifists, represented in the time of the last war by Johanan ben Zakkai, and now by Akiba. They held that the most important element in Judaism was study, and all they asked of the world was the opportunity to pursue it. They would even yield to restrictions on the observance of the Law, provided their schools were not closed. They were the leaders of the party which Josephus called the Pharisees, but which was in reality the Hillelite wing of that sect.

These various groups were not, however, sharply defined

organizations, as had been the parties of the Second Commonwealth. They merged gradually into one another, and there were many people whom it was difficult to allocate among them. Yet the fundamental divisions were clear, and comprised all the possible responses which a subject people can make to repression: submission, armed resistance, non-violent resistance and philosophic adjustment. Although under the circumstances the division could not be as distinct for the contemporary as for the historian, Akiba seems to have recognized it. Being, however, a rabbi rather than a sociologist, he recorded not the fact, but a theological idea which it suggested. The attitudes taken by the various parties reminded him of the responses of men to divine punishment. "Some, like Abraham, ordered to sacrifice his son, submit in silence; others, like Job in his pains, make violent protests; still others, like Hezekiah in his illness, plead for mercy; and a fourth group, like David punished for the sin of Bath Sheba, kiss the rod." [49]

While the scholars, like the people at large, were finding themselves in the various factions, the conclave assembled once more in Ludd to determine on a national policy. Apparently Ishmael did not attend; either because the Romans would not permit it, or because he was preoccupied with his revolutionary preparations. But he had already given his opinion, which was unquestionably accepted by his nationalist followers. There was no purpose in resisting the Roman decrees for the moment; the edicts which they issued had to be obeyed, no matter what Jewish law they contravened. The moderate Nationalists, who hoped for rescue by God rather than by force, were aghast at this doctrine. Did not the Book of Daniel record that its hero had courted martyrdom by the recitation of prayers when that had been made a capital offense? Was not the history of Israel filled with the names of illustrious men and women who had given their lives for an iota of the Law? Standing between the two groups, Akiba insisted that the practical problem could not be solved before the scholars agreed on the basic theory of the place of observance in Judaism. The militant nationalists had denied the obligation of martyrdom; but how could they justify this position? Surely they did not intend to imply that in the choice between God's Law and Caesar's the Jew had a real alternative. It was obvious that insistence on the ceremonies would lead to the annihilation of the Jews, for the Romans were apparently serious in their determination to destroy Judaism. Yet even if it involved national suicide, could obedience to God be refused? From his own point of view, no such drastic ultimatum was presented. The plebeians had always held that study was more important than observance; and it was entirely logical for them to maintain that should observance lead to the destruction of the Torah it would defeat its own purpose. The patricians had, however, always opposed this view. We have already seen how their leaders, Shammai and Simeon ben Gamaliel I, took the view that intellectual debate was a waste of time.[50] Elisha ben Abuya had repeated the principle in his pious youth; and Eleazar of Modin had objected when Joshua found references to study in Scripture.[51]

Perhaps Akiba admitted that he had himself not fully comprehended the significance of the controversy between the older teachers until the crisis had made it clear. Only now did he realize why Johanan ben Zakkai could prefer the foundation of the academy at Yabneh to the preservation of the Temple at Jerusalem. The decision had been a corollary of the proposition that Judaism was first and foremost a system of knowledge, and only incidentally a series of ceremonies.

Akiba insisted that a vote be taken on the principle involved, before the practical question of resistance or non-resistance be decided. This put the militant nationalists in a quandary; for they dared not repudiate their older teachers; and yet to follow Tarfon and Jose the Galilean, who drew the logical conclusions from the statements of Shammai and Simeon ben Gamaliel, was equally impossible. Finally the members of the conclave developed a formula which saved their tradition and yet adjusted it to the momentary need. "Study," they said, "is important, for it alone can lead to observance." [52] In other words, it was well to forego the observance of the Law for the moment, in order to preserve the academies which were needed to guide future generations.

With the theoretical question settled, the conclave approached the much more awkward practical problem: what was to be done about the Roman edicts, were they to be obeyed or resisted? The decision which had just been reached implied that it was not necessary to risk martyrdom for the sake of observance. Yet, Akiba urged, there were obviously some religious practices which were so basic to life that survival without them was a self-contradiction. Judaism was, it is true, a system of knowledge—but knowledge of what? Of God and His law. If, then, the Jew was ordered to worship idols, how could his desire to perpetuate the Law justify him in yielding, as Ishmael had maintained he might do? The fundamental purpose of the Law was that "man should live by it." How could anyone propose that a Jew, commanded by a tyrant to commit murder, should obey because of his love for the Law! And equally important with the recognition of God and the sanctity of life, Akiba considered the purity of the home. Could a Jew submit to unchastity, even at the threat of death? Akiba therefore proposed this rule: "While most of the commandments may be violated to save one's life, three groups of laws must be preserved at all costs and at all times. They are those which forbid idol-worship, murder and the infringement of chastity." [53]

His disciple, Meir, who took part in these crucial deliberations and already showed his future patrician sympathies, insisted that the protection of property was as important as the protection of life and home. "A man must be prepared to accept martyrdom rather than rob his neighbor," [54] he said. But Akiba's view, which put life and home and the worship of God in a class by themselves, prevailed. This famous decision of Ludd was destined to become the fundamental policy of the Jews in all the centuries that have followed. At various times, parts of the Law had to be abandoned; but never the Study of the Law, and never the three cardinal principles of the existence of the one God, the sanctity of life and the purity of the home.

It is highly probable that the severity of the recent enactment against the Jews was related to the Emperor's expected return to the East. Rufus may well have feared that the revolutionary activity of the nationalists, of which he was aware, but which he could not suppress, would reach his master's ear. Unable to deal directly with the seditious propaganda, he sought to abolish the ceremonies which in his opinion were its principal support. To the Jews, on the other hand, the arrival of the Emperor, which occurred in the year 130, seemed a most opportune occasion to present their petitions and their grievances in person. They could not forget that at his accession Hadrian had removed their arch-oppressor, Quietus; they conveniently overlooked the fact that that was done for personal reasons, and not out of respect for their feelings. They may even have hoped that the Emperor on receiving their

submission might grant them their heart's desire, the rebuilding of the sanctuary. Wherever he had come on his journey
through the East he had been greeted as Savior, Benefactor,
Rebuilder. It was natural that the people should expect him
to be as kind to Judea as he had been to Achaea, Libya,
Bithynia and a dozen other places.

While the scholars and teachers who saw the world from
the perspective of Judea were giving free rein to these opti-
mistic dreams, the Emperor was leisurely making his way
through other larger provinces. He visited Antioch, the capital
of Syria, and Palmyra, the ancient Arabic kingdom in the
midst of the desert; but finally he turned back and arrived at
Philadelphia, the capital of Ammon, in Transjordan. Thence
apparently he went directly to the ruined city of Jerusalem.[55]

It must have been obvious to Hadrian that the Romans had
committed an act of unjustified waste in razing Jerusalem to
the ground. The interests of the empire demanded the re-
establishment of the great wealth-producing metropolis which
was the center of the country's commerce, industry and religion. He could see clearly that Caesarea, the seat of the
Roman governorate, could never become a second Jerusalem.
The traditions which made the ancient city so holy were an
integral part of its being, and could be transferred to no other
center. Hadrian decided to grant the request of the Jews and
to rebuild their city.

He also granted them a temple. But—and in this he displayed the same blindness that had been the cause of so many
tragedies in the history of this people—the temple, like so
many others he had founded, was to be dedicated to the worship of himself, as identified with the Capitoline Jupiter![56]

Perhaps he anticipated a little dissatisfaction or disappointment among the people that their full request for the restora-

tion of their own special faith had not been granted. But after all, in his own eyes, his gift outweighed by far the insignificant details of ritual and theology. He was granting them their city, which was their economic and spiritual life, and a temple which would ultimately dim the glory of both Solomon's and Herod's structures. That this peculiar people, whom he now met, were more concerned about their theology than about their bread, and that the Temple ritual meant more to them than the finest structure, the pagan militarist could not realize. He did not know that when the Emperor Caligula had ordered the erection of his statue in the Temple, thousands of Jews had presented themselves in a delegation to Petronius, the Governor of Syria, asking that they be slain in cold blood before the edict was carried out. Centuries before, the Jews, who had tamely submitted to every other form of oppression, had broken out into open revolt when their Sanctuary was defiled by Antiochus. It was to this people that the Roman Emperor was now offering the poisoned gift of a pagan temple, where the heathen Jupiter would be worshiped in the form of Hadrian's statue!

The Jews understood the Roman as little as he understood them. He regarded their devotion to their traditional cult as mere obstinacy; they considered his desire for a temple dedicated to himself as megalomania. Both were in error. The Emperor's policy was based on principles of prudence and statesmanship as fundamental as the Jews' ideals of faith and piety. It was to the interests of the Empire that Jerusalem be reëstablished as a commercial, religious and educational center; but it was equally important that the ideas which prevented its complete spiritual integration with the Empire be forgotten. The Empire needed a city on Mount Zion; but it could not be Jerusalem. It had to be Aelia Capitolina, indicating in its very name (taken from that of the Emperor) its new function as an outpost of Rome.

Thrown into consternation by the Emperor's decision, and misunderstanding his motives, the Jews, it is reported, decided to send a representative to intercede with him. The record which tells of this interview, a letter purported to have been sent by Hadrian to his brother-in-law, is not altogether clear, and there are even grounds for suspicion of its authenticity. But the incident it relates is, in itself, altogether probable. The Jews sent Akiba, then in his ninetieth year, to interview the mighty potentate, who had already left their country and was now in Egypt.

Hadrian was not at all impressed with Akiba's pleas and arguments. Aside from the diversity of interest, the ideological gulf between the two men was impassable. Vespasian had been won over by the flatteries of Josephus; Caligula, by the cleverness of Agrippa; Antony and Augustus, by the cunning of Herod; but what incense could the deeply pacifist monotheist, Akiba, bring to the altar of the great soldier who believed that the Empire's safety demanded his recognition as a god? From the sage's imperfect Greek, and his interpreter's confused ideas, the Emperor gathered that Judaism was a variant of the Egyptian faith, and he could not see why the perverse Palestinians should cling so tenaciously to their especial brand of the worship of Serapis.

The effect of this pronouncement on Akiba was crushing. The last hope for improved relations with Rome had disappeared; the teachings of his whole lifetime, that a pacific attitude toward the Empire would call forth reasonable treatment from it, were refuted by the event. Suddenly he felt the burden of his four score and ten years. The heavy disasters which he had borne with fortitude and resignation—the death

of his son and his son-in-law, the loss of his masters, the desertion of his colleagues and the disciples—fell upon him with
renewed weight. He must have asked himself why he had
undertaken the heavy responsibility of a conference with the
master of the world. Would it not have been better to send a
younger man, perhaps a patrician, who could impress the
Emperor with his own wealth and position?

For the first time in his life he began to be uncertain of his
views. Endowed with extraordinary powers of introspection
and self-examination, the old sage must have wondered
whether his intellectual powers, which had so long resisted
the years, had not failed him at last. His memory, once so
retentive, was of recent years clearly weakening. He could
recall that when he had rendered a decision a little time before, his colleague, Yeshebab, said to him: "Do you not
remember that both of us were sitting at the feet of Joshua
when he decided otherwise?" [57] Akiba had paid little attention to the incident at the time, merely reversing himself, and
accepting Yeshebab's tradition. But as he looked back at the
event he could see in it a graver portent. He noticed that for
some time his dialectical powers, too, had been impaired. The
arguments which in his prime (which he reached at the unusual age of sixty) had come to him with such rapidity and
ease, had to be formulated with slower and more painful
deliberation of late. Surrounded by younger and more vigorous minds, who were almost unanimous in their opposition
to him, the teacher felt, perhaps, the same doubt of his prescience that any less gifted man might feel about a vivid
recollection challenged by numerous other observers.

If these were indeed his reflections, they did him wrong.
But decades were to pass before his pacifist policy was vindicated. Meanwhile, uncertain of his political abilities, Akiba

also lost faith, and perhaps interest, in the juristic struggle which had occupied so much of his life. Of him who had so courageously led the war on the patricians, with the formidable Gamaliel and Eliezer at their head, it could now be said with truth that "Akiba respected wealth." [58] More than once when those who remembered his youthful ardor expected a clear and definite exposition of the plebeian view, he offered compromises between the opposing views of the Shammaites and the Hillelites.[59] In one memorable instance, he accepted Eliezer's opinion and rejected that of Joshua, although the latter represented the interests of the trading groups of Jerusalem.[60] Once he amazed his disciples when he declared a chair which they thought he would consider pure, defiled.[61] On three occasions he declined to give any reply to students who asked for guidance in the Law.[62] Finally, at a meeting of the conclave, he publicly renounced certain plebeian views which had for decades been repeated in his name. Judah ben Ilai, his faithful disciple, records the strange scene. A number of human bones had been discovered and they were brought into the academy to determine whether they were defiling. Several physicians, including one especially famous Theodorus, who had been consulted by the sages, stated that the bones were derived from several bodies, and that neither the skull nor the spine of any one skeleton had been preserved. A vote was then taken and Akiba, who was asked to give his opinion first, said, "I consider them pure." Whereupon all the other sages cried out, "Since you, who were the one who always insisted that such bones, from several bodies, were impure, have changed your mind, there is no need for any further discussion," and the bones were declared pure.[63]

Simeon ben Yohai, who was with Akiba in his last days when, before their final extinction, his spiritual and intellectual energies burst into brief and dazzling activity, challenged the truth of this story. "Until the day of his death," Simeon said, "Akiba considered such bones impure; whether he changed his mind after he died," he added, with his usual asperity, "I do not know." Nevertheless, the detailed description of the meeting which is given by Judah leaves no doubt that Akiba did publicly vote against the convictions which he had defended throughout his life, and that only afterward, in prison, did he revert to his earlier opinions.

In his wretchedness and perplexity, Akiba lost the mellowness which had characterized him throughout his mature lifetime, and treated his students, whom he dearly loved, with a harshness that amazed them. When one of them offered an argument of which he disapproved, he cried, "You have dived into deep waters seeking for pearls, but you brought up a potsherd." [64] When the nationalists asked him for Eliezer's opinions on certain questions, he shouted, "Be silent! I will not tell you what he said regarding this!" [65] Once a young man, Judah ben Nehemiah, defeated Tarfon in an argument, and openly showed his exultation. Akiba, seeing the happy glow on the victor's cheek, said to him in words which might rather have suited Eliezer ben Hyrkanos, "Your face glows because you have refuted the old sage. I doubt whether you will live long!" Judah ben Ilai records the incident and adds: "This happened at the Passover season. When I returned for the Pentecost and asked for Judah ben Nehemiah I was told that he had died." [66]

He was equally impatient with his colleagues. Once he, Tarfon and Eleazar ben Azariah were discussing the tragic situation of their people. The pious Tarfon remarked that the trouble with the Jews was their irreligion and their lack of anyone who was in a position to reprove the others. Eleazar ben Azariah, the famous preacher, gave it as his opinion that "there was no one in this generation who is able to accept reproof." Akiba, hearing the remarks, said sharply, "The real difficulty is that there is no one alive who knows *how* to offer reproof!" [67]

But the blow which had all but prostrated the old scholar stimulated the masses of the people to furious action. A decree of wholesale extermination could hardly have aroused them more than the news of the Emperor's decision to establish his pagan sanctuary on Mount Moriah. The fanaticism which had been held in check for decades broke loose. A new Antiochus ruled the world, ready to stretch forth his thrice defiled hand against the sacred shrine itself. Surely now God would awaken to the needs of His people, and reveal Himself through them as He had through the Maccabees three centuries earlier.

As the excitement grew, Ishmael and Simeon cast off the secrecy under which they had heretofore carried on their activities. The Romans arrested them and condemned them to death, even before the revolution had broken out. Their faith endured to the last. While they were being led to the execution, they merely commiserated with each other on the fate which prevented them from sharing in the glory awaiting their people. Akiba, speaking over their graves, warned his hearers to expect no miracles. "Prepare yourselves for suffering," he cried to the weeping multitude. "If happiness were destined to come in our time, none deserved better to share in it than Rabbi Simeon and Rabbi Ishmael. But God, knowing what distress is in store for us, removed them from our midst, as it is written, 'The righteous is taken away from the evil to come'" (Isa. 57:1).[68]

The discouraging words were without effect. The leadership of the rebellion passed from the intellectual sages, Ishmael and Simeon, to Simeon bar Kokba, a soldier and strategist, who at once set out to organize the straggling bands of patriotic peasants into a regular army. His first few victories aroused wild enthusiasm among the people, who saw in him not only a second Maccabee, but the Messiah. The private and public fortunes of a nation were staked on the personal prowess and military genius of the unproved leader.

Akiba himself did not long resist the contagion of Messianism. When he saw Roman legions yield to untrained Judean youths, new hope blossomed in his heart. "Yet once, it will be a little while," he quoted from Haggai (2:6), "and I will shake the heavens and the earth, and the sea, and the dry land." [69] He went so far as to encourage the popular delusion concerning the miraculous rôle to be played by the new leader and applied to him the verse (Num. 24:17), "The star hath trodden forth out of Jacob." [70] Once he even said outright, "This is the Messianic King."

The dismal response of one of his friends, "Akiba, grass will grow out of your jaw and the Messiah will not yet have come!" shows that some of the sages were still sane enough to realize the hopeless inequality of the struggle.[71]

The story of the denouement is well known; how in a little more than three years the Romans destroyed the last vestige of Jewish resistance, how in their fury they drenched the land with blood, slaughtering hundreds of thousands of people, how they sold tens of thousands into slavery, forbade the few remaining Jews to observe any of their ancestral customs and took the children forcibly out of their religious schools and put them to manual labor. Hundreds of scholars fled to Babylonia, but many still felt that their duty was in Palestine.

A contemporary sage, Nathan the Babylonian, describes the conditions in Palestine in these words: "The expression in the Decalogue, 'Those who love Me and observe My commandments,' applies to the people who live in Palestine and offer their lives for the Law. 'Why art thou being taken to execution?' 'Because I circumcised my son.' 'Why art thou being taken to crucifixion?' 'Because I read the Torah or ate the *Mazzot.*' 'Why art thou being beaten a hundred stripes?' 'Because I took the *Lulab.*'" [72]

The practical annihilation of the Jewish community in Judea left the Romans free to proceed with their plans for the paganization of the Holy City. The temple where Hadrian was to be worshiped as the personification of Jupiter was erected on Mount Moriah, and the statue of the Emperor placed within it.[73] At a short distance, on the spot which the Christians consecrated as the grave of Jesus, another temple, dedicated to Venus, was established.[74] The city was called Aelia Capitolina, and only Gentiles were permitted to live in it or even to approach it.[75] The province, too, was renamed. It was no longer Judea; it had become Philistinian Syria, or, more briefly, Palestine.

The prohibition against the settlement of the Jews in Aelia did not extend to Gentile Christians. One of the most permanent results of Hadrian's edict therefore was the transformation of the character of the Christian community in Jerusalem. The leaders as well as the main body of the Church until the time of Bar Kokba had been Jews. From that time onward, they were Gentiles.[76] But Aelia could hardly exercise the influence or authority which had belonged to Jerusalem. In spite of all the efforts of the Romans, it remained a small village of no consequence either politically or religiously. Once a year, on the ninth of Ab, the anniversary of the destruction of their Temple, the Jews would gather there, apparently by special permission, to bewail the loss of their ancient glory. Otherwise, as Tertullian says, "they might look on the city, but with their eyes afar off." [77]

The name Aelia persisted for many centuries. So completely had the former name been obliterated that one of the governors of the province in the fourth century no longer could identify Jerusalem; and even in the early Arabic centuries the town was called Iliya. The country's new name, Palestine, has survived until our own day.

The fact that Akiba was not imprisoned shows that he had not implicated himself actively in the rebellion. Like other Jews, he could observe the Law only in secret; but he was permitted to move about, and apparently even to give instruction. Clearly, the Roman generals who were trying to destroy Judaism root and branch did not at this time share the opinion of some modern historians that Akiba himself was the secret instigator of the whole rebellion and that his wide travels, ostensibly for the Sanhedrin and the Law, were really made to foment sedition. But his personal safety gave the old sage little comfort. "The verse, 'And I will break the pride of your power' (Lev. 26:19), applies to the heroes of Israel who were like unto Joab ben Zeruiah," he said.[78] "Isaac's words, 'The voice is the voice of Jacob, and the hands are the hands of Esau' (Gen. 27:22), describe our generation, when the voice of Jacob cries out because of what the hands of Esau (Rome) have done to him." [79] Bereft of pupils and colleagues, he looked over the fearful ruins of Israel's glory. Eliezer's prophecy had been fulfilled with regard to his colleagues; what was to be his own destiny?

X. THE APOTHEOSIS

IT was not long before the loyalty of Akiba and his colleagues to the principle of study was to be put to the ultimate test. The savagery of the repressions grew from month to month. It was probably in the year 134, just before the capitulation of Betar, that the Romans issued their drastic decree, forbidding not only the practice, but also the study of the Torah. Now Akiba knew that he had reached the end of compromise. He had counseled the people to accept the Roman gift of a Temple when that had been offered; he had warned them not to be disappointed when the offer was withdrawn; he had asked them to sacrifice the right to observe the Law, in order that its study might be perpetuated. But the last stronghold, the innermost shrine of all was to be defended at all costs. If the study of the Torah was abolished, there was no further purpose in living. And so, at the age of ninety-five, the compromising pacifist once more took up the weapons of non-resistant war. Calmly he gathered his students, gave his decisions, delivered his lectures. Gatherings in secret, he both disdained and feared. They were unworthy of the dignity of the Torah; and were certain to raise the suspicion of political activity. He had always taught in the open, in the shade of a tree; and he would continue to do so. He made only one compromise with necessity. He invited his disciples to dine with him; and they discussed the Law during their meal.[1]

A casual remark which he made at one of these gatherings

reveals his serenity, his intellectual youthfulness and his enduring faith, in this last period of his life. He disregarded the havoc of the moment, and thought only of the future. The Romans were a passing phenomenon, about which he could do nothing. Palestine's farms, her trees and her children, were his primary concern. "Those who raise crop-destroying cattle, those who chop down good trees, and those who teach children dishonestly, will never see a blessing," he said.

When his old antagonist, Pappias, warned him that he was courting death by continuing to teach so publicly, Akiba replied with the parable of the fishes and the fox. The fox, coming to the river's bank, suggested to the fishes that they might find safety from the fishermen by coming on the dry land. But the fishes replied, "If in the water which is our element, we are in danger, what will happen to us on the dry land which is not our element?"

"So, too," continued Akiba, "If there is no safety for us in the Torah which is our home, how can we find safety elsewhere?" [2]

Akiba could not have expected to continue teaching for long. Soon he was seized by the soldiers and carried off to prison. The Romans, still respecting his learning, his reputation and his distinguished personality, perhaps also remembering his pacifist and conciliatory teachings, hesitated to put him to death. They kept him in confinement for three years, treating him with consideration, even with courtesy. He was allowed the attendance of his disciple, Joshua ha-Garsi, who waited on him; and was permitted to enjoy the visits of Simeon ben Yohai, who had returned from Zidon to be near the Master in his affliction. "Continue to instruct me," Simeon begged of him.

At first reluctant, out of fear that he might endanger his

pupil's freedom and even his life, Akiba finally yielded to his importunities, "My son," he said, "more than the calf wants to suck, the cow wants to suckle!" And he taught him.[3]

Convinced at last that there was no point in trying to conciliate the oppressor, Akiba decided to bring the calendar, which had been neglected for a decade, into order. He added an intercalary month to each of three successive years—an unprecedented procedure—until Passover, which had been thrown back into January, once more occurred in its appropriate season.[4] He gave his visitors secret instructions, intended to mitigate the rigors of the Law for the harassed survivors of the persecution. In one decision, he rejected a tradition which had developed naturally in plebeian Jerusalem but was entirely unsuited to the new conditions of Jewish life. This tradition required persons who had been authorized by a husband to arrange his divorce to write the necessary document in person. It was not sufficient for them to supervise the writing. The provincial sages, living in communities where the ability to write was far from universal, had always objected to this rule. Now, when the government had declared the practice of Jewish ceremonies a state offense, it was frequently necessary to obtain the sanction of the husband for divorce and to postpone the writing for some more convenient time. Hence, Akiba felt compelled to accept, perhaps as an emergency measure, the provincial view to which he had always objected.[5]

Although he pursued these audacious activities secretly, Akiba must have known that the Romans would soon learn of them. When this happened, he was merely transferred to a prison in distant Caesárea, where no one but his servant-pupil, Joshua ha-Garsi, was permitted to attend him.

And still he carried on. The impoverished and leaderless

community made unheard-of sacrifices to obtain decisions from Akiba during these days. When one difficult question arose, they hired a man at a cost of four hundred *zuz* to make his way into the prison and get Akiba's opinion.[6] On another occasion stratagem had to be used. Since the Romans had forbidden the Jews to observe any of their ceremonies, the rite of *halizah* had been carried out in private, and the scholars wondered whether under those circumstances it was valid. One of them took a peddler's basket and daringly went up and down before the jail, crying, "Needles for sale! Needles for sale! What is the Law regarding a private *halizah?* Needles for sale; needles for sale!"

Akiba, hearing the noise, replied from his jail, "Have you any spindles? It is permitted." [7]

Even in his new prison, Akiba continued to observe every detail of the Law. His pupil-servant, Joshua ha-Garsi, brought him daily a small quantity of water, half of which he would drink, keeping the remainder for his ritual washing. One day the guard, meeting Joshua, inspected his pitcher, and cried: "You have too much water. Are you trying to wash away the walls of the jail?" With these words, he seized the vessel and poured out half of its contents.

When Joshua at last came to his master and presented what was left of the precious liquid, Akiba's face fell. "Joshua," he said, "you know that I am an old man, and my life depends on you!" Joshua then told him what had happened. "Let me have the water, so that I may wash," said Akiba.

"There is not enough left for your drink," Joshua cried, "and how can any be spared for washing?"

"What can be done?" Akiba said. "The Law requires that we wash when we awake and before we eat. It is better that I should die than that I should transgress the words of my colleagues." And he declined to taste a morsel until he was given sufficient water to wash his hands.[8]

Finally Akiba was brought to trial; his judge was to be his former friend, Rufus. There was no possible defense against the charges; Akiba had violated the Law by offering instruction to his disciples. Yet Joshua ha-Garsi, standing in the open Court, at a little distance from the prisoner, and in front of the grim Roman general, prayed that somehow the aged scholar might be saved. But even as the half-smothered words came from his mouth, he noticed a cloud covering the sun and the sky. "I knew then that our prayer was useless," he said, "for it is written, 'Thou hast covered Thyself with a cloud, so that no prayer can pass through'" (Lam. 3:44).[9]

Akiba was found guilty and condemned to death. Still attended by his faithful Joshua, he retained his courage and his strength of mind until the very end. The popular story tells that the Romans killed him by tearing his flesh from his living body. As he lay in unspeakable agony, he suddenly noticed the first streaks of dawn breaking over the eastern hills. It was the hour when the Law requires each Jew to pronounce the *Shema*. Oblivious to his surroundings, Akiba intoned in a loud, steady voice, the forbidden words of his faith, "Hear, O Israel, the Lord is our God, the Lord is One. And thou shalt love the Lord thy God with all thine heart, and with all thy soul, and with all thy might." [10]

Rufus, the Roman general, who superintended the horrible execution, cried out: "Are you a wizard or are you utterly insensible to pain?"

"I am neither," replied the martyr, "but all my life I have been waiting for the moment when I might truly fulfill this commandment. I have always loved the Lord with all my might, and with all my heart; now I know that I love him with all my life." And, repeating the verse again, he died as he reached the words, "The Lord is One."

The scene, indelibly impressed on the eyes of Joshua ha-Garsi, became part of Jewish tradition. The association of the *Shema* with the great martyr's death made its recitation a death-bed affirmation of the faith, instead of a repetition of select verses; and to this day the pious Jew hopes that when his time comes he may be sufficiently conscious to declare the Unity of his God, echoing with his last breath the words which found their supreme illustration in Akiba's martyrdom.

APPENDIX

I. AKIBA'S PRINCIPLES
IN RELATION TO CLASS DIFFERENCES

A. AKIBA'S PLEBEIAN STANDARDS

In most of the controversies which arose out of Akiba's application of his juristic principles, his opponent was Ishmael; though in
some instances, the patricians were led by Tarfon, Eleazar ben
Azariah or Jose the Galilean.[1] Some of his disagreements with
these teachers arose simply out of their different experiences and
surroundings. Akiba, for instance, maintained that the lot for a
house, unless otherwise specified in the deed of sale, must be not
less than four cubits by six (about seven feet by ten and one-half).
Ishmael, hearing this opinion, exclaimed: "That is not a house, but
a stable. If one undertakes to build a stable, it may be four cubits by
six; a small house is six cubits by eight; a large house eight cubits by
ten; a triclinium ten by ten. The height in each case being half the
sum of length and width." [2]

Akiba applied the same modest standards of his class to other
questions of law, such as the division of property among the heirs.
The patrician sages held that no garden could be profitably oper-
ated if it were less than half a *Kab* (about 1500 square feet) in area;
therefore, they refused to sanction the division of an estate unless
each heir received at least this minimum. Akiba, accepting the
lower standards of the poorer, more individualistic plebeians, said
that the minimum was a quarter of a *Kab*.[3]

On the other hand, the fact that the plebeian estates were as a
rule barely large enough to support their owners, made Akiba, and
other scholars of his class, averse to the compromise principle of
equal division which were favored by the patricians.

Thus, if a man and wife died in an accident and there was no way of ascertaining which of them died first, the Shammaites held that the wife's property as well as her dower, should be divided equally between her heirs and those of her husband.[4] For, if she died first, her property had been inherited legally by the husband in the few seconds by which he survived her, and from him rightfully it descended to his family; whereas if he died first, it belonged to her and her family. Since the truth could not be ascertained, equal division seemed appropriate. But the Hillelites, whose tiny estates could not readily bear division even according to their lower standards of living, developed the principle of the *status quo*. So far as concerns the property of the wife, the legal presumption favors her relatives, they said; but the dower right, being uncollected, remains in the hands of the husband and his heirs. The Hillelites, however, agreed that if a man and his mother were killed in such an accident the properties should be divided between his children and her heirs; Akiba, alone, taking an extreme plebeian position, said that even then the principle of presumption must be followed.

In one special case, Tarfon had introduced an interesting, characteristically humanitarian variation in the Shammaitic position. If a man dies leaving behind him a small estate, which becomes the subject of litigation between his heir, his wife and his creditor, Tarfon would solve the problem by "giving it to the poorest among them." Akiba, hearing this view, said: "The law is not charity; the property must be given to the heir, for both the wife and the creditors can collect only if they take an oath that they were not paid during the lifetime of the deceased, while the heir need take no such oath." [5]

Akiba transferred the doctrine from law to ethics when he challenged the reasonableness of the extreme humanitarian position adopted by his colleague, Ben Petira. The question which divided the scholars was purely academic, but the answers are for that reason especially illuminating. "If two men, traveling in the wilderness, lose their way, and are left with only a single cup of water, which is owned by one of them; and the cup is so small that if divided between the two of them both must die of thirst, but if one takes all, he may survive until he can reach safety, what is to be done?" Ben Petira said: "Let them both drink and die, and let not the owner of the cup stand by while his neighbor is perishing." But Akiba said, "The Scriptures command, 'That thy brother may live with thee' (Lev. 25:36); from this we infer, that thy life has precedence over thy brother's life." [6]

His plebeian point of view probably also accounts for an interesting controversy between him and Tarfon regarding the disposal of lost-and-found articles. The Law demands that the finder of an article which is identifiable keep it until the owner claims it. However, an animal which must be fed but gives no return may be sold. The question arises, May the money obtained from this sale be used by the finder pending the discovery of the owner? Tarfon, thinking of the wealthy who could always lay their hands on money, says, "The finder may use the funds; but if they are lost he is responsible." Akiba, with his poor plebeians in mind, maintains, "He must not use the money; and if he loses it by accident, he is not responsible." [7]

In the matter of purely ceremonial law, he ruled, as we have noticed, that a poor man whose meal consists only of some cooked vegetables must recite the full Grace. The patrician sages maintained that a meal without bread called only for the shorter benediction.[8] It is permitted, he taught in opposition to Ishmael, to spend the money of the second tithe on such plebeian dishes as locusts and mushrooms.[9] Like the poorest artisans in the market place of Jerusalem who, living in a rich vine country, were strangers to the juice of the grape, he considered wine a luxury, and ruled that the tiniest amounts fell within the ceremonial law.[10] On the other hand, he objected to Ishmael's exhortation "to beautify the commandments, by the purchase of a fine *lulab*, fine fringes, or a fine *sukkah*."[11] The first fruits which were brought to Jerusalem must not be bedecked with any costly products from foreign countries.[12] Nor would he agree that vessels of bone or precious glass are free from the law of impurity.[13]

In an attempt to make the ceremonial law easier for small landowners, Akiba practically abolished the biblical prohibition against mixed planting. In a series of far-reaching decisions, he surrounded the prohibition with mitigations which limited it to the largest fields. But, characteristically, he insisted that where the law did apply it must be carried out in its full rigor: "Not only must mixed species not be planted; but he who permits them to grow of themselves transgresses the law." [14]

His sympathy for the small farmer went so far that he exempted him from part of his obligations to charity; but he would not grant total exemption to the poorest landowner. And so, strangely enough, whereas Joshua had limited the rule of "borders" (*peah*) to large farms, while Eliezer and Tarfon had included smaller farms, Akiba said, "Any land, no matter how small, must have some part set aside for the poor." [15]

Since the Temple was destroyed and the Levites no longer had any official function, Akiba felt that their tithe should cease to be binding on small farmers. While therefore earlier teachers urged the people to gather in their harvest early so as to have the tithe ready betimes, Akiba ruled that grain which has not been garnered in time is free from the tithe.[16] He went further and maintained that the grain is free from tithes unless it is stored in a protected barn. If it is stored in a court to which two people have keys, it is unprotected and free from tithes.[17] These interpretations effectually abolished the whole system of tithes. Even such famous scholars as Judah the Patriarch and Jose the son of Judah ben Ilai adopted Akiba's devices and interpretations to free themselves from this obligation. In vain did Judah ben Ilai, who was Akiba's pupil, chide them, pointing out that Akiba himself had never taken advantage of his own rules. "He used to purchase herbs and grain in order to give tithes from every species," Judah said.[18] But his was a futile cry; Akiba's innovations answered the new conditions and could not be argued away.

The sin of the sons of Samuel (I Sam. 8:3), he said, consisted in their use of force to collect more than was due them as their tithe.[19] Such an interpretation could only have been an indirect protest against contemporary abuses.

B. THE DEFENSE OF TRADERS

We have already observed that the articulate plebeians of ancient Palestine were largely traders and artisans; and we must therefore be prepared to find Akiba's philosophy tinged with ideas especially suitable to the needs of these classes.

One of the principles which he voiced bears a strange resemblance to the modern commercial opposition to "putting the government into business." Akiba objected vigorously to the commercial use of sanctuary funds. The cost of the daily sacrifice in the Temple was defrayed from the voluntary annual tax of half a shekel paid by each adult male Jew. Toward the end of the Second Commonwealth there was generally an annual surplus which Temple officials invested in oil, wine and flour to be sold, at a profit, to pilgrims. These enterprises were a grievous infringement on the rights of private traders; for Temple commodities, besides being, in all probability, cheaper, had the advantage of convenience and prestige. Ishmael defends the practice on the grounds of precedent; Akiba opposes it. "Temple funds and charity funds," he said, "must not be used commercially." [20]

In the same spirit are both of Akiba's rulings on the tithes. There were two tithes in ancient Palestine. The first was handed over to the Levites. The second had to be carried by the farmer to Jerusalem, to be eaten there by himself and his family, or else given away. In a sense, then, the second tithe was not really a tithe, but a device to bring the population to Jerusalem at least once a year. Farmers living at a distance from Jerusalem were, however, permitted to commute the second tithe into cash, which they had to spend in Jerusalem. Akiba ruled that only regularly minted currency could be used for this commutation. Ishmael, thinking only of the farmers, maintained that any coins were satisfactory.[21]

Ishmael had also permitted provincial tenant-farmers, renting their land from owners resident in Jerusalem, to substitute the second tithe for their annual payments. Thus they evaded both the tithe and the journey to Jerusalem.[22] The landowner lost nothing through this arrangement; the only sufferer was the merchant of Jerusalem, who had one customer instead of many. Akiba refused to accept this ruling.

C. THE TRADITIONS OF JERUSALEM

Much of Akiba's polemic against his master, Eliezer ben Hyrkanos, had originated in the special interests and traditions of the plebeians of Jerusalem. This metropolitan point of view dominated also in his controversies with the younger scholars. Jerusalem differed from rural Judea, not only in its social organization as a large city, but in its climatic conditions. Situated on a high plateau, it is definitely colder than the lowlands, where most of the prosperous provincials had their farms. During the Passover week, many Jerusalemites would still be using fire to warm their houses, while the farmers of the coastal plain no longer needed it. Hence it came about that when the city people destroyed their leaven before the Passover—in accordance with the rule set down in Exodus 12:15—they burned it, while the country people, who usually had no fire available, buried it, or tossed it into the sea, or ground it to dust. A series of patrician scholars beginning with Judah ben Bathyra and ending with Simeon ben Yohai, who derive their traditions from provincial life, insist on the admissibility of the rural custom, while Akiba and his urban followers deny this.[23]

Lack of water has played a greater part than climate in the history of Jerusalem. Only in our own day, has the problem of the city's water supply been solved. There are few important springs in the neighborhood, and the rainfall is definitely below the average of the remainder of the country. To make matters worse, the rainy reason begins in Jerusalem some weeks later than in the lowlands.[24] The result of this combination of circumstances is that August and September, which were months of great rejoicing in the vine producing lowlands, because of the harvest and the ingathering, were periods of concern in the capital, where the water had to be measured by drops. The wealthy, of course, were always provided for, somehow; but in the poorer sections of Jerusalem, the last months of the summer brought considerable privation.

It was natural, therefore, that while Sukkot, which falls in September, was primarily observed in the country as a feast of thanksgiving, the poorer artisans and traders of Jerusalem used it to emphasize their dependence on the rains. Centuries before Akiba, the Hasideans and the Pharisees had instituted special rain ceremonies for the Sukkot week, which the Sadducees opposed so furiously that on one occasion a civil war ensued.[25] In the second century c.e. this controversy, like all the others, had been conveniently settled in favor of the Pharisees by the death of the Sadducee party; but while provincials and patricians accepted the Pharisaic teaching as a matter of practice, they continued to deny its theological basis. As represented by the School of Ishmael, they still held that the "world is judged" for rain, as for everything else, on Rosh Ha-Shanah.[26] Akiba, however, energetically defended the view of the earlier Jerusalem plebeians. "The Law says, bring barley on Passover, because it is the time of barley, so that the grain may be blessed; bring the first wheat on Shabuot which is the wheat season, so that the fruits may be blessed; pour libations of water on the festival of Sukkot, which is the season of rains, so that the rains may be blessed for you, as it is written, 'And it shall come to pass that everyone that is left of all the nations that came against Jerusalem shall go up from year to year to wor-

ship the King, the Lord of Hosts, and to keep the feast of tabernacles. And it shall be that whoso of the families of the earth
goeth not up to Jerusalem to worship the King, the Lord of Hosts,
upon them there shall be no rain'" (Zech. 14:16).[27]

The point of Akiba's remark lies in the last phrase. Everybody
agreed that it was appropriate to pray for the barley harvest on
Passover and for the fruits on Shabuot. Sukkot, the third of the
pilgrimage holidays, must also look forward and not backward;
it is not only a time of thanksgiving for the ingathering which
is completed, but of petition for the rains which are to come later.
This logical argument is reinforced by the citation from Zechariah
in which Sukkot is definitely associated with rain.

While the plebeians of Jerusalem thus disagreed with both
patricians and provincials in regard to the essential meaning of
Sukkot, they were as anxious as any other Jews to observe the
customs which Scripture prescribed for the festival. Their almost
pathetic efforts to carry out in their crowded slums the law requiring booths for the festival have already been described. They
were put to similar straits in their observance of another rustic
ceremony connected with the festival.

It was customary for the Sukkot pilgrims, marching in procession round the Temple altar, to carry a cluster of vegetable products, consisting of a citron, a palm branch and some myrtle and
willow twigs. This custom, like many others, had spread from
the Temple to the Synagogue, and was universally observed in
Palestine. But while citrons or palm branches were expensive,
willows could be had for the gathering in the country, and the
villagers made a display of them. The same was done by the
richer townspeople. But the urban plebeians, grateful if they could
fulfill the barest letter of the Law, usually had to be satisfied with
the single twig of myrtle and another of willow. Ishmael and
Tarfon, representing the country tradition, declared this modest
bouquet inadequate, while Akiba defended it.[28]

The scarcity of wells in the neighborhood of Jerusalem explains

Akiba's view that water which has become turgid, either with clay or mud, is still fit for ritual immersion.[29] Ishmael denied this. Similarly, Akiba permitted the use of melted snow for purification, but Ishmael, representing the practice natural to inhabitants of the warmer lowland where snow was almost unknown, and water quite plentiful, opposed him. Akiba reports, however, that after Ishmael had settled in the village of Azziz, in the vicinity of Hebron, the highest point in Judea, where snow was as plentiful as in Jerusalem, he changed his mind on the subject. "All his life he used to argue against me," Akiba remarked with relish, "but the people of Medeba (in Transjordan) testified that when they asked his advice about the construction of a pool for purification, he said to them, 'Go out and collect snow and construct your pool.'" [30]

A most illuminating controversy between the sages concerned "machine" labor on the Sabbath day. All Jews agreed that household work was forbidden on the Sabbath even if no human or animal labor was involved. Thus a housewife could not leave her bread in the oven at sunset on Friday if it was insufficiently baked, nor could she permit her pot to remain on the fire to complete its cooking.[31] There was considerable disagreement however, regarding occupational work which was automatic; the plebeian Hillelites permitted a dyer to let his materials soak in the cauldron during the Sabbath if he did not touch them, and to set a trap for animals or a net for fish on Friday, even though the capture would ensue automatically on the Sabbath day. The rural Shammaites, to whom such work was also part of household activity, forbade this.[32] The extraction of fruit juices, on the other hand, which was ordinary household work in the city, was done on an industrial scale in the country. The urban plebeian conceded the principle for wine and oil, but demurred in the case of garlic, unripe fruits and certain oleaginous grains. Hence we find Akiba, usually lenient in such matters, declaring that it is forbidden to let the juice of fruits and vegetables continue to flow on the Sabbath; while Ishmael, his opponent, maintains that it is permitted.[33] The rabbinic record significantly adds that the "custom of the priests was in accordance with Ishmael's views." [34]

In the litigation which was constantly arising between the ancient patrician families and the new class of de-urbanized traders and artisans who, driven from Jerusalem by the Romans, sought to settle on the land, Akiba's sympathies naturally were altogether with the latter. When they bought a house, they frequently neglected to specify, for instance, that the well, which supplied the water, went with it. The provincial judges, guided by fixed precedents, and taking no account of the helpless inexpertness of a townsman buying rural properties, held that only what was mentioned in the deed was bought. Akiba could not deny that the weight of precedent favored the seller; but he raised a new question. The well, being unmentioned in the deed, might remain the property of the original seller, but how was he to reach it? The patricians said that the reservation of the well implied a right of way to it; but this Akiba denied. Nothing had been said about the well explicitly, and it was quite sufficient that it should not be transferred with the rest of the field. To claim with it a passage across the property was preposterous. Thus the craftiness of the seller overshot its mark, and at best he could only exact an additional payment for the well he could not use.[35]

On the other hand, Akiba said, if a person *buys* a well, which is situated in the middle of a field, and neglects to acquire at the same time a right of passage to it, that must be attributed to oversight, and the use of the way is allowed him. The other sages said that the purchase of a well does not carry with it any other rights.

In general, Akiba laid down the rule that "a vendor sells with generosity," and must be presumed to have given away all the necessary appurtenances to the property disposed of; his opponents maintained the traditional view, inherited from a harsher age, of *caveat emptor*. The controversy which began with the well spread to the trees, pigeon houses and other rural properties.

In a number of other controversies, Akiba's urban point of view is recognizable, though not so obviously. He maintained, for instance, that the Israelites in Egypt had collected the blood of the paschal lamb into vessels, such as were doubtless used in Jerusalem when an animal was slaughtered in one's house; Ishmael, adhering to provincial tradition, said that "a hole was made in the threshold into which the blood was poured." [36]

In his defense of the urban population, Akiba opposed the rule, upheld by Eliezer ben Hyrkanos, which would have freed imported grain from the law of *hallah*. This law, enunciated in Numbers 15:19 ff, demands "the first of the dough" as a gift for the priests. So small was the amount involved, and so pious were the women who did the household baking, that this particular perquisite of the Aaronids survived when all the others disappeared. Even outside of Palestine where there was never any legal obligation to make the gift, Jewish women continue to separate a portion of dough as their mothers have done for centuries. Since the sacred portion may be eaten only in purity, and the Diaspora contains no undefiled priests, the offering is thrown into the fire.

Akiba was deeply conscious of the reverence and affection which attached to this institution. His colleagues had taught that a person who was unable to prepare his dough "in purity" would do better to knead it in small measures which were free from the obligation of *hallah*. "No," said Akiba, "it is better to separate it in impurity than to avoid it; for just as the portion separated in purity is called *hallah,* so is that separated in impurity; but if a person prepares the dough in small quantities, he will have no share in the commandment." [37]

He took issue with the majority who denied that the priestly portion could be offered from a small quantity of dough. The minimum he said, had been fixed so as to free smaller quantities from any obligation; but if the poor housewife who has only a single *kab* (two quarts) of dough wants to fulfill the commandments, she may do so. The other sages denied that a portion separated from *kab* could properly be called *hallah*.

Realizing how deeply rooted the custom was among the Palestinian masses, Akiba refused to free imported grain from this obligation. Besides, to have done so would have placed a definite taint on the foreign product, thus increasing the demand for Palestinian wheat and barley which was insufficient to meet the country's needs. The resulting rise in price would have been welcomed by the farmer, but the plebeians of the city would have been the sufferers.

The problem also had a reverse side. The Palestinian farmers not only tried to monopolize the home market, they also wanted to establish a preference for their wares among the Jews of the neighboring countries and provinces. Hence they insisted that their grain was subject to the laws of *hallah* even when it was taken out of the country; its sanctity was inherent and remained with it wherever it went. This too Akiba denied.[38]

D. THE DEFENSE OF THE SHEPHERDS AND CATTLE DEALERS

The shepherd class, Akiba's own, also benefited from his legislative efforts, as is evident from the instances which follow.

The Bible demands that the owner of an ox which has strayed into a neighbor's field recompense the farmer "of the best of his field and of the best of his vineyard" (Exod. 22:4). Traditionally, this was taken to mean that the damaged section of the field was to be considered not inferior to the best of the remainder. The burden of proof to the contrary lay with the owner of the ox. But this interpretation, obvious to those who established it, was absurd in the eyes of Akiba. In his opinion, this was an unjustified reversal of the rule which places the onus of proof on the plaintiff. Hence Akiba rejected the traditional interpretation, saying, "The passage only commands that the damages be paid out of the defendant's best lands." [39]

It was in accord with this view that Akiba demanded a trial

by twenty-three judges, before an ox which had killed a man could be stoned.[40] But his defense of the plebeian interest overshot the mark when he ruled that a man injured by an ox could not collect damages in excess of the value of the animal.[41]

Perhaps it was his shepherd origin, too, that accounted for Akiba's peculiar leniency with regard to the law of meat and milk. Urban scholars generally were very severe on this point.[42] Akiba maintained that the biblical prohibition against the uniting of meat and milk is limited to the meat of cattle. But even such a mixture might be sold to Gentiles, he said; it was prohibited only for Jews. In both of these views, he was opposed by the majority of his own faction, as well as by Ishmael; and tradition has not followed him on this point.[43]

E. THE ATTACK ON THE PRIESTS

Akiba's friendship for the shepherds, combined with his hostility to the priests, inspired a series of lenient decisions with regard to the firstlings of cattle. If a sheep gives birth to twins, Jose the Galilean insists that both belong to the priest. Tarfon maintains that only one need be given to the priest; but, he says, the Aaronid may have his choice of either one. Akiba says that the priest, like anyone else who tries to collect a claim against another, must prove his case. Since he cannot produce any evidence that either is the true firstling, he must be satisfied with the inferior animal.[44]

If the firstling has had to be removed through an operation, it must be considered of doubtful status, according to Tarfon and the same rule applies to any natural born lamb which follows it. Akiba, however, says that they both unquestionably belong to the shepherd and not to the priest.[45]

The Shammaites had held that only priests may eat the flesh of the firstling; and the earlier Hillelites, who disagreed with them, had insisted that any Israelite might partake of it. But Akiba said that there was no limitation in the matter at all. Even a pagan might eat of the firstling.[46]

But what shocked the priests even more than his halakic opinions with regard to their privileges were his aggadic imputations against the character and position of their eponym. He held, for instance, that not only Miriam, but also Aaron, had been stricken with leprosy because they had slandered Moses. "Whether you be right or wrong," Judah ben Bathyra retorted when he heard this, "you are destined to give account before God for such an interpretation. If you are right, the Torah has concealed his shame, and you have revealed it; and if you are wrong, you are simply slandering a saint." [47]

A similar controversy arose from the custom which required the priests to bless the people after the sacrifices in the Temple. Ishmael remarked, "The priests bless the people, but who blesses the priests? To answer this the Scriptures say, 'And I shall bless them' (Num. 6:27), meaning that while the priests bless their fellow-Israelites, God Himself blesses the priests." Akiba could not brook this ascription of a special privilege to the priests, nor was he willing to agree that the blessing of the people is entirely dependent on the ecclesiastics. "No," he said, "the verse means rather that priests bless the Israelites, and God confirms their blessing." [48]

Ishmael probably believed he was conferring an honor on Abraham, the father of the Hebrew people, by making him a high priest; Akiba, believing that this posthumous promotion did more honor to the priesthood than to Abraham, denied it to the patriarch.[49]

II. AKIBA IN THE PHARISAIC TRADITION

A. THE ADMISSION OF THE PLEBEIANS INTO THE GEROUSIA

It can hardly be doubted that the Great Assembly convoked by Simeon the Righteous was intended to take the place of the general meetings of the whole community which were customary in older times (cf. Menes, *Die Vorexilischen Gesetze Israels,* pp. 88 ff.), and which the Book of Deuteronomy makes mandatory once in seven years (Deut. 31:10). These gatherings were intended to serve as a check on the "heads of the families." The rabbinic tradition which associates the Great Synagogue with Ezra and Nehemiah has this much historical value, that that gathering, too, is described as one in which Levites or plebeians took part (see Neh. 10:9); and it may have served as precedent for Simeon's Assembly. The historical reasons for Simeon's establishing the new departure cannot be discussed here. But it is sufficient to note that in the letter of Antiochus III, the Great, which is generally accepted as authentic (cf. Ed. Meyer, *Ursprung u. Anfaenge d. Christentums* II, 126), and is cited in Josephus *Ant.* XII, 3:3 the "scribes of the Temple and the singers of the sanctuary" are expressly mentioned as being free from certain taxes. This can only mean that the scribes were already recognized members of the Sanhedrin. A second Great Assembly of all classes of the people was convoked about a century later, to establish the authority of Simeon the Hasmonean. The First Book of Maccabees (14:28) explicitly states that "in a Great Assembly (Gk. *ekklesia megale;* original Hebrew, doubtless, *keneset gedolah*) of priests and people and princes of the nation and of the elders of the country," Simeon was declared the leader and high priest, "forever until a faithful prophet should arise."

The expulsion of the Pharisees from the Sanhedrin under John Hyrkan, and their restoration under Queen Salome, are well attested and generally recognized. But seen in the perspective of general history, both events were more than sectarian victories; they were parts of the continuous struggle of the scholars for a voice in the government of the people. From the time of Queen Salome, the place of the plebeians in the Sanhedrin was secure. (For the whole discussion, cf. S. Zeitlin, *The Second Jewish Commonwealth*, pp. 38 ff.)

B. THE PRINCIPLE OF BI-PARTISAN LEADERSHIP AMONG THE PHARISEES

In his *Meqomah shel ha-halaka behokmat yisrael*, a small pamphlet of incalculable importance for the study of Jewish history, Professor Louis Ginzberg has shown (pp. 14 ff.) that the division of the Pharisees into two opposing schools antedated the time of Hillel and Shammai, and in fact originated at the very beginning of the Pharisaic movement. He also proved that it was this division which lay at the basis of the leadership of the Pharisaic movement by "pairs" of scholars for more than one hundred and fifty years. Each member of the "pair" represented a faction. (See Mishna *Abot,* chap. 1, and Mishna *Hagiga,* chap. 2).

It can be demonstrated, however, that this system of dual leadership did not come to an end with the last of the "pairs," Hillel and Shammai, but continued until the end of the tannaitic period.

Hillel's immediate successor was apparently Gamaliel I, a plebeian, like Hillel himself. For reasons given above (p. 7) Gamaliel had no associate. But it is instructive to note that when the proposal was made to appoint an associate to him, the person to whom the position was offered was Akabiah ben Mahalalel, a patrician. The factional affiliations of Akabiah have been recognized by I. H. Weiss (*Dor Dor ve-Dorshav* I, 176). Perhaps, however, it will be well to examine the evidence more fully.

(1) In two recorded norms, he insisted on severities with regard to the ritual purity of women which are similar to those elsewhere

defended by the Shammaites (Cf. Mishna *Eduyot* 5:6, with Mishna *Niddah* 2:7). Quite aside from this textual evidence, it is clear that the severities he imposed would hardly have concerned the patrician women or their polygamous husbands, but would have involved great hardships for the plebeian women, who were engaged in trade and work from which they had to desist in a state of impurity, and would also have required restraint for their husbands.

(2) A third norm ascribed to him (Mishna *Eduyot, ibid.*) concerns special priestly privileges with regard to the firstlings. Like other patricians, Akabiah defends the rights of the priest.

(3) A fourth norm concerns the equality of status between proselytes, former bondswomen and natural born Israelite women. The majority of the sages insist that they be treated alike; Akabiah makes a distinction between them, at least so far as the Ordeal described in Numbers 5:11 ff. is concerned.

(4) In a fifth rule, he limited the law of Scripture which permits any passerby to eat "to his satisfaction" of the grapes or the grain of his neighbor's field (Deut. 23:25-26) to workers in the field or vineyard (*Midrash Tannaim* 23:25, p. 153). The generous, original rule allowed of no such limitation (see commentaries on Deuteronomy, *ad loc.*). In fact, we are explicitly informed that the disciples of Jesus "plucked ears of corn" of the fields through which they passed when they were hungry (Matt. 12:1; Mark 2:23; Luke 6:1). And to this day the custom prevails in Palestine (Robinson, *Biblical Researches in Palestine* I, 493, 499; for similar Arab hospitality, cf. Doughty, *Arabia Deserta* I, 520; II, 152). Yet there must have been attempts to limit it even before the time of Akabiah, for the Sect of Damascus takes account of the rule permitting only workers to eat the food. In view of the record in the Gospels, it seems probable that the more niggardly custom prevailed among the landowners near large urban centers, whose visitors would have denuded field and vineyard, like so many locusts, if they were permitted to eat their fill. It remained for Akabiah, representing this group of landowners, to formulate a universal rule.

(5) The final evidence of his patrician sympathies is to be found in his almost Sadducean theology (see above, p. 159).

The plebeians, who controlled the Sanhedrin, were prepared to recognize Akabiah as associate to Gamaliel if he would renounce some of his extreme views. He declined to do this; and Gamaliel remained the sole leader of his day.

We have observed in the text that both Simeon ben Gamaliel I, and Gamaliel II, were Shammaites, and that in their time the Hillelites were led by Johanan ben Zakkai, and Joshua ben Hananya.

With Simeon ben Gamaliel, the House of Hillel reverted to its original plebeian attitude. He had all the humor, the humility and the character of his famous ancestor. When his son, Judah, destined later to become the Nasi, complained of the preferment given at school to the son of Simeon ben Yohai, the patient father consoled him with these words, "My child be not wroth. He is a lion, and the son of a lion; you are a lion, but the son of a fox (*B. Baba Mezia* 84b). In part this humility was doubtless a result of his reduced circumstances. The Romans, who had massacred all the household of Gamaliel II during the war of Bar Kokba and the Hadrianic persecution (*B. Sotah* 49b), had doubtless also confiscated the Nasi's estates. Simeon ben Gamaliel possessed no slaves, as his father did; nor, so far as can be seen from the record, did he own large fields or vineyards. On the contrary, his mode of life gives every evidence of simplicity, and even of poverty.

His closest friends in the academy were not Simeon ben Yohai and Meir, the patricians, but Judah ben Ilai and Jose ben Halafta, the plebeians (*Tosefta Demai* 3:14, p. 50; *B. Sukkah* 26a; *B. Pesahim* 100a). In fact, Meir once joined in a conspiracy to remove Simeon ben Gamaliel from his office (*B. Horayot* 13b).

His decisions, like these external facts of his life, give evidence of plebeian leanings. He held, for instance, that a dyer or a baker could not be ejected from his shop by the owner before he had lived there for three years (Mishna *Baba Mezia* 8:5); he declined to insist with his colleagues that a merchant remove the sediment from his scales every thirty days (Mishna *Baba Batra* 5:10); he freed mechanics from any claim for injury resulting from their work on highways, not only while they were engaged at their tasks, but during the thirty days when they were preparing their materials (Mishna *Baba Mezia* 10:5); he was lenient in his decisions regarding the Samaritans, saying that "with regard to those laws which they accept, the Samaritans are more rigorous than the Jews" (*B. Gittin* 10a); he maintained that a slave can say to his master, "either support me or free me" (*ibid.* 12a); and further that "it was as commendable an act to redeem slaves as to free Israelites from pagan captivity" (*ibid.* 37b). All of these decisions are essentially in the spirit of Akiba and the plebeian faction.

His contemporaries were, of course, aware of his plebeian leanings, and appointed a patrician, Nathan the Babylonian, as his associate. Nathan's patricianship is obvious first from his family connections, for he was the son of the Babylonian Head of the Exile (*Horayot* 13b). But in addition, it is clear that Nathan belonged to the School of Ishmael. This can be seen from the fact that he reports an incident in Ishmael's life as though he had been an eye witness to it (*B. Shabbat* 12b); but more especially from the frequency with which his name occurs in the tannaitic midrashim of the School of Ishmael, although he is hardly mentioned in the similar works from the School of Akiba (see Hoffmann, *Einleitung in d. halach. Midrashim,* pp. 39, 88). He further actually cites Ishmael in *B. Pesahim* 67b; also the patricians, Eliezer ben Hyrkanos, in *Pesahim* 48a; Jose, the Galilean, in *Menahot* 38b; and Tarfon, in *Zebahim* 97a.

Nathan, who survived Simeon, continued to hold office with Judah the Patriarch I, who was also classed as a plebeian.

This analysis of the factional tendencies of the various scholars may be summarized in the following table of Pharisaic leaders from the year 170 B.C.E. to 220 C.E. (The patrician member of each pair is indicated by an asterisk).

TABLE I

	NASI	AB BET DIN
170-162 B.C.E.	Jose ben Joezer*	Jose ben Johanan
162-ca. 149 B.C.E.	*Interruption because of the persecutions and wars*	
149-109 B.C.E.	Joshua ben Perahya*	Nittai of Arbel
109-76 B.C.E.	*Interruption due to persecution of Pharisees*	
76-60 B.C.E.	Simeon ben Shatah	Judah ben Tabbai*
60-39 B.C.E.	Shemayah	Abtalyon*
39-ca. 20 B.C.E.	*Interruption due to Herod's persecution*	
20 B.C.E.-20 C.E.	Hillel	Menahem* Shammai*
20-50 C.E.	Gamaliel	(Associateship offered to Akabiah ben Mahalalel*)
50-70 C.E.	Simeon ben Gamaliel*	Johanan ben Zakkai
70-80 C.E.	*Interruption due to Roman Conquest*	
80-116 C.E.	Gamaliel* (Eleazar ben Azariah* appointed *ad interim* during Gamaliel's removal)	Joshua ben Hananya
116-ca. 145 C.E.	*Interruption due to disordered times*	
145-ca. 170 C.E.	Simeon ben Gamaliel	Nathan*
170-217 C.E.	Judah I	Nathan* (while he lived; position left vacant thereafter)

The evidence of bi-partisan leadership which this table offers us, is supplemented by other records. It can be shown that it was a definite policy of the Pharisees to have plebeians and patricians represented, equally so far as was possible, on the various commissions which were appointed by the Sanhedrin. Thus Josephus expressly tells us that the commission sent to investigate his activities in Galilee consisted of two patricians and two plebeians. "The scheme agreed upon," he tells us, "was to send a deputation comprising persons of different classes of society but of equal standing in education. Two of them, Jonathan and Ananias, were from the lower ranks and adherents of the Pharisees; the third, Joazar, also a Pharisee, came from a priestly family; the youngest, Simeon, was descended from high priests." (*Life,* 39).

Of the recorded rabbinical commissions sent to Rome, we know that one consisted of Eliezer, the patrician, and Joshua, the plebeian (*Yer. Sanhedrin* 7:19, 25a; Gamaliel did not count, since his appointment to the office of Nasi was the subject of the mission); the second, of Gamaliel and Eleazar ben Azariah as patricians, and Joshua and Akiba as plebeians (see above p. 136); the third, of Simeon ben Yohai, the patrician, and Eleazar ben Jose, the plebeian (Meilah 17a).

When, during the period of Gamaliel's removal from office, a commission was appointed to negotiate with Dosa ben Arkenas, the leader of the Shammaites, for an agreement on certain rules, it consisted of Tarfon and Eleazar ben Azariah of the patricians, and Joshua and Akiba of the plebeians (*Yer. Yebamot* 1:6, 3b, line 2; Tarfon's name is omitted in *B. Yebamot* 15a).

Apparently the same principle applied in the last days of the Commonwealth to the judges of Jerusalem, for the Mishna records that "there were two judges of decision in Jerusalem: Admon and Hanan ben Abishalom." (Mishna *Ketubot* 13:1). A study of their decisions shows that Admon was a patrician and Hanan a plebeian. In fact, this is evident from a mere perusal of the record which gives two decisions of Hanan and informs us that he was supported in both by Johanan ben Zakkai, and opposed by the high priestly families and Dosa ben Arkenas, the Shammaite. On the other hand, two of Admon's decisions are explicitly supported by Gamaliel II.

An analysis of the issues involved, however, offers more conclusive evidence for their class associations. The cases are all listed in Mishna *Ketubot* 13:1 ff. and may be summarized as follows:

1. A woman whose husband had left for distant parts came to court to ask for maintenance from his estate. According to the law, she was entitled to this remedy, provided the court was assured that the husband had made no provision for her. As she could offer no evidence to this negative fact, the court was urged to impose an oath upon her, stating that she was without means. But Hanan, loyal to the plebeian principles which were opposed to unnecessary oaths, particularly by women, gave her the income without adjuration.

2. In a similar case, the woman had been supported by another man during her husband's absence from home. When the husband returned, the generous friend demanded that he be reimbursed. Hanan would not grant the claim, although the facts were admitted. The decision which may seem, at first, a patent perversion of justice, was in reality based on far-reaching social considerations. Just because plebeian women were emancipated, the sages who represented that group were particularly fearful of any dangerous friendships between the sexes. We have observed above (p. 191) what steps Akiba took to prevent emancipation from leading to sexual irregularities. The same principles were followed by the School of Hillel generally (cf. Mishna *Yebamot* 15:1 ff.) and in a series of four important decisions by Joshua ben Hananya in particular (Mishna *Ketubot* 1:6 ff.). Hanan felt that the judge who desired to maintain the traditional standards of chastity could not encourage close relations between the wife of an absent husband and male "friends." The man who helped a woman under the circumstances acted irregularly; the appropriate remedy would have been an appeal to the court for provision from her husband's property. To permit him to be repaid would encourage others to take similar care of women whose husbands had left, and this might lead to forbidden intimacy.

3. The issue of feminine chastity reappeared in another case, which came before Admon. A man died leaving insufficient property to support both his sons and his daughters, and Admon was called upon to arrange the division. The ordinary rule which gave the inheritance to the sons but charged them with the support of their sisters, was of course inapplicable, since the necessity of maintaining the daughters would leave the sons without any income for themselves. The plebeians, fearing that the girls would be driven to a life of infamy, insisted that they be given preference; but Admon, adhering to the aristocratic, landowning psychology of the son's priority, said: "Shall he be deprived of his rights because he is a male?" and gave the property to the sons unconditionally.

4. The fourth problem involved again the plebeian aversion to oaths. A man was brought to court on a claim for certain barrels of oil. He admitted receiving the barrels, but denied that they had contained oil. Since no witnesses or documentary evidence were available, the decision had to depend, in Jewish law, on the credibility of the litigants. Now the law requires a defendant who admits part of a claim and denies the rest, to confirm his statements under oath, whereupon the decision is issued in his favor. But in this instance, the plebeian sages denied that the defendant should be obliged to take an oath, for, they said, his admission has nothing to do with the claim. The suit is for barrels of oil; the admission concerns barrels, but is an absolute denial of the claim for oil. The casuistic quibble, for it is nothing more, could only have been raised by judges who would go any length to avoid the imposition of an oath. But Admon, as a landowning aristocrat, did not share their prejudices, and insisted on the usual oath.

5. A man of small means, anxious to improve himself socially and financially, had won the hand of the daughter of a wealthy patrician, and had been promised a large dowry. When the time for the wedding came, the bride's father refused to keep his promise. The husband, unable to secure the property, also declined

to accept the wife. But since in ancient Palestinian custom betrothal bound the woman to the husband, she was prevented from marrying anyone else. The poor girl thus found herself ground between two opposing wills; her husband would not accept her without the property, the father would not give her any dowry. She appealed to Admon for redress, asking that the husband either release her or marry her. In those days, before the advent of modern romanticism, plebeian sympathies were all with the husband who, his comrades held, had simply been made the victim of a fraudulent contract. But Admon, agreeing as usual with the men of property, decided for the girl.

In other important civil decisions, Admon showed himself sympathetic to the rural landowning classes against the rising city merchants. One of the litigations gives us, incidentally, a striking picture of the unruly, chaotic times, when physical force was rapidly supplanting the normal jurisdiction of the community.

6. A man's farm had been seized by a brigand who was sufficiently influential with the governor to prevent his being driven away through ordinary legal process. Later a purchaser appeared, wanting to buy the field but apprehensive about the robber's title to it. To allay his suspicions, the powerful bandit had the effrontery to compel the original owner, his victim, to witness the deed of sale which he issued for the field. Nevertheless, the original owner afterward brought suit against the purchaser to recover his property. The plebeians, taking the view of the defrauded innocent purchaser, held that in acting as witness to the sale, the original owner had waved his rights. But Admon, knowing that once such a precedent were established any number of bandits would use it to confirm their wrongful titles, said, "The original owner may say, I was willing to witness the sale, because I knew I could recover the land from the purchaser, but was unable to do anything against the robber."

7. Like so many others under suspicion, the owner of an estate had had to flee to a distant country, and had had no time to make provisions for his property. During his long absence, the path which led from the main road to his farm had been absorbed by the neighbors and was no longer recognizable. The plebeians, having little sympathy for these returning revolutionaries, said the owner must buy a road from one of the neighboring farmers or "let him fly in the air." Admon said he may claim from his neighbors the shortest possible right of way from the road.

Finally, two other decisions show that Admon's approach to commercial matters was that of a typical rural judge, unaccustomed to the intricate business relations of the city.

8. A man borrowed money from another and later bought a field from him. When the lender brought suit for the loan, the borrower claimed that it had been paid; and as evidence, said: "If I had owed you the money, would you have sold me the property without demanding payment at once?" Admon, accustomed to regard a loan as purely a matter of personal kindness, upheld the claim. But the plebeian scholars held that it was invalid. The lender might have tried to collect his money, they said, unsuccessfully, and welcomed the opportunity to sell the borrower real estate which he would afterward be able to seize for debt.

9. *A* sued *B* for a debt and presented in evidence a duly executed note. *B* admitted the validity of the note, but claimed he had paid it off and had simply failed to obtain the document from *A*. As proof of his statement, he brought forward a note showing that *A* had recently borrowed money from him. "Why should *A* have asked me for a loan," he said, "if I was in debt to him? Would it not have been more natural for him to demand repayment of the loan I owed him?" *A* did not deny his indebtedness to *B*, but he insisted that *B* was also indebted to him. Admon sustained *B*'s

claim, feeling certain that no one would borrow money from his debtor, and that therefore A's note must have been paid off before he received the loan from B. But the plebeian sages, knowing the ways of the city market, held that each note was valid and should be enforced.

A consideration of all the evidence adduced seems to me to establish the fact that the Pharisees recognized the two factions in their midst, and also that they consciously chose their leaders with an eye to the equal representation of the opposing groups.

C. THE USUAL AGE FOR MARRIAGE AMONG THE PLEBEIANS

Any doubt regarding the custom of late marriage among the plebeians is removed by a consideration of the remarks in the Testaments of the Twelve Patriarchs, Testament of Issachar 3.5 ff., where the author obviously tries to comfort the wifeless husbandman. "Therefore," the author says, "when I was thirty-five years old, I took to myself a wife, for my labor wore away my strength and I never thought upon pleasure with women; but owing to my toil, sleep overcame me." (R. H. Charles, tr.). This corresponds very closely to Hesiod's advice to the Boeotian peasant, given half a millennium earlier, but doubtless applicable throughout antiquity: "Bring home a wife to your house when you are of the right age, while you are not far short of thirty years, nor much above; this is the right age for marriage" (Works and Days, lines 695-97; Evelyn White, tr.).

D. THE SHAMMAITIC INCLINATIONS OF GAMALIEL II

Gamaliel's descent from Hillel, and the fact that after his removal from office he somewhat changed his policy, have helped to conceal both from talmudic scholars and modern historians his definitely Shammaitic inclinations. But the records leave no room for doubt on the subject.

(1) He married the widow of his brother, who had died without children, although another wife of the same brother was his daughter. This is a Shammaitic practice which was most severely denounced by the Hillelites (*B. Yebamot* 15a). The explanation offered by the Babylonian Talmud that his daughter was sterile and, therefore, her marriage to his brother was really void, cannot possibly be accepted.

(2) Simeon ben Gamaliel reports that his father would not permit laundry to be sent to a pagan for wash after Wednesday, which is precisely in accordance with Shammaitic opinion (Mishna *Shabbat* 1:9; cf. *Sifre* Deuteronomy 203).

(3) The Mishna itself records that Gamaliel followed Shammaitic practice in three matters (*Bezah* 2:6). But the enumeration given there is not exhaustive, as can be seen from examples 1 and 2, which are not included in the Mishna.

(4) In a series of momentous decisions regarding the rights of married women, Gamaliel sided with Eliezer against Joshua (Mishna *Ketubot* 1:6-9). The fact that Gamaliel and Eliezer accept the woman's claim and Joshua rejects it must not blind us to the essentially Shammaitic nature of their view. It was characteristic of the plebeians that they distrusted women in such matters (cf. Mishna *Yebamot* 15:2 ff).

(5) In Mishna *Ketubot* 8:1 ff, Gamaliel indicates his sympathy with the Shammaitic tendency to augment the wife's authority over her property rather than to limit it in accordance with Hillelite principles. With regard to Examples 4 and 5 it is important to bear in mind that among the plebeian city groups for whom the Hillelites and Joshua legislated the laxity of sexual morals and family ties was more pronounced than among the upper middle classes of the city and the provincial groups whom the Shammaites and Eliezer considered. It was because of the "freedom" of the plebeian woman when she was the possessor of property that the Hillelites made every effort to limit her rights.

(6) Shammaitic custom attached great importance to the *ma'amar* or formal betrothal of the widow who was bound to

Levirate marriage (*B. Yebamot* 51b). The reason for this is obvious. Among the patricians and rich provincials, it frequently happened that a man died leaving more than one wife. No one could predict which of them the Levir would choose as his wife until he had indicated his selection through some ceremonial. Hence it became customary for him to offer the wife whom he intended to espouse some token of *ḳiddushin* or betrothal. When he did this, she was as much his wife as any other betrothed woman might be. The Talmud points out (*B. Yebamot, loc cit.*) that Gamaliel occupied exactly the same position. The fact that some plebeian teachers expressed moderate sympathy with this view (*ibid.*) cannot be offered as evidence, of course, against its definitely Shammaitic nature.

(7) Like the Shammaites, Gamaliel opposed the admission of the poor into the academy. The statement cited in the text about the poor student being compared to the unclean fish is ascribed in *Abot of R. Nathan* to Gamaliel the Elder, but this name is frequently used for Gamaliel II (cf., e.g., *Tosefta Shabbat* 7(8):18, p. 119; see reference to parallel passage in *Yer., ibid.*). But quite aside from this, Gamaliel's refusal to admit all those "who were not within as without" (see p. 128) indicates his opposition to the usual Hillelite liberality of instruction. This has already been noticed by Jacob Reifmann, in *Bet Talmud* IV, 47 ff.

(8) In Appendix II,B, we have indicated that Gamaliel sided with the patrician Admon in several important recorded decisions.

(9) Finally, there is the evidence adduced in II,B to show that in the selection of representatives of the two groups, Gamaliel was always classified as a patrician.

E. COMPARATIVE MONTHLY RAINFALL IN VARIOUS PARTS OF PALESTINE

My learned friend, Dr. A. Baruch, the government meteorologist at Tel Aviv, Palestine, has furnished me the following tables of average monthly rainfall in various parts of Palestine (the amounts are in millimeters):

TABLE II

MONTH	COAST		VALLEY OF JEZREEL	
	Haifa	Tel Aviv	Nazareth	Jerusalem
September	2	3	0	0.7
October	26	28	19	11
November	96	67	86	60
December	163	162	180	146
January	168	131	161	169
February	99	81	116	128
March	61	47	94	104
April	30	20	26	43
May*	8	3	6	7
Total for the year	655	542	688	669

* The amounts in June, July and August are insignificant.

Jerusalem is thus better watered than the coastal plain and has almost as much rainfall as Nazareth. Its total of 669 mm. compares very favorably with 420 mm. at Gaza, 615 at Hebron, 487 at Tiberias, and 440 at Menahmiah.

The tables make it abundantly clear that in October the rainfall for the Judean lowlands is twice as much as that for Jerusalem. Hence we find that Eliezer, the scholar of Ludd, holds that on the first day of Sukkot, i.e., about the fifth of October, one should begin to insert in the prayer the words: "He who causeth the wind to blow and the rain to descend." Joshua, living at Jerusalem, where Sukkot normally should occur in the dry season, says that the words are inserted only on the last day of the festival (Mishna *Ta'anit* 1:1). While the men of Jerusalem wished for rain as the winter was about to set in, and made special prayers and ceremonies for it, since they needed it for drink, they did not want it to come down till the festival had passed. Its early descent would not only destroy their festival booths but would drive all the visitors back home to complete their farm-labor before the rainy season started in earnest.

Similarly at Passover, which occurs in Jerusalem before the rainy season is over, the metropolitan Jews were no longer anxious for its descent. Their cisterns full, they were fearful that continued rains would make the pilgrims anxious to hurry away from the city. They ceased the insertion of the words, "He who causeth the wind to blow and the rain to descend," on the first day of Passover, and ceased praying for rain on the last day. But Meir, representing the rural farmers, who still needed the late rains, to prevent the burning of their crops under the semi-tropical sun, says, "One prays for rain until the end of Nisan," fully nine days after the close of the Passover festival. (*Ibid*. 1:2). Meir in this follows the principle laid down by an earlier rural teacher, Judah ben Bathyra (*Yer., ad. loc.,* 64a).

F. AKIBA'S AND ISHMAEL'S RULES OF INTERPRETATION AND THEIR DOCTRINES OF THE REVELATION

In his own school, Akiba endeavored to prove the superiority of his method of interpretation through experiment, as it were. He would take up various known and recognized decisions, and ask how they could be derived from Scripture. He would first indicate possible demonstrations through the traditional rules, and would refute each of them. He would then triumphantly conclude by what he considered a convincing and irrefutable argument according to his own methods. But in the conclave, he preferred wherever possible to use his opponents' dialectic, so as to beat them on their own ground. One such argument with Johanan ben Nuri has been preserved. After Akiba had unsuccessfully tried to prove his point by methods which Johanan would have accepted, he suddenly cried out, "You have refuted the logical argument; but what can you say in reply to the verse itself?" (*Sifra Behukotai, perek* 9:11, 113). Unfortunately, however, what Akiba called the verse, was his *interpretation* of it.

One of the greatest tributes to Akiba's brilliance and pedagogic effectiveness was the curious intrusion of his terminology into the vocabulary of his opponents. Parallels to this phenomenon can be cited from other fields of science and learning; but it is extraordinary to find Ishmael speaking of "inclusions" instead of "generalizations," and several times citing a rule which was invented by Akiba as support for his argument. For instance, the principle, *en ribui ahar ribui ela lemaet,* "two generalizations must be taken as a limitation," is ascribed to Akiba in *Sifra Zav, pereḳ* 11:4, 34d; but to Ishmael in *Sifre* Numbers 124, p. 155, *Midrash Tannaim* 16:9, p. 93, and 25:3, p. 163. In fact during one argument, Akiba took advantage of Ishmael's use of his terminology to further his own side of the debate. "If the verse includes what you admit it does, it includes also what I find in it," he said (Mishna *Shebuot* 3:5).

Akiba's use of superfluous letters and words as bases for new laws necessarily implied that everything found in the Five Books of Moses was literally dictated by God. This theological doctrine did not at all surprise the ancients; indeed it was so widely held that it formed the strongest foundation for Akiba's system. But Ishmael tried to fortify his position with the assertion that generally Moses, like the other prophets, received from God only the substance or idea, which he put into words. This view was supported, Ishmael believed, by the fact that sometimes Scripture says, "This is the *word* (*ha-dabar*) which the Lord hath commanded" (Num. 30:2; Lev. 17:2). These verses indicated that elsewhere Moses received from God not words, but ideas.

This amazing disagreement between the schools has left unmistakable traces in the extant tannaitic *midrashim*. See, e.g., *Meḳilta* of R. Simeon 12:1, p. 6 (and note of Hoffmann, *ibid.*); 19:3, p. 94; 20:22, p. 114; *Sifra, Aḥare, par.* 6:2, 83c; *Sifre,* Numbers 153, p. 198; *Sifre,* Deut. 83; *Midrash Tannaim* 13:2, p. 63; *Ibid.* 18:15, p. 111. From these sources we may infer that the School of Ishmael held that the revelation of Moses was not essentially different from that of prophets, except in so far as in specified cases he repeats the word which came to him, and in those cases he uses the expression, "This is the word"; while the School of Akiba held that the expression, "Thus saith the Lord," when used by Moses implied a verbatim quotation, but when used by the prophets had no such significance.

This difference between the schools is clearly reflected in their disagreement in the interpretation of Exodus 20:22. *Mekilta* of R. Ishmael (*Jethro, Bahodesh,* chap. 9, Horowitz-Rabin p. 238, Lauterbach II, p. 274) explains the verse as follows: "Thus shalt thou say to the children of Israel—in the language in which I speak to thee, in the Holy Language." It is obvious from this statement that the School of Ishmael believed that the only limitation which God imposed on Moses' words was that they should be in Hebrew. The School of Akiba, however, as represented in the *Mekilta* of R. Simeon (20:22, p. 114) maintains that the verses required Moses to speak to the Children of Israel in the precise words which he received from God. According to this *Mekilta,* he was required to speak "in the holy language, and in this sense, and in this order, and with these divisions, and in these sections, 'according to everything which the Lord commanded,' neither omitting nor adding."

It is true that the Mekilta of R. Ishmael, *Jethro, Bahodesh* chap. 2, (Horowitz-Rabin p. 207, Lauterbach II, p. 201, quotes the *baraita* in almost exactly the form in which the *Mekilta* of R. Simeon has it, both here, and in the commentary on 19:3, p. 94. But there can hardly be a doubt that the correct version of the *baraita* of the School of Ishmael is that found in the *Mekilta* of R. Ishmael, chapter 9, and that the form in chapter 2 has been changed under the influence of the School of R. Akiba or its texts.

Akiba's insistence that all tradition was implicit in the Holy Writ led to a fundamental modification of the Pharisaic position regarding the Oral Law. For centuries plebeian scholars had insisted that their traditions, derived from their teachers through successive generations leading up to Moses on Mount Sinai, had equal validity with the Written Law. When they were asked how they justified the water libations on the Feast of Tabernacles, or whence they knew that Shabuot occurred on the fiftieth day after the first day of Passover, or why glass and metal ware should come under the ordinary rules of Levitical impurity, they said that this was their tradition; and that ended the discussion. After Hillel had spent a whole day trying unsuccessfully to prove to the Bene Bathyra that the Passover sacrifice must be offered even if the fourteenth day of Nisan occurs on a Sabbath, he scored a victory when he uttered the words, "This is my tradition from my masters, Shemaya and Abtalyon!" (*Yer. Pesahim* 6:1, 33a; cf. *Tosefta, ibid.*, 4:1 (11), p. 162; and *B. ibid.*, 66a.) There could be no further argument. The Sadducees and the later Pharisaic patricians might ask how it came about that *their* teachings had told them nothing of such unwritten traditions. They might ask themselves inwardly why these unwritten traditions always took forms which were adapted to the needs of plebeian Jerusalem, and opposed to the interests or desires of patricians and provincials, but they could not disprove what the plebeians asserted to be a fact. What Hillel said to the Bene Bathyra, "Alas that you have not studied under Shemaya and Abtalyon!" had doubtless been anticipated by many others of his sect and faction before him. As one of the sages remarked, "We do not say to a person who has no evidence, 'Come and testify,' but to him who has evidence." It became an accepted part of the Pharisaic theology that their traditions formed an Oral Law, as authoritative and revealed as the Written Law itself.

But Akiba's efforts to democratize the Law were not at all helped by this doctrine of the Oral Law, for his rules had no foundation in tradition. It was, as we have observed, this necessity which had made his methods of interpretation so vital and indispensable a part of his whole program. But having invented his method to discover *new* rules, he also used it to justify the old ones. Hence he no longer needed the traditional distinction between Written and Oral Law; everything was either expressed or implied in the script. His colleagues interpreted the words, "These are the statutes and ordinances and laws (*torot*) which the Lord made between him and the children of Israel on Mount Sinai by the hand of Moses" (Lev. 26:46) to mean that "two laws (*torot*) were given to Israel, the one in writing, the other orally." But Akiba could not accept this. "Have we only two *torot?*" he asked. "There are many *torot.* There is the *torah* of the whole burnt offering, and of the meal offering, and of the guilt offering, and of the peace offering, and of impurity." (*Sifra Behukotai, per.* 8:12, 112c.)

G. AKIBA AND THE PRAYER FOR THE KINGDOM OF GOD

A number of years ago, I pointed out in the *Jewish Quarterly Review,* N.S. XVI (1925), p. 17, that the prayer for the Kingdom of God in the service of the New Year's Day must have been added late in the first or early in the second century c.e. The evidence I then adduced for this was the fact that in Mishna *Rosh Ha-Shanah* 4:5, the order of the benedictions on Rosh Ha-Shanah is given in two variant forms, the one ascribed to Akiba, the other to Johanan ben Nuri. The two statements are, however, identical, except in so far as relates to the prayer for the Kingdom of God. By a critical analysis of the text, I came to the conclusion that both Akiba and Johanan ben Nuri are citing an older norm, which knew nothing of any prayer for the Kingdom of God; and that each of them inserted the mention of that prayer where he considered it proper. I am now able to offer further evidence in support of the theory then propounded.

In a *baraita* cited in *B. Rosh Ha-Shanah* 32a, and found also in *Sifra Emor, par.* 11:3, 101 d, Eliezer, describing the prayers of Rosh Ha-Shanah, makes no mention of *Malkuyot,* the prayer for the Kingdom of God. Akiba, who disagrees with him in some details, also mentions the prayers but omits any reference to *Malkuyot.* The only conclusion to be drawn from the fact that Akiba fails to mention the *Malkuyot* in this *baraita,* while he does mention it in the statement quoted in the Mishna, is that the *Malkuyot* came into existence sometime during Akiba's lifetime.

H. THE TRAJAN DECLARATION

The singular difficulty which modern historians have experienced in their attempt to reconstruct the relation of the Emperors Trajan and Hadrian to the Jews is due to the confused and colored traditions which have been preserved by both Jewish and Christian writers. The rabbinic sources of our information about the matter are as follows:

1. *Megillat Ta'anit,* ed. Hans Lichtenstein, in Hebrew Union College *Annual* VIII-IX 346: "On the twelfth day in it (the month of Adar) is Tiryon Day."

2. *Yer. Ta'anit* 2:13, 66a; *Megillah* 1:6, 70c: "The day on which Julianus and Pappus were executed abolished the Tiryon Day."

3. *Genesis* R. 64:7, p. 710: "In the time of Rabbi Joshua ben Hananya the Government ordered the Temple to be rebuilt. Thereupon Julianus and Pappus set up tables from Acre unto Antioch to supply the needs of those who would return from exile. The Samaritans, however, said to the Government: 'Let it be known now unto the king that, if this city is builded and the walls are finished, they will not pay tribute, impost or toll.' [Ezra 4:13]. . . . He said to them, 'What then shall we do?' They said, 'Send them an order to change the sanctuary from its place, or to make it five cubits larger, or five cubits smaller, and then they will of their own accord withdraw.' Thereupon the whole community gathered into the valley of Rimmon. When they came together they began to weep, and wished to rebel against the government. They [the leaders] said, 'Let some wise man arise and quiet the community. Let Joshua ben Hananya arise, for he is the sage of the Law.' He thereupon arose and said, 'A lion who had captured some prey, and caught a bone in his throat, offered reward to anyone who would remove the bone. An Egyptian crane, which has a long beak, thereupon came and removed the bone. When, however, the crane asked for its reward, the lion replied that it might boast that it had entered the mouth of a lion and

escaped in peace. So,' Joshua concluded, 'it is enough for us that we came to this people in peace and have escaped in peace.' "

4. *Sifra Emor perek* 9:5, 99d; *Mekilta* of R. Simeon 21:13, p. 125; *Semahot* 8:15, p. 164; Scholion to *Megillat Ta'anit loc. cit.*: "When Trajan seized Julianus and Pappus in Laodicea, he said to them, 'If you belong to the people of Hananiah, Mishael and Azariah, let your God come and save you from my power.' They replied, however, 'Hananiah, Mishael and Azariah were worthy, and Nebuchadnezzar was fit to have a miracle performed through him. But you are a wicked king and are unfit to be the instrument of a miracle. We, too, are deserving of death, and if you fail to slay us God has many executioners, lions, bears, serpents and scorpions who will come upon us. But if you slay us, God will demand our blood at your hands.' It is said that he had no opportunity to leave the place before there came a pair of officers from Rome and they broke his head with axes and hatchets."

These traditions, standing alone, would indicate that the promise to undertake the building was made under Trajan. Nothing less than such a promise could possibly justify the establishment of a Trajan Day. The theory that this festival was established in honor of Trajan's death is clearly contrary to the statement in *Yerushalmi,* cited above, that it was abolished because of the execution of Julianus and Pappus by Trajan. Graetz's theory that Julianus and Pappus were not actually executed, but were saved by this miraculous intervention from Rome, is clearly opposed to the text he uses. *B. Ta'anit* 18b and *Semahot* 8:15 expressly state they were executed; and the others imply the fact. It is true that in all the sources Trajan and Quietus, who was his tool, are confused. Trajan died with remarkable suddenness, Quietus was executed. The later sages simply telescoped the two events into one.

Of the Greek and Roman sources, the most important is, of course, Epiphanius (*De Mensuris et Ponderibus* 14) who, admittedly confused in his tradition, yet apparently drew on reliable records, which he simply failed to interpret correctly. (Cf. W.

Weber, *Untersuchungen zur Geschichte d. Kaisers Hadrianus,*
p. 205, note 732). He maintains that Hadrian, having arrived in
Jerusalem, planned "to rebuild the city but not the Temple." He
adds a detail, which could hardly have been invented, and yet is
recorded in no other source, that the project was entrusted to
Aquila, the proselyte. All this happened, he says, in the forty-
seventh year after the destruction of the Temple, i.e., in 116-117.
It was then that Hadrian, having reëstablished the city, called it
Aelia after himself.

Since we know from Dio Cassius that the rebuilding of Jerusalem and its renaming occurred as a result of Hadrian's visit in
130, it is obvious that we cannot accept Epiphanius's statement as
it stands. It is clear that he has confused the promise to rebuild
the Temple made by Trajan, and the actual rebuilding under
Hadrian. He had a tradition regarding the former, and the latter
was well attested by historians. What more natural than that he
should combine the two, and seek to reconcile the difficulties in
some manner.

The references to the rebuilding of the Temple in Chrysostom
(*Orat. adv. Judaeos,* V. 10, Migne, P. G. col. 897), Georg. Cedrenus
(*Historiarum Compendium,* ed. Bekker, p. 437), and Nicephorus
Callistus (*Eccl. Hist.* III. 24, Migne, P. G. 145, 944) speak only
of the attempt of the Jews to rebuild the Temple and do not there-
fore come under consideration.

It is doubtful whether the statement in *Chronicon Paschale* (ed.
Dindorf I, p. 474) that Hadrian, before founding the new city
called after him, destroyed the Temple of the Jews—implying that
some progress toward its reconstruction had been made—deserves
credence. But if it has any authority at all, it corroborates the
suggestion that an offer had been made to the Jews to rebuild their
sanctuary.

Further evidence that it was Trajan who made the offer is given
in the development of the story in the text. See, however, Graetz,
Geschichte IV, 126, 411 ff; J. Juster, *Les Juifs dans l'Empire*

Romaine II, 189 ff; Schuerer,[4] *Geschichte des jüdischen Volkes* I, 671 ff; S. Krauss, *Revue d. Etudes Juives* 30:211; Lagrange, *Le Messianisme chez les Juifs,* p. 309; Derenbourg, *Histoire de la Palestine,* p. 408 ff.; Volkmar, *Einleitung in die Apokryphen,* I, *Judith,* p. 83 ff; B. Bokser, *Pharisaic Judaism in Transition,* p. 25, note 60.

I. THE IDENTITY OF ISHMAEL'S COLLEAGUE, SIMEON

Some mediaeval copyists have identified this Simeon with Simeon ben Gamaliel, whom they accordingly substituted for him in the list of the Ten Martyrs (see *Mekilta,* ed. Horowitz-Rabin, p. 313, variant reading from *Yalkut ha-Makiri;* cf. also *Mahzor Vitry,* p. 544; also the reading of three mss. of *Semahot* in ed. Higger, p. 153; *Midrash Psalms,* ed. Buber, 9:13, 45a; *Lament. R.* chap. 2, verse 2). This identification was easily refuted by modern scholarship, but those substituted can hardly be called superior. Simeon ben Azzai, who is I. H. Weiss's choice, (*Dor Dor ve-Dorshav* II, 132) is expressly described as having died a natural death (*Tosefta Hagiga* 2:3, p. 234, and parallel passages). None of the writers on the subject have taken notice of the fact that the Simeon mentioned precedes Ishmael *in every list.* We must therefore look for a Simeon who is older than Ishmael. Now, while there were many Simeons who were younger than Ishmael, or at least inferior to him in rank, like Ben Zoma, Ben Nannos and Simeon ha-Temani, there was, so far as our records go, only one in that generation who was his senior, Simeon ben Nethanel, the disciple of Johanan ben Zakkai, and the colleague of Eliezer and Joshua.

While this Simeon did not play any very important rôle in the history of the *halaka,* he did contribute more than is usually credited to him. For whenever we find the expression "R. Eliezer and R. Simeon say" we may be certain that the Simeon referred to is none other than Simeon ben Nethanel. The expression occurs in Mishna *Shekalim* 3:1 and-Bekorot 9:5; Yoma 5:7; *Rosh ha-Shanah* 1:1; *Yebamot* 6:3, 4; *Tosefta Yoma* 4(3):7, 8, p. 187; *ibid. Menahot* 5:14, p. 518.

It is usually assumed that the Simeon referred to in these passages is Simeon ben Yohai, but obviously he could not be cited so frequently as a colleague of Eliezer, who was his master's master. To escape this difficulty copyists resorted to the device of writing Eleazar instead of Eliezer and supposing that Eleazar ben Shammua, Simeon ben Yohai's colleague, is the person intended. But Eleazar ben Shammua would obviously be mentioned after Simeon ben Yohai, who was both older and more famous, and not before him. Other copyists have made the emendation of Eleazar ben R. Simeon, which is easily proven to be unacceptable.

But we know that Simeon ben Nethanel's views were close to those of Eliezer, as can be seen from a comparison of *Abot* 2:13 with Mishna *Berakot* 3:4. They were related by marriage, and both were originally *am ha-arez*. It is altogether natural to suppose that they would agree on a number of points and would be mentioned together, in the order in which they occur. That Simeon is cited without the appellative, ben Nethanel, need not surprise us at all. It was doubtless assumed by the compilers of the early traditions that everyone would understand that the colleague of Eliezer was his brother-in-law and not some much younger Simeon. Cf. also Mishna *Abot* 2:13, where Simeon ben Nethanel is obviously referred to, and yet cited merely as Simeon. It is probable that Simeon ben Nethanel is also intended in Mishna *Shebiit,* 9:5, where he disagrees with Eliezer, Joshua and Gamaliel II; Mishna Horiot 1:2 where he disagrees with Eliezer. (There can be no doubt this is Eliezer ben Hyrkanos since Akiba and Ben Azzai disagree in the interpretation of his words; Simeon's view is given before that of Eliezer in order to bring the latter in immediate conjunction with the commentaries of these later scholars). In Mishna *Negaim* 14.9 = *Sifra Mezora, per.* 3:11, he again disagrees with Eliezer.

FOOTNOTES

I. THE GRAVE ON THE HILLTOP

1. Jewish War, II.9.1; Antiquities XVIII.2.3; *Yer. Shebiit* 9.8.
2. *Yer., ibid.*
3. The older legend places Akiba's grave in Caesarea (*Midrash Mishle*, chap. 9).
4. *B. Sanhedrin* 86a.
5. *Numbers R., Naso,* chap. 9; *Bekorot* 58a.

II. IN THE DEPTHS

1. Quoted by Philo, *Legatio ad Gaium* 36(281), ed. Cohn et Reiter, VI,206; cf. also *ibid.* 31(216), p. 196; and *In Flaccum* 7(46), p. 128, line 27 (same volume).
2. Mishna *Shekalim* 4.2 ff.
3. Mishna *Yoma* 1.1.
4. *B. Sanhedrin* 11b; *Tosefta, ibid.* 2.6, p. 416; cf. *Midrash Tannaim* 26.13, p. 176.
5. *B. Pesahim* 88b.
6. Mishna *Bikkurim* 3.4.
7. *B. Ketubot* 17a.
8. Mishna *Sotah* 7.8.
9. Acts 5.34.
10. *B. Sanhedrin* 20a.
11. *B. Ketubot* 49b.
12. *B. Baba Batra* 91b. For the normal price of grain in Palestine see Krauss, *Talmud. Archaeologie* p. 378, and note 449, on p. 700; cf. also Mishna *Peah* 8.7; *Erubin* 8.2; *Baba Mezia* 5.1, all of which imply that four seahs for a *sela* is the normal price. In *B. Baba Batra* 91a, the price of two seahs for a *sela* is declared as that of a famine justifying emigration from Palestine. See also II Kings 7.7, and commentaries.
13. *B. Baba Batra* 21a.
14. Dalman, *Arbeit u. Sitte in Palaestina,* III, 154 ff.

15. Olmstead, *History of Palestine and Syria,* p. 46 ff.; see also Nelson Glueck, "Recent Archaeological Work in Palestine," *Yearbook of the Central Conference of American Rabbis,* XXXIX, 3 f.

16. Some evidence to support this statement so far as the Rabbinical period is concerned, is presented in Appendix I, A. Regarding the earlier periods, Professor W. F. Albright writes me as follows:

> "I cannot find any definite statement by myself or any other scholar of competence to the effect that the hill-country of ancient Palestine was poorer than the Coastal Plain and the Plain of Jezreel. Yet there can be no doubt that this was true in nearly all periods. In the fourth and the early third millennium B.C.E. we find the hill-country very thinly occupied in comparison with the plains; cf. my observations in the *Journal of the Palestine Oriental Society,* VIII (1928), 251 and the references in notes 2 and 4. Subsequent excavations and discoveries have fully confirmed this picture. The hill-country was, in fact, largely wooded down to the beginning of the Iron Age, when the Israelites occupied it more intensively. In the Iron Age, from 1200 to 600 B.C.E., we find the same difference between the wealth and prosperity of the hill-country and of the Coastal Plain. By this time, however, the prosperity of the latter is no longer dependent upon a comparatively small maritime trade and sporadic caravan traffic, in addition to the rich grain fields, but is supported largely by a vastly expanded sea traffic. There continues to be a striking difference between the wealth of towns in the Coastal Plain and in the hill-country, as illustrated by excavations."

17. Cf. Kittel, *Gesch. des Volkes Israel* II, 56 ff; Olmstead, *History of Palestine and Syria,* p. 127; Cambridge Ancient History, IV, 60 ff; Weber, *Religionssoziologie,* III, pp. 27, 63.

18. See above, notes 15 and 16.

19. Krauss, *Talmudische Archaeologie* I, 19 ff.

20. *Ibid.* I, p. 122; for a further discussion, see Jeremias, *Jerusalem* II A, p. 38.

21. *Sifre* Deut. 76; *Tosefta Arakin* 4.27, p. 548; *B. Hullin* 84a.

22. *Tosefta* and *Hullin, ibid.*

23. Mishna *Berakot* 6.8.

24. *B. Nedarim* 49b.

25. This explains the controversy between the Schools of Shammai and Hillel regarding the necessity of inserting fringes in a "sheet" which is used as a garment. The Shammaites, being the wealthier class, did not use linen garments for daily wear and considered them free from the law of fringes; the Hillelites, among whom the use of a linen *sadin* as a garment was usual, believed that it ought to be treated like any other garment (see Mishna *Eduyot* 4.10).

26. *B. Nedarim, ibid.*

27. Mishna *Hallah* 2.3.

28. *Yer. Sanhedrin* 7.19, 52d. The games there described as being played in Rome were obviously known in Palestine.

29. A legend widely repeated in medieval works (*Mafteah* of *R. Nissim, Berakot* 27b; *Menorat Ha-Maor* III.5, 3b; *Yohasin,* s.v. *Akiba*) tracing Akiba's ancestry to the Canaanite general, Sisera, is of course without foundation.

30. *Abot* 5.21.

31. Cf. Mishna *Baba Batra* 6.4.

32. See Appendix II, C.

33. *B. Pesahim* 49b.

34. *B. Ketubot* 62b; *Nedarim* 50a; *Yer. Shabbat* 6.1; *Abot of R. Nathan,* chap. 6 (14b ff).

35. Mishna *Yadaim* 3.5.

36. *B. Ketubot* 63a.

37. *Yer. Shabbat* 6.1, 7d; *ibid. Sotah* 9.16, 24c; *B. Shabbat* 59b; *ibid.* Nedarim 50a.

38. *Leviticus R.* 7.3.

39. See Guedemann, *Erziehungswesen d. Juden* I, pp. 50, 272; also Abrahams, *Jewish Life in the Middle Ages*[1], p. 351.

40. *Abot of R. Nathan,* I, chap. 6; II, chap. 12; 14b, 15a.

41. *Tosefta Parah* 3.8, p. 632.

42. See Budde, "The Nomadic Ideal in the Old Testament," in *New World,* December, 1895; published in German in an expanded form in *Preussiche Jahrbücher,* 1896; and Flight, "The Nomadic Idea and Ideal in the Old Testament," in *Journal of Biblical Literature,* 42 (1923), 158 ff.

43. See above, notes 15 and 16.

44. Compare Dalman, *Arbeit u. Sitte in Palaestina,* I.1, p. 41.

45. Max Weber, *Religionssoziologie* III, 37; M. Lurje, *Studien zur Gesch. d. Wirtschaftlichen u. sozialen Verhältnisse im Israel.-jüd. Reiche,* p. 16; and cf. Genesis 4.17,20-22; where the origin of cities is ascribed to the landless nomads who were related to the itinerant smiths and artisans. See also commentaries, *ad loc.*

46. *Sifre* Deut. 352, 145a.

47. Cf. *Abot* 1.1.

48. For a thoroughgoing and convincing discussion of his date and identity see G. F. Moore, in *Jewish Studies in Memory of Israel Abrahams,* p. 348 ff.

49. *Abot* 1.2.

50. See Josephus, Antiquities XII.3.3. See also Appendix II, A.

51. The most curious instance of this preference for Greek names is that of Alexander Jannaeus's wife, whose name in Hebrew was *Shelomit.* This was Graecized into *Salampsio.* The poor Jews, unable to pronounce this strange word, and yet apparently not daring to call her *Shelomit,* corrupted the name still further into *Shelemtzia, Shelentzia,* and similar forms. The name was apparently characteristic of priestly families (Klein, *Jüdisch-palaestinisches Corpus Inscriptionum,* p. 12).

52. For this, see further M. Katzenelson, in *Monatsschrift f. Gesch. u. Wisssenschaft d. Judentums,* 1899, p. 1; 1900, p. 433.

53. Mishna *Yebamot* 1.4.

54. *B. Erubin* 13b.

55. See Appendix II, B.

56. This Passover was remembered for generations as "the Passover of crushing" because so many pilgrims were crushed to death on it (*B. Pesahim,* 64b).

57. *B. Shabbat* 17a.

58. *Ibid.* Another reference to Shammaitic ascendancy at this time may be found in *Tosefta Shebiit* 3.10, p. 64.

59. *Tosefta Hagiga* 2.11, p. 236.

60. *B. Sanhedrin* 11a, bottom.

61. Mishna *Erubin* 6.1.

62. *B. Baba Mezia* 59b.

63. *Tosefta Aboda Zara* 3.10, p. 464. For *Rabban Gamaliel,* there, we must read *Rabban Simeon ben Gamaliel;* Simeon ben Nethanel

could hardly have been old enough to marry while Gamaliel was still living.

64. *Tosefta Yoma* 1.6, p. 180; *Sifra Emor, par.* 2.1, 94c; Josephus, War IV.3.8.

65. Compare Mishna *Bezah* 2.6.

66. Mishna *Abot* 1.15.

67. *Ibid.* 1.17.

68. *Ibid.*

69. Mishna *Keritot* 1.8.

70. Life 38.

71. War II.20.3.

72. Mishna *Shabbat* chap. 1, end; *Babli and Yerushalmi, ad loc.;* Graetz, *Geschichte der Juden* III, 2, p. 802 ff; cf. also *Menorah Journal,* 1936, p. 143.

73. This is certainly implied in Josephus's Life 38. The omission of any reference to Simeon in War II.20.4, must be intentional.

74. The right of the priests to the tithes was open to some question; see below, p. 83.

75. Josephus's statement that John was "poor at the opening of his career" (War II.21.1) is contradicted by his own statement (Life 10) which represents John as one of the leading citizens of Gishcala before the revolution, and an adherent of the upper-class peace party. This has been noted by Simhoni, in his notes to the Hebrew translation of Josephus, p. 445.

76. War III.5.8; see also Laqueur, *Der jüd. Historiker,* p. 126 f., and and Thackeray's masterful treatment of the whole subject in *Josephus, The Man and the Historian,* p. 25 ff.; as well as his *Introduction to Josephus,* War, Bks. I-III, in the "Loeb Classical Library," p. x.

77. Josephus, War I.1.2.

78. *Sifre* Deut. 357, 150a.

79. Mishna *Sanhedrin* 5.2.

80. *Abot of R. Nathan* II, chap. 31 (34a).

81. *Midrash Tannaim,* p. 58.

82. *Midrash Tannaim* 20.8, p. 120; cf. *Sifre* Deut. 192, 110a.

83. See below, p. 257.

84. *Abot* 2.8.

85. *B. Rosh Ha-Shanah* 18a.

86. *Yer. Shabbat* 16, end, 15d.

87. *Abot* 2.8.

88. *B. Pesahim* 26a; cf. *Lamentations R.,* Proemium 12.

89. *Mekilta Jethro, Bahodesh,* chap. 11, 74a, Horowitz-Rabin p. 244, Lauterbach II, p. 290.

90. According to tradition (*Sifre* Deut. 357, 150a), he must have been more than one hundred years old at this time, for it is said that he was 120 years old when he died, about fourteen years later. But this is doubtless an extravagance, intended to emphasize the resemblance between Johanan and Moses. The same is true regarding the similar tradition about Akiba (*ibid.*) and that current in the early Christian community about Symeon son of Clopas, the second Bishop of Jerusalem (Eusebius, *Hist. Eccl.* III.32).

91. See *B. Gittin* 56a; *Lamentations R.* 1.31.

92. Josephus, War IV.6.3. The surrender of Johanan must be placed in the spring or summer of the year 68, before the siege of Jerusalem had actually begun, but after Vespasian had made all preparations for the final attack. The tradition which makes Johanan surrender to Vespasian rather than to Titus is thus verified. The fact that the news of the revolt in the West reached Palestine soon after Johanan's surrender naturally laid the basis for the legend that it was Johanan rather than Josephus who prophesied Vespasian's election as Emperor.

93. See Josephus, War I.1.2; and II.16.4; cf. also Thackeray, *Josephus, The Man and the Historian,* p. 28. The same condition, of course, encouraged the rebels a generation earlier; cf. Philo, *Legatio ad Gaium* 31(216), ed. Cohn et Reiter, VI, p. 196.

94. Cf. *ibid.* VI.2.1; and VI.6.3. The statement of the fourth century writer, Sulpicius, who maintains that Titus was in favor of the conflagration, cannot be accepted in view of these statements of Josephus, who would hardly dare misrepresent his patron's views. See Wilhelm Weber, *Josephus u. Vespasian* 72 f; cf. however, Thackeray, *op. cit.,* p. 48; and introduction to his edition and translation of the War, in "Loeb Classical Library," p. xxv.

95. Mishna *Rosh Ha-Shanah* 4.1; *Babli, ad. loc.*

96. *Abot of R. Nathan,* chap. 4, 11a.

97. *R. Berakot* 28b.
98. *Ibid.*

III. AMONG THE FOOTHILLS

1. This is implied in the fact that neither Johanan ben Zakkai nor Gamaliel II is mentioned in connection with Akiba's first application for admission as student; see Ginzberg, art. Akiba, in Jewish Encyclopedia.
2. *Sifre* Deut. 41.
3. *Yer. Yebamot* 4.12, 6a. *B. Baba Mezia* 85a; *Tosefta Ketubot* 5.1, p. 266.
4. *Yer. Sotah,* end; *B. Sanhedrin* 11a; *Canticles R.* on chap. 8.9.
5. *Sifra Emor, par.* 1.12; *Semahot* 4.6, p. 117; *B. Zebahim* 100a.
6. *B. Gittin* 56a; *Yebamot* 15b. This is implied in Zadok's observance of the Hillelite severity though he was a Shammaite.
7. *B. Ta'anit* 21a.
8. In the Babylonian Talmud he is called Papus; See *Mekilta Beshallah, Massekee Vayehi,* chap. 6, Horowitz-Rabin p. 112, Lauterbach I, p. 247; *B. Berakot* 61b.
9. *Yer. Sotah* 9.10 (cf. also *B. Baba Kamma* 80b).
10. *B. Berakot* 27b; cf. also *B. Yebamot* 16b; *Yer. ibid.,* chap. 1, end; *B. Hagiga* 3a.
11. *Yer. Hagiga* 2.1, 77b.
12. Mishna *Berakot* 1.3; *Tosefta, ibid.,* 1.4, p. 1.
13. Mishna *Shabbat* 19.1; From Mishna *Pesahim* 6.2 it is obvious that Joshua, as well as Akiba, disagrees with Eliezer in his view.
14. Mishna *Shabbat* 1.9.
15. See Appendix I, C.
16. *B. Shabbat* 19a.
17. Cf. *Harvard Theological Review,* XXII, p. 219. For similar Shammaitic views, cf. *B. Kiddushin* 43a, where Shammai declares that the agent's personality merged with that of the principal.
18. Cf. Genesis 1.27; 5.2; 9.6; Lev. 25.6,7,10,42,55; Deut. 29.9,10,11; Job 3.19; 31.13,14,15.
19. *Abot of R. Nathan* I, chap. 3, 7b.
20. *Mekilta of R. Simeon* 16.4, p. 75.
21. This particular part of Akiba's life, his relation to Eliezer, Joshua, and Tarfon has to be reconstructed from scattered references in the

talmudic works, and from what we know of the general character of the men.

22. *Yer. Shabbat* 6.1.

23. In *B. Ketubot* 62b, the time is given, in the usual exaggerated form, as twelve years.

24. For a record of the institution during the Middle Ages, see Guedemann, *Erziehungswesen d. Juden* I, 267 ff.

25. *B. Ketubot* 62b.

26. *Sifre* Num. 99, p. 98.

27. *Abot of R. Nathan,* chap. 6, 15a.

28. *Ibid.*

29. *Leviticus R.* 34.16; *Pesikta Rabbati* 25, 126b; *Masseket Kallah,* end, ed. Higger, pp. 156, 207.

30. *Yer. Nazir,* 7.1, 56a; *Semahot* 4.19, p. 125; *Derek Erez,* in Higger, *Massektot Derek Erez,* 7.6, p. 131.

31. *Semahot* 9.3, p. 169.

32. *Tosefta Shebiit* 4.21, p. 67; *Yer. Bikkurim* 2.5, 65b; *ibid. Rosh Ha-Shanah* 1.2, 57a; *B. Rosh Ha-Shanah* 14a.

33. *Sifre* Numbers 75, p. 70; *Yer. Yoma* 1.1 38d; *ibid. Megillah* 1.12, 72b; *ibid. Horayot,* chap. 3, 47d; cf. also *Sifra Nedaba par.* 4.5; *Tosefta Zebahim* 1.8, p. 480; *ibid. Mikvaot* 1.19, p. 654; *Yer. Terumot* 8.2, 45b; *B. Kiddushin* 66b; *ibid. Zebahim* 13a.

34. *Abot of R. Nathan* chap. 6, 15a.

35. Nehemiah 10.39a, which contradicts both 10.38, and 10.39b.

36. Cf. Numbers 18.8 ff; *Sifre* Num. 119, p. 142, where the twenty-four priestly emoluments are enumerated.

37. Josephus, *Life* 12 (63); 15 (80); *Against Apion* I.22 (188); *Antiquities* IV.4.3. So also *Jubilees* 13.25; but contrast *Tobit* 1.6. A complete list of references can be found in Strack-Billerbeck, *Kommentar z. N.T.,* IV, 656 ff.; cf. also E. Kaufmann in *Ziyyunim,* (memorial volume for Simhonj), p. 101.

38. See Leviticus 21.1 ff.

39. *B. Yebamot* 86b; *Yer. Ma'aser Sheni* 5.5, 56b.

40. Cf. *Yer. Shebiit* 4.2, 35b; *B. Yebamot* 15a; Mishna *Berakot* 1.3.

41. Mishna *Makkot* 1.10.

42. Mishna *Menahot* 12.5; *Sifra Nedaba par.* 8.7, 9b.

43. Cf. Loew, *Die Flora der Juden,* II, p. 289; Dalman, *Arbeit u. Sitte*

in Palaestina IV, 177 ff.; Krauss, *Talmudische Archaeologie*, II, 216; Felix Goldmann, *Der Ölbau in Palaestina zur Zeit der Mishnah*, p. 6; and see Gen. 49.20; Deut. 33.24; *Sifre* Deut. 355, 147b; 148a; *Midrash Tannaim, ad loc.* p. 220-21; Mishna *Menahot* 8.3; *Tosefta ibid.* 9.5, p. 526; *B. ibid.* 85b; Josephus, War II.21.2.

44. *B. Shabbat* 17a.
45. *Ibid.* 26a.
46. Mishna *Terumot* 9.2.
47. Mishna *Yebamot* 15.7.
48. Mishna *Keritot* 5.2; *Sifra Hobah, par.* 12.1, 26b.
49. Cf., e.g., Mishna *Shebiit* 3.10.
50. *Mekilta Jethro Amalek*, chap. 2, Horowitz-Rabin p. 198; Lauterbach II, p. 183.
51. *B. Sanhedrin* 51b.
52. *B. Pesahim* 22b; *Tosefta Shebuot* 1.7, p. 446; of *Yer. Berakot* 9.7; *Yer. Sotah* 5.7.
53. *Sifre Zutta* 6.12, p. 243; Mishna *Nazir* 7.4.

IV. THE STEEP ASCENT

1. Mishna *Pesahim* 6.1; *Babli* and *Yerushalmi*, 6.4, 33c; *Tosefta ibid.* 5.1, p. 163; *Sifre Zutta* 9.2, p. 257.
2. Cf., e.g., *Tosefta Shekalim* 3.17, p. 179.
3. *Sifre Zutta* 19.16, p. 312.
4. Mishna *Pesahim* 9.2; *Tosefta, ibid.* 8.2, p. 168; *Sifre* Num. 69, p. 64; *Sifre Zutta* 9.13, p. 260.
5. *B. Sukkah* 27b.
6. *Mekilta Bo, Pisha*, chap. 17, Horowitz-Rabin, p. 69; Lauterbach I, p. 157; *Mekilta of R. Simeon* 13.10, p. 35; cf. the reading of *Yer. Erubin* 10.1, where, as frequently happens, the name of Hillel has been substituted for that of Shammai.
7. *Mekilta of R. Simeon, loc. cit.* In *B. Menahot* 36b, the opposite view is ascribed to Akiba in another controversy with Jose the Galilean; but the reading of the Palestinian *Mekilta of R. Simeon* must be given preference.
8. See above, p. 85.
9. Some such half observance of the law on the part of the *am ha-arez*

is implied in Mishna *Kelim* 9.2; *Ohalot* 5.1,2,3,4; see commentaries there and the illustrating discussion in *Tosefta Ohalot* 5.11, p. 603.

10. Mishna *Eduyot* 4.6; cf. *B. Yebamot* 15b; and *B. Shabbat* 17a.

11. *Sifra Shemini, par.* 8.5, 55b; *B. Pesahim* 16a.

12. *B. Sukkah* 27b.

13. Mishna *Eduyot* 8.4.

14. *B. Baba Mezia* 81b.

15. Jubilees 49.10.

16. *B. Berakot* 9a; *Mekilta Bo, Pisha,* chap. 6, Horowitz-Rabin p. 19, Lauterbach I, p. 46; *ibid.* chap. 5, Horowitz-Rabin pp. 17-18, Lauterbach I, p. 42; *ibid.* chap. 18, Horowitz-Rabin p. 74, Lauterbach I, p. 167; *Mekilta* of R. Simeon 12.8, p. 11; *Sifre* Deut. 133; *Yer. Berakot* 1.3; cf. also Mishna *Pesahim* 1.9 and *Babli, ad loc.* 120a; where the opinion of the patricians is assumed as basis for an anonymous norm.

17. Cf. also *Tosefta Pesahim* 10.12, p. 173 where Gamaliel is reported to have remained awake all the night of Passover. But obviously in this he followed the Hillelite tradition; cf. also Mishna *Berakot* 1.1.

18. Mishna *Berakot* 1.1. For Akiba's view, see *B. Berakot* 7b. In *Tosefta, ibid.* 1.1, and *Yer. ibid.* 1.3, Simeon is cited as authority for the statement, but *Babli* shows that he only transmitted Akiba's opinion.

19. Mishna *Peah* 7.7; *Sifra, Kedoshim, per.* 3.1, 88a.

20. *Sifre* Deut. *ad loc.; B. Yebamot* 47b; *Semahot* 6.13, p. 141.

21. *Mekilta* of R. Simeon 13.5, p. 32.

22. *Mekilta Bo, Pisha,* chap. 14, Horowitz-Rabin, p. 48, Lauterbach I, p. 108; *Sifra, Emor, perek* 17.11, 103b; the reading of which is to be accepted in preference to that found in *B. Sukkah* 11b.

23. Mishna *Sukkah* 1.6; 2.3; 2.7.

24. Mishna *Sotah* 9.3,4.

25. *Sifra, Shemini, Miluim,* 35, 45d.

26. *Sifre Zav, par.* 8.1, 36a; *ibid. Shemini, per.* 10.5,6, 55c; *et al.*

27. *Yer. Yebamot* 13.2, 14c; *Abot of R. Nathan* I, chap. 16, 32a; compare Ginzberg, *Eine Unbekannte Jüdische Sekte,* p. 32.

28. *B. Ta'anit* 25b; *Yer. ibid.* 3.4, 66c.

29. *Sifre* Deut. 32, 73b; *Mekilta, Jethro, Bahodesh* chap. 10, Horowitz-Rabin p. 241, Lauterbach II, p. 281; *B. Sanhedrin* 101a.

30. Cf. Mishna *Pesahim* 9.6; *Yebamot* 8.4.

31. Mishna *Sotah* 5.2; *Sifra Shemini par.* 7.12, 54b.

32. Mishna *Nedarim* 10.6; *B. ibid.* 74b.

33. *Yer. Horayot* 3.7, 48a; *Leviticus R.* 5.4; *Deuteronomy R.* 4.8.

34. *Yer. Pesahim* 2.7, 29c.

35. *Mishna Bekorot* 4.4.

36. *Tosefta Mikvaot* 1.17, p. 653; *B. Kiddushin* 66b.

37. *Tosefta Makshirin* 2.14, p. 675; *Yer. Sotah* 6.1, 21a.

38. *Abot of R. Nathan* I, chap. 26, 41b. Cf. the text in *Abot of R. Nathan* II, chap. 33, 36a, and Mishna *Abot* 3.13, which have been used as a basis for emending the superior text of *Abot R. Nathan* I.

39. Mishna *Abot* 4.25; *Abot of R. Nathan* I, chap. 24, 39a.

40. *B. Baba Kamma* 74b.

41. *Sifre* Deut. 16, 68b.

42. *Ibid.*

43. *Leviticus R.* 23.4.

44. *Sifra, Kedoshim, perek* 4.9; *Arakin* 16b; and cf. *Sifre* Deut. 1, where the story is softened.

45. See Appendix II, D.

46. Reifmann in *Bet Talmud* IV, p. 47, notices the contrast between Gamaliel's actions and the teachings of the Hillelites in this matter.

47. *Abot of R. Nathan* I, chap. 40, 64a.

48. Mishna *Sotah* 9.15. "Since the Temple has been destroyed, the scholars have become as the scribes, the scribes as the court assistants, and the court assistants like the peasants."

49. *B. Berakot* 16b; *Yer. Sukkah* 2.1, 54d; *Midrash Proverbs* 9.21; *Mekilta Bo Pisha,* chap. 17, Horowitz-Rabin p. 68, Lauterbach I, p. 154; *Semahot* 1.11, p. 101; *Yer. Niddah* 1.5, 49b; Mishna *Sukkah* 2.1.

50. *B. Sanhedrin* 104b.

51. *Tosefta Baba Kamma* 9.30, p. 366; *B. Shabbat* 151b; *Yer. Baba Kamma* 8.10, 6c.

52. *B. Sanhedrin* 11a; *Yer. ibid.* 1.2, 18c; *Semahot* 8.7, p. 152.

53. *Sifre* Numbers 4, p. 7; *Sifre Zutta* 5.10, p. 237; *B. Baba Kamma* 113a; *Tosefta, ibid.* 10.17, p. 368; *Yer. ibid.* 9.15, 7a; *Yer. Aboda Zara* 2.4, 41b. It is obvious that Akiba's removal to Zifron was not simply a trip like that to Nahardea, since his views are said to

have changed during that time, and since it is used as a special date in his life. I believe that the whole situation justifies the conjectures made in the text.

54. *Cant. R.* chap. 1. This interpretation of the exclamation sounds more reasonable than the supposition that Akiba was simply outside the physical walls of the academy.

55. Mishna *Rosh Ha-Shanah* 2.8,9.

56. See Mishna *Rosh Ha-Shanah* 1.6, B. *ibid.* 22a; *Yer. ibid.* 57b.

57. *Tosefta Berakot* 4.15, p. 10; compare also *Tosefta Demai* 6.24, p. 56.

58. B. *Baba Mezia* 59b; *Yer. Moed Katan* 3.1, 81d.

59. A similar controversy arose with regard to the purification of metalware, which was also used by the wealthy but uncommon among the poor; see Mishna *Kelim* 14.7. It is interesting that in these instances Eliezer is lenient, although generally he, like his brother Shammaites, inclined toward rigorous interpretations of the Law.

60. Mishna *Eduyot* 5.6.

61. *Bekorot* 36a.

62. B. *Berakot* 27b; *Yer. ibid.* 4.1, 7c; *Ta'anit* 4.1, 67d.

63. Mishna *Sotah* 5.2; *Yadaim* 4.1 ff; and commentaries *ad loc.; B. Berakot, loc. cit.*

64. *Yer. Yebamot* chap. 1, end, 3b; *Ibid. Sotah* 3.3, 19a (in the name of R. Johanan) "the voice announcing that the decision was with the Hillelites was uttered in Yabneh." The story of the visit of the scholars to Dosa shows that this decision was not reached before the removal of Gamaliel.

65. Mishna *Eduyot* 1.5.

66. B. *Berakot* 28a; *Yer. ibid.* 4.1, 7d.

67. For the number thirty-two, see *Tosefta Mikvaot,* end, p. 661; *Yer. Yebamot* 1.1, 2c; *Sotah* 2.5, 18b; *Kiddushin* 3.5, 64a. For the increase to seventy-two at this time, see Mishna *Yadaim* 3.5.

68. *Tosefta Kelim Baba Batra* 2.4, p. 592. Eighty-five names are attached to the pronouncement recorded in Nehemiah, chaps. 9 and 10.

69. The office of *hakam,* later held by Meir, (B. *Horayot* 13b), may originally have been created for Eleazar, or it may have existed from still earlier times, and Eleazar now appointed to fill it.

70. B. *Niddah* 24b.

71. Mishna *Ma'aser Sheni* 2.6; *Keritot* 3.7; *Negaim* 7.4; *Sifra Hobah*, *pereḳ* 1.8.

72. *Yer. Pesahim,* chap. 4, end, 31b; *B. Kiddushin* 27a; *Mishna Ma'aser Sheni* 5.9.

73. *Yer. Peah* 4.6, 18c; *ibid.* 8.6, 21a; *ibid. Ma'aser Sheni* 5.6, 56c.

74. See *B. Yebamot* 98a; 121a; *ibid. Rosh Ha-Shanah* 26a; *Yer. Yebamot* chap. 16, 15d. Whether he went to Media is doubtful; cf. *Beraḳot* 8a, but see Ginzberg, article "Akiba," in Jewish Encyclopedia.

75. *Tanhumah,* ed. Buber, *Naso, par.* 13, 16a.

76. *B. Beraḳot* 60b.

77. *Yer. Pesahim* chap. 4, end, 31b; *Esther R.* 2.3.

78. *Abot of R. Nathan* I, chap. 3, 9a; *Ecclesiastes R.* 11.1.

79. *B. Yebamot* 121a; *Yer. Yebamot* chap. 16, 15d.

80. *Meḳilta Bo, Pisha* chap. 18, Horowitz-Rabin p. 73, Lauterbach I, p. 166; *Yer. Kiddushin* 1.7, 61a; anonymously in *Tosefta ibid.* 1.11, p. 336 and *B. ibid.* 29a.

81. *B. Shabbat* 156b. The biblical *zedaḳah* meaning righteousness came to be interpreted as "charity" in rabbinic times, for the gifts of the poor were considered their just due. The literal translation of the verse is, "Righteousness delivereth from death."

82. *Canticles Zutta* 1.15, p. 19.

83. *Ibid.,* p. 17.

84. *Midrash Psalms* 65.4, 157a.

85. *Abot of R. Nathan* I, chap. 3, 8a.

86. *B. Pesahim* 112a.

87. *B. Ketubot* 50a; *Araḳin* 28a; compare *Yer. Peah* 1.1, 15b.

88. *Abot of R. Nathan* II, chap. 12, 15a; *B. Yebamot* 62b, and *Ketubot* 63a; *Genesis R.* 61.3, p. 660; *Ecclesiastes R.* to chap. 11.6; but *Tanhumah, Hayye Sarah, par.* 6, ed. Buber, *par.* 8, 61b, give the number as three hundred.

V. ON THE HEIGHTS: AKIBA AND HIS SCHOOL

1. There are numerous references to this voyage. Cf. Mishna *Ma'aser Sheni* 5.9; *Erubin* 4.1; *Tosefta Yom Tob* 2.12, p. 204 (according to reading of *ed. pr.* and Ms. Vienna); *Sifra Emor, per.* 16.1, 102a; *B. Sukkah* 23a; *ibid.* 41b; *B. Makkot* 24a; *Sifre* Deut. 43; *Lament. R.*

chap. 5, on verse 18; *Yer. Erubin* chap. 1, 19b; *Sukkah* 2.4, 52d; *Abot of R. Nathan* I, chap. 14, 32a.

2. The two journeys must not be confused; for Eliezer ben Hyrkanos who was a member of the first, being at the time the foremost scholar in the academy, did not accompany the second, which left for Rome after his excommunication. See *B. Horayot* 10a (the incident narrated there must have occurred before Johanan ben Nuri's appointment as overseer, and hence before Akiba's earliest days in the academy); *Genesis R.* 13.9, p. 118; *Deut. R.* 2.24; *Yer. Sanhedrin* 7.19, 52d. It is especially noteworthy that in the records of this voyage, Eliezer and Joshua are mentioned *before* Gamaliel, who was not yet Nasi. It must have been on this first trip, too, that Joshua discovered the young Jewish captive whom he redeemed and who later became a prominent scholar. A child taken captive in the year 70 would have been quite a mature man by the time of Akiba's visit in 95; but in the year 80, he would be just about the age implied in the story (*Tosefta Horayot* 2.5, p. 476; *Yer. ibid.* 3.7, 48b; *B. Gittin* 58a; *Lamentations R.* chap. 4, on verse 2).

3. Mishna *Erubin* 4.1; *B. ibid.* 43a; *Yer. ibid.* 4.1, 21d.

4. *B. Ta'anit* 7a.

5. *Tosefta Aboda Zara* 6(7).7, p. 479; *B. ibid.* 54b.

6. *Exodus R.* 30.9.

7. See Thackeray, *Josephus, The Man and the Historian,* p. 35.

8. See War IV.5.2; contrast *Pesahim* 57a, "Woe unto me for the House of Hanan, woe unto me of their whisperings!" See also Josephus's own description of Hanan in Antiquities XX.9.1; and Life 39. See notes of Simhoni to the Hebrew translation of Josephus, p. 442; and Thackeray, *op. cit,* p. 135.

9. Thackeray, *op. cit.* p. 65.

10. *Ibid.* p. 14.

11. War III.9.5.

12. Thackeray, *op. cit.* p. 52.

13. *Ibid.* p. 16.

14. Contrast War II.8.2 ff. with Antiquities XVIII.1.3 ff.

15. See above, Note 8.

16. Thackeray, *op. cit.* p. 100 ff.

17. Antiquities VI.12.7.

18. *Ibid.* X.11.7.
19. Cf., e.g., his revised version of the events in the cave of Jotapata, War III.8.7—"He, however, (should one say by fortune or by the Providence of God?) was left alone with one other." See also Antiquities, X.11.7, end.
20. Peroration to the Antiquities.
21. *Ibid.* and Against Apion I.9.
22. Peroration to Antiquities.
23. Against Apion II.38.
24. *Derek Erez R.* chap. 5, in Higger *Massektot Derek Erez, Pirke Ben Azzai,* chap. 3, p. 183 ff. For the identification with Josephus, see *Revue des Études Juives* 23, p. 318; 36, p. 309; *Monatsschrift* 1877, p. 355; Bruell, *Jahrbücher,* 4, p. 41; Vogelstein-Rieger, *Geschichte d. Juden in Rom,* I, p. 29 note 3.
25. *Sifre* Deut. 43.
26. *Tosefta Yom Tob* 2.12 p. 204.
27. *Sifre* Deut. 357, 150a.
28. *B. Gittin* 67a; *Abot of R. Nathan* chap. 18, 34a.
29. Mishna *Megillah* 1.4 ff. Other such compilations occur in Mishna *Kiddushin* 1.7 ff., *Hullin* 1.4 ff.; *Arakin* 2.1 ff; *Niddah* 6.2 ff. For the demonstration that the form is of ancient origin, see Ginzberg in *Hoffmann Festschrift,* p. 311 ff.
30. Cf. J. Brill, *Mebo Ha-Mishnah,* p. 118.
31. Mishna *Sanhedrin* 3.4; *Tosefta Ma'aser Sheni* 2.1, p. 88; 2.12, p. 89; (cf. *Yer. ibid.* 3.7, 54b); *Tosefta Arakin* 5.15, p. 550.
32. Cf. e.g., Mishna *Gittin* 9.10; *Kelim* 20.6.
33. Thus, for example, Mishna *Hullin* 3.1, in which *pesukat ha-gargeret* (an animal whose trachea has been torn from its throat) is listed as *terefah,* follows the view held by Akiba in Mishna *Hullin* 2.4, and there opposed by Yeshebab. We know from that Mishna that Akiba ultimately accepted Yeshebab's opinion, yet the form of Mishna *Hullin* 3.1 retains his earlier view. It is obvious from *Tosefta Hullin* 2.9, p. 502, that Yeshebab gave his opinion "in the name of Joshua" after Joshua ben Hananya had died, i.e., when Akiba was an old man. This is thus one of the instances where we can actually date a Mishna; Mishna *Hullin* 3.1 was formulated in Akiba's middle age.

34. The same applied to the text of the prayers, which were likewise memorized, as I have shown in *Jewish Quarterly Review, N.S.* XIX, p. 211 ff.

35. *Sifre* Deut. 48.

36. *B. Menahot* 29b.

37. *B. Aboda Zara* 5a.

38. See *Canticles R.* chap. 8, on verse 2; *Lament. R., Proemium* 23; *Ecclesiastes R.* chap. 6, on verse 2; and chap. 12, on verse 7; and Epiphanius, *Adversus Haereses* xxxiii.9 and xv, end.

39. R. Johanan; *B. Sanhedrin* 86a.

40. *Pesikta of R. Kahana, Parah,* 39b; *Pesikta Rabbati* 14, ed. Friedmann 64b.

41. *B. Berakot* 43a.

42. *B. Sotah* end; *Tosefta ibid.* 15.3, p. 321; compare Mishna *ibid.* 9.15 and *Yer. ibid.* end, 24c; compare also *Yer. Shekalim* 5.1, 48c.

43. *Midrash Mishle,* chap. 9, 31b; *Midrash Eleh Ezkerah* in Yellinek, *Bet. Ha-Midrash* II, 67 f., and Eisenstein, *Ozar Ha-Midrashim,* II, 441.

44. *B. Erubin* 46b.

45. *Sifra Zav perek* 11.6; *B. Menahot* 89a; *Niddah* 72b; *Zebahim* 82a; cf. also *Sifra Emor, par.* 7.2, 98a.

46. Mishna *Bekorot* 6.6; *B. ibid.* 40a; *Tosefta ibid.* 4.8, p. 539.

47. *B. Gittin* 90a.

48. *B. Ketubot* 29b.

49. *B. Baba Batra* 56b; *Tosefta Ma'aser Sheni* 1.13, p. 87; *ibid., Ohalot* 5.8, p. 602.

50. *Abot of R. Nathan* chap. 19, 35a.

51. *Derek Erez Rabbah,* chap. 3; Higger, *Massektot Derek Erez, Pirke Ben Azzai* chap. 1, p. 155.

52. *Abot of R. Nathan* I, chap. 25, 41b, and see editor's notes *ad loc.*

53. *Tosefta Yebamot* 8.4, p. 250; *B. Yebamot* 63b; *Genesis R.* 34.14, p. 326.

54. *B. Ketubot* 63a.

55. *B. Bekorot* 58a.

56. Cf., e.g., *Sifra Nedaba per.* 2.12, 4a; *Mekilta, Bo, Pisha, Proemium,* Horowitz-Rabin p. 5, Lauterbach I, p. 13. *Sifre* Numbers 103, p. 101

(where Ben Azzai should replace *ha-Temani*); *Midrash Psalms* 65.4, 157a.

57. Mishna *Ta'anit* 4.5; *Tosefta Shebiit* 2.13, p. 63; *ibid. Yoma* 1.13, p. 182.

58. *Tosefta Shekalim* 2.8, p. 176.

59. *Tosefta Berakot* 7(6).2, p. 14; *B. ibid.* 58a; *Yer. ibid.* 9.2, 13c.

60. Mishna *Abot* 4.1.

61. *Sifra Kedoshim par.* 3.9, 90b.

62. *Tosefta Hagiga* 2.3, p. 234; *Yer. ibid.* 2.1, 77b; *B. ibid.* 14b; *Canticles R.* to chap. 1, verse 4.

63. *B. loc. cit.*

64. Mishna *Sotah* end.

65. *Yer. Hagiga, loc. cit.*

66. *Tosefta, Yer. and B., ibid.* The catastrophe probably explains the story in *Genesis R.* 61.3, p. 660, and parallel passages, of the destruction of Akiba's first pupils and the difference between them and the second group.

67. *Tosefta Mikvaot* end, p. 660; *Sifre* Num. 124, p. 158.

68. *Yer. Shebiit* 4.5, 35b.

69. *Yer. Ketubot* 11.3, 33b.

70. *Sifra Tazria per.* 13.2, 68b.

71. *Hullin* 49a.

72. *Yer. Shekalim* 3.1, 47d; *ibid. Rosh Ha-Shanah* 1.1, 56d.

73. *B. Sanhedrin* 32b; *Tosefta Shabbat* 3(4).3, p. 113; *Semahot* 2.5, p. 103.

74. *B. Pesahim* 112a.

75. *Yer. Sotah* 2.4, 18a; *B. Erubin* 13a; *B. Berakot* 10a.

76. *B. Shabbat* 118b.

77. *B. Nedarim* 49b; cf., for his inner happiness, *B. Shabbat* 25b.

78. The first five are described as Akiba's disciples in the classic passages: *B. Sanhedrin* 11a; *ibid.* 86a; *Genesis R.* 61.3, p. 660. For Johanan, see *Yer. Hagiga* 3.1, 78d; for Benjamin, *Tosefta Kiddushin* 5.4, p. 342; for Hanina, see *Leviticus R.* 21.8.

79. Cf. Hoffmann, *Zur Einleitung in die halachischen Midraschim,* p. 38 ff; cf. *Yer. Ma'aserot* 5.4, 51d, where he is described also as a disciple of Akiba.

80. *B. Nedarim* 40a.

81. *B. Sukkah* 45b; *Yer. Berakot* 9.3, 13d; *Genesis R.* 35.2, p. 300; *Pesikta of R. Kahana, Beshallah,* 88a.

82. *Ibid.*

83. *Sifre* Deut. 31; *Sifre* Numbers 95, p. 95; *Sifre Zutta* 11.21, p. 272; *Tosefta Sotah* 6.7, p. 304; *Yer. Ta'anit* 4.8, 68c.

84. *B. Niddah* 16b; *Leviticus R.* 21.8; *Pesikta of R. Kahana, Ahare* 176b.

85. *Yer. Sanhedrin* 1.2.

86. *B. Gittin* 67a.

87. For Simeon, Meir and Judah, see *B. Sanhedrin* 86a; Jose is generally credited with the editorship of the Mishna *Kelim* and it is doubtless from his collection that Mishna *Hullin* chap. 8 is derived. See *ibid.* par. 2, and *B. ibid.* 104b. Contrast also the opening phrases of that chapter with those of the chaps. 5,6,7,10,11,12.

88. *B. Gittin* 60b.

89. See Hoffmann, *Zur Einleitung in die halachischen Midraschim,* p. 41 ff; compare Albeck, *Untersuchungen über die halakischen Midraschim,* p. 126 ff.; whose discoveries do not, however, set aside the Hoffmann's theory, as he supposes.

90. *Sifre* Numbers 2, p. 5.

91. *Ibid.* 131, p. 169.

92. Compare Weiss, *Dor Dor ve-Dorshav* II, p. 114 ff.

93. *Sifre* Numbers 112, p. 121; *B. Sanhedrin* 90b; cf. *Yer. Yebamot* 8.1, 8d; *ibid. Nedarim* 1.1, 36c.

94. See *Baraita* of the Thirteen Hermeneutic Rules in introduction to the *Sifra;* and compare Hillel's seven arguments with the Bene Bathyra listed in *Tosefta Sanhedrin* 7.11, p. 427; *Abot of R. Nathan* I, chap. 37, p. 110.

95. See above, chap. IV, note 31.

96. *Sifra Zabim, par.* 5.5, 79a; *Yer. Yoma* 2.5, 40a.

97. *Genesis R.* 1.14, p. 12; 22.2, p. 206; cf. *B. Hagiga* 12a.

98. *B. Sanhedrin* 99a; *Tosefta Ohalot* 16.8, p. 614; *Ibid. Parah* 4.7, p. 633.

99. *B. Erubin* 54b; *Mekilta Mishpatim* chap. 1. Horowitz-Rabin p. 246, Lauterbach III, p. 1.

100. *Sifre* Deut. 48.

101. *Tosefta Zabim* 1.5, p. 476.

102. *Tosefta Yoma* 5(4).11, p. 189; *B. Pesahim* 109a.

103. *Semahot* 8.13, p. 160.
104. *Leviticus* R. 21.8; *Pesikta of R. Kahana, Ahare,* 176b; *B. Ketubot* 62b.
105. *Genesis* R. 61.3, p. 659; *Ecclesiastes* R. chap. 11, to verse 6; *Abot of R. Nathan* I, chap. 3, II, chap. 4, 8a,b.
106. *Canticles* R. chap. 1, to verse 3; cf. *B. Sanhedrin* 68a; *Abot of R. Nathan* I, chap. 25, 41a.

VI. ON THE HEIGHTS: AKIBA'S JURISTIC PHILOSOPHY

1. *Yer. Sanhedrin* 1.1, 18a.
2. Mishna *Shabbat* 6.10.
3. *B. Berakot* 5b. Even if the usual interpretation be accepted, that he carried about the bone to console others who had suffered, it is altogether probable that the idea came to him from a custom of less altruistic origin. Cf. also Mishna *Yadaim* 4.6.
4. This seems to me the most natural interpretation of the curious leniency of the Shammaites with regard to such bones "from two bodies." See Mishna *Ohalot* 2.2,6,7; 3.1,5; *Hullin* 72a; *Sifra Emor* 2.4, 94d; the identity of Dosa's views with those of Ishmael were pointed out by as eminent and early an authority as R. Johanan (*Hullin* 124b).
5. *Tosefta Yoma* 3(2).2, p. 185; cf. *ibid. Parah* 3(2).3, p. 631.
6. *Tosefta Berakot* 3.3 (p. 5).
7. *Sifre* Deut. 171; *Midrash Tannaim* 18.10, p. 110; *Tosefta Shabbat* 7(8).14, p. 118.
8. Mishna *Sanhedrin* 10.1.
9. *Sifre* Deut. 84; for the interpretation of the passage see *Proceedings of the American Academy of Jewish Research,* 1932-33, p. 43.
10. *Tosefta Shabbat, loc. cit.; Yer. Berakot* 6.8, 10d.
11. *Ibid., et B. Berakot 53a.* The explanation that the wish for good health would involve an interruption of lecture is far-fetched and an obvious afterthought.
12. *Tosefta Shekalim* 2.1-2 (p. 175); the reading of *Sifre* Deut. 79, must be corrected in accordance with that of the *Tosefta.*
13. *Tosefta Berakot* 3.2, p. 5; in Mishna *Abot* 3.12 the maxim is ascribed to Hanina ben Dosa.

14. *B. Berakot* 62a; *Yer. ibid.* 9.8, 14c; *Derek Erez* in ed. Higger, *Pirke Ben Azzai,* chap. 5, p. 220.

15. *B. Berakot* 8b. The talmudic text has the "Medes" where I read "the Easterners." In this I follow the text of *Pesikta of R. Kahana, Parah,* 33b; and many of the Mss. of *Genesis R.* 74.2, p. 859; cf. also *Numbers R.* 19.3. In these sources, however, the apothegm is attributed to Simeon ben Gamaliel II. This does not, however, make the ascription to Akiba improbable. Simeon ben Gamaliel is not known as a traveler; and it is altogether probable that he repeated this maxim of Akiba, as others of his generation were wont to repeat other teachings of the great master. It is, however, improbable that Akiba traveled as far as Media (see above chap. IV, note 74).

16. *Derek Erez, Pirke Ben Azzai,* chap. 5, ed. Higger, p. 215.

17. *Derek Erez, ibid.,* chap. 7, p. 232.

18. *Ibid.* p. 231.

19. *Abot of R. Nathan* I, chap. 3, 8a; cf. *Tosefta* 9.31, p. 366, and *B. Shabbat* 105b, where the maxim is ascribed to Johanan ben Nuri.

20. *Abot of R. Nathan, loc. cit.*

21. *Ibid.* chap. 26, 42a.

22. Mishna *Yebamot* 12.3.

23. *Tosefta Berakot* 3.5, p. 6.

24. *Tosefta Megillah* 4(3).16, p. 226; *Yer. Ketubot* 7.5, 31b.

25. *Tosefta Baba Mezia* 6.17, p. 385.

26. *Abot of R. Nathan,* chap. 11 (23b).

27. Josephus, Antiquities XIII.10.6; XX.9.1.

28. *Tosefta Makkot* 1.1, p. 438; *B. ibid.* 2b.

29. *Sifra Kedoshim, per.* 6.1, 90b; *B. Sanhedrin* 63a.

30. *B. Makkot* 12a; *Baba Kamma* 90b; cf. *Tosefta ibid.* 3(2).7, p. 441. For a further leniency with regard to unintentional homicide see Mishna *Makkot* 2.7. Cf. further Mishna *Sanhedrin* 10.6; *Tosefta Sanhedrin* 14.3, p. 436; 14.6, p. 437; *Sifre* Deut. 94, 95, 96; *Midrash Tannaim* 13.17, p. 68.

31. *B. Baba Kamma* 90b; *Tosefta Sanhedrin* 12.3, p. 433.

32. Mishna *Baba Kamma* 8.6.

33. *Semahot* chap. 2, p. 102.

34. Mishna *Eduyot* 2.10. For Akiba's method of listing analogies as

proofs of the point he wishes to make, cf. *Tosefta Sukkah* 3.18, p. 197, and discussion regarding it given above.

35. This is doubtless the significance of the controversy between Akiba and Ishmael in *Sifre Numbers* 112, p. 121, line 11. Cf. also Mishna *Sanhedrin* 10.3 ff; *Tosefta ibid.* 13.9 ff, p. 435.

36. *Yer. Kiddushin* 1.9, 61d.

37. *B. Sanhedrin* 81a; *ibid. Makkot* 24a; *Midrash Psalms* 15.7, 60a.

38. *Sifra Hobah, par.* 12.8, 26d.

39. Mishna *Sanhedrin* 10.1; *Abot of R. Nathan* chap. 36, end, 55a.

40. *B. Shabbat* 25a.

41. *Sifra Mezora,* end; *B. Shabbat* 64b; *Yer. Gittin,* end, 50d.

42. Mishna *Niddah* 8.3.

43. Mishna *Gittin* 8.10.

44. For Eliezer ben Hyrkanos's view see *Tosefta Gittin* 9(7).1, p. 333; *B. ibid.* 83a; *Yer. ibid.* 9.1. Eliezer's view that a writ of divorcement which frees the wife to everyone except one special person is valid is obviously a result of his Shammaitic doctrine that the natural basis for divorce is adultery and the suspicious husband may therefore rightly deny his wife the freedom to marry the suspected man. The view of Eleazar of Modin is implied in the statement that Moses did not divorce his wife but merely sent her home, whereas according to Joshua he actually divorced her (*Mekilta Jethro* chap. 1, Horowitz-Rabin p. 190, Lauterbach, II, p. 167; the text of *Mekilta of R. Simeon* must be corrected according to that of *Mekilta* as is obvious from the context). For the view of Ishmael see *Midrash Tannaim* 23.15, p. 148, and Hoffmann's note explaining the passage.

45. *B. Sotah* 17a.

46. *Abot of R. Nathan* I, chap. 26, 42a.

47. *Ibid.* chap. 3 (8a).

48. Mishna *Yebamot* 4.12, 13; compare also *Tosefta Yebamot* 6.5, p. 247; 11.6, p. 253.

49. *Abot of R. Nathan* II, chap. 35, p. 85.

50. Mishna *Nedarim* 11.4; cf. also *B. Ketubot* 66a; Mishna *Ketubot* 3.3 and *Sifre Zutta* 5.24, p. 276; *Tosefta Sotah* 2.3, p. 294; *B. Sotah* 19b.

51. Mishna *Sanhedrin* 3.4.

52. *B. Gittin* 89a; for his severities in case of unintended bigamy, see

Tosefta Gittin 8(6).6,7, p. 332-33; *Yer. Yebamot* 10.5, 11a; 8.7, 49c.

53. *Tosefta Sanhedrin* 12.10, p. 433.

54. *Mishna Yadaim* 3.5.

55. *Abot* 3.13.

56. See *Harvard Theological Review* XXII, p. 219 ff.

57. Mishna *Gittin* 4.5.

58. Cf. the Akibite *Midrashim, Mekilta of R. Simeon* 21.2, p. 118; *Sifre* Deut. 118 (see the reading of *Midrash Ha-Gadol* in *Midrash Tannaim* p. 85); with the statement of Ishmael in *Mekilta of R. Simeon, loc. cit.,* p. 118, line 26, that the slave described in Exodus is identical with the one spoken of in Deuteronomy 15.12, where the "Hebrew who is sold into bondage by the court" is discussed. See further the citation from the *Mekilta* on Deuteronomy in *Midrash Tannaim* p. 85; and compare the reading of *Midrash Ha-Gadol* to Leviticus, p. 643, where a *baraita* from the School of R. Ishmael (and therefore not found in the *Sifra*) is cited to the same effect. Cf. further *B. Kiddushin* 14b.

59. *Mekilta Mishpatim* chap. 3, Horowitz-Rabin pp. 257-58, Lauterbach III, pp. 25-26.

60. *Sifra Behar, per.* 9.1, 110b; *Yer. Kiddushin* 1.2, 59b; *Abadim* 2.8, ed. Higger (Seven Small Treatises) p. 58.

61. *Tosefta Keritot* 1.17, p. 562; Compare *Sifra Kedoshim, per.* 5.1, 89c; *B. Keritot* 11a.

62. *B. Sotah* 3b.

63. *B. Kiddushin* 24b; *Abadim,* end, ed. Higger, p. 60; cf. *Mekilta Mishpatim,* chap. 9, Horowitz-Rabin p. 279, Lauterbach III, p. 71.

64. Mishna *Baba Kamma* 8.9.

65. *B. Sanhedrin* 76a.

66. *Yer. Nazir* chap. 9, 57d; *Semahot* 14.10, p. 207; *Tosefta Baba Batra* 1.11, p. 399; cf. *Midrash Tannaim* 19.14, p. 115.

67. Mishna *Horayot* 2.5.

68. *B. Baba Mezia* 113b.

VII. ON THE HEIGHTS: AKIBA'S PHILOSOPHICAL AND POLITICAL IDEALS

1. *B. Sanhedrin* 38a. Jose is here cited without any further appellative. For similar citations of other older sages, see below, Appendix II, I.

In *B. Hagiga* 14a, the statement is ascribed to Jose the Galilean, but it is hardly likely that he would be cited simply as Jose.

2. *Mekilta Jethro Bahodesh* chap. 9, Horowitz-Rabin p. 238, Lauterbach II, p. 275.

3. *Mekilta Bo, Pisha,* chap. 1, Horowitz-Rabin p. 6, Lauterbach I, p. 15. It must be noted that the correct reading in this passage would be rendered "as though with a finger." (See notes of Horowitz, *ad loc.*)

4. *Sifra, Nedabah, perek* 2.12; *Sifre* Numbers 103, p. 101.

5. *Mekilta, Beshallah, Vayehi* chap. 6, Horowitz-Rabin p. 112, Lauterbach I, p. 247; *Genesis R.* 21.5, p. 200; *Canticles R.* to chap. 1, verse 9. Cf. Job. 4.18; 5.1, 15.15; 25.3; and the speeches of Elihu in 33.23.

6. Enoch 45.1.

7. Acts 23.8.

8. *Midrash Psalms, ad loc.* (221b).

9. *B. Yoma* 75b.

10. *Tosefta Hagiga* 2.2, p. 234; *B. ibid.* 14b.

11. Cf., e.g., *B. Yoma* 54b; *Genesis R.* 12.11, p. 109; 13.9, p. 118; for older discussions of the same type see *Genesis R.* 1.15, p. 13.

12. Mishna *Hagiga* 2.1; but see especially *Yer. ad. loc.,* 77a, where this rule is distinctly ascribed to *Akiba.*

13. Mishna *Negaim* 2.1.

14. *Mekilta Mishpatim* chap. 10, Horowitz-Rabin, p. 286, Lauterbach, III, p. 87.

15. Mishna *Aboda Zara* 1.2.

16. *B. Baba Kamma* 113a; comp. *Sifre* Deut. 16.

17. *Midrash Tannaim* 16.18, p. 97.

18. *Ibid.* 1.22, p. 11; cf. *Sifre* Deut. 20; where the passage is cited anonymously.

19. Compare Ishmael's pointed question to Joshua about the nationalist boycott against the Romans during the Rebellion of 66-70, in Mishna *Aboda Zara* 2.5, and Joshua's evasiveness.

20. *Mishna Eduyot* 2.9.

21. *Tosefta, ibid.* 1.14, p. 456.

22. *Masseket Kallah,* in Higger, *Massektot Kallah,* p. 156.

23. *B. Aboda Zara* 55a. It was Akiba's strong feelings on this point

which led him to identify Zelophehad with the "gatherer of sticks" (Num. 15.33). The Scriptures remark that Zelophehad "died in his own sin" (Num. 27.3). Since Akiba did not admit that a man could die "for his own sin," but held that his life span was fixed by his father, he was compelled to maintain that the sin for which Zelophehad died was a capital offense and that he was executed by the court (B. Shabbat 96a).

24. Cf. Schechter's note to his edition of the fragment of Mekilta on Deuteronomy in Jewish Quarterly Review, 1904, p. 452 ff., and accepted by Hoffmann in Midrash Tannaim p. 62, note 9.

25. Josephus, War II.8.4.

26. Mishna Abot 3.15.

27. Canticles R. to chap. 3, verse 5.

28. Mekilta Beshallah, Vayassa, chap. I, Horowitz-Rabin p. 158, Lauterbach I, p. 248.

29. Mishna Abot 4.2.

30. B. Sukkah 52a; Genesis R. 22.6, p. 210.

31. B. Kiddushin 81a.

32. Genesis R. 26.6, p. 252.

33. Mekilta Beshallah, Vayehi, chap. 6, Horowitz-Rabin p. 112, Lauterbach I, p. 248, for other references see above p. 341, note 5.

34. Mishna Abot, loc. cit.

35. Genesis R. 62.2, p. 674; Canticles R. to chap. 6, verse 2; Ecclesiastes R. to chap. 5, verse 11.

36. Sifra Shemini, par. 8.7, 52b.

37. Mishna Abot 3.15.

38. Genesis R. 33.1, p. 298; Pesikta of R. Kahana, Shor, 73a; Leviticus R. 27.1.

39. Sifre, Deut. 32, Midrash Tannaim 6.5, p. 26; Mekilta Jethro, Bahodesh chap. 10, Horowitz-Rabin, p. 239, Lauterbach II, p. 277.

40. Sifre, loc. cit.

41. Leviticus R. 13.4; 35.6; Pesikta of R. Kahana, Shimu 117a; Canticles R. on chap. 1, verse 4; cf. B. Hagiga 9b.

42. Genesis R. 28.7, p. 266.

43. B. Sanhedrin 97b (Joshua); 102a (Jose); cf. also Tosefta Ta'anit 4(3).9, p. 220.

44. *B. Gittin* 56a; *Lamentations R.* chap. IV, to verse 2; see also *Tosefta Shabbat* 16(17).8, p. 135; Josephus, *War* II, 408 ff.

45. This seems to me to be the implication of *Sifre* Deut. 70.

46. *Tosefta Shekalim* 1.7, p. 174.

47. *Tosefta Gittin* 1.4, p. 324.

48. *Yer. Berakot* 9.7, 14b; *ibid. Sotah* 5.7, 20d.

49. Mishna *Shebiit* 8.10; *Yer. Gittin* 1.5, 43c; Cf. further *B. Kiddushin* 75a.

50. *Tosefta Kiddushin* 5.4, p. 342; cf. Mishna *Yadaim* 4.4.

51. *Sifra Kedoshim, perek* 4.12; *Yer. Nedarim* 9.3, 41c; *Genesis R.* 24.7, p. 236; for the correct interpretation of the passage, cf. G. Kittel, *Probleme d. Palaestinischen Spaetjudentums u. d. Urchristentums,* p. 116; Bacher, *Aggada d. Tannaiten* I, p. 420; Oppenheim in *Bet Talmud* IV, p. 256.

52. *Genesis R.* chap. 34, p. 326; *Tosefta Yebamot* 9.4, p. 250.

53. Mishna *Abot* 3.14.

54. *Mekilta Jethro, Bahodesh* chap. 2, Horowitz-Rabin p. 207, Lauterbach II, p. 202.

55. Mishna *Sotah* 8.5; *Sifre* Deut. 197; *Tosefta Sotah* 7.22, p. 309. *Midrash Tannaim* 20.8, p. 120. For Jose's opinion see *Sifre* Deut. 190. The words attributed to him in *Sifre* Deut. 197 must be emended accordingly, as is indicated in *Proceedings of the American Academy of Jewish Research* 1931-32, p. 40.

56. *Mekilta of R. Simeon* 5.23, p. 170.

57. Mishna *Sanhedrin* 10.3; *Sifra Behukotai, per.* 8.1, 112b; *Lament. R.* chap. 1 on verse 1.

58. *B. Rosh Ha-Shanah* 31a.

59. *Sifre* Numbers 76, p. 70.

60. Mishna *Yoma,* end.

61. *Mekilta Beshallah, Shirah,* chap. 3, Horowitz-Rabin p. 127, Lauterbach II, p. 26.

62. *Mekilta Bo, Pisha,* chap. 14, Horowitz-Rabin p. 51, Lauterbach I, p. 114; *Sifre* Numbers 84, p. 82; *Yer. Sukkah* 4.3, 54c.

63. *Sifre* Deut. 346.

64. *Mekilta Bo, Proemium,* Horowitz-Rabin p. 5, Lauterbach I, p. 13.

65. *Mekilta of R. Simeon* 4.16, p. 169.

66. *Abot of R. Nathan* I, chap. 26, 41b.

VIII. A PERILOUS SUMMIT

1. The date is fixed by considerations which are presented below. See also Appendix II, H.
2. *Abot of R. Nathan,* chap. 6, 15a.
3. *Tosefta Ketubot* 4.6, p. 264.
4. See above p. 23.
5. *B. Nedarim* 50a; *ibid. Aboda Zara* 10a.
6. *B. Hagiga* 25a. There may be a reference to these purifying ashes in *Tosefta Makshirin* 3.15, p. 676.
7. In discussing Hadrian's plan for reconstructing Jerusalem, Mommsen (*Provinces of the Roman Empire,* II, p. 243) remarks, "He certainly did not do them [the Jews] the honor of fearing them." And yet clearer studies of the situation in the East shows that that is just what Hadrian, and his predecessors, did. The whole Roman policy toward the Jews was dictated by a realization of the danger involved in any unrest in Palestine. See above, pp. 67 ff.
8. *Megillat Ta'anit,* ed. Lichtenstein, in *H.U.C. Annual* VIII-IX, pp. 321, 346; cf. also p. 272. See Joel, *Blicke in die Religionsgeschichte* I, p. 15; also see Appendix II, H. Contrast the statement in *Monatsschrift f. Gesch. u. Wissenschaft d. Judentums,* 1854, p. 139.
9. *B. Gittin* 56b.
10. *Mekilta Beshallah, Amalek,* chap. 2, end, Horowitz-Rabin p. 187, Lauterbach II, p. 161. *Pesikta of R. Kahana, Zakor,* 29a.
11. *Pesikta Rabbati* 1, 4a; *Midrash Psalms* 90.17, 197a.
12. See *Jewish Quarterly Review,* N.S. XIX (1929) 221 ff. The words "the early years of Hadrian" on p. 222, *ibid.,* should be corrected, as I now realize, to "the later years of Trajan." My conviction that the benediction was established in connection with Trajan's promise has grown as I came to realize that not only Eliezer, but also Ishmael, died before the Bar Kokba revolt was at an end; yet both of them mention the benediction. On the other hand, it was unknown in Gamaliel's early days when he and Akiba in their discussions speak only of "three benedictions" in the Grace (Mishna *Berakot* 6.8; *Tosefta Berakot* 4.15, p. 10). There was only one event which occurred in the years between Akiba's admission to

the Academy and Gamaliel's death which could justify such an addition to the old formula of Grace, and that was Trajan's announcement.

13. Mishna *Pesahim* 10.6.

14. Compare *Revue des Études Juives* 1932, p. 22; and *Jewish Quarterly Review*, N. S. XVI (1925), p. 35, note 86; where evidence is offered to show that the mention of this benediction in Mishna *Tamid* 5.1 is an early gloss.

15. *Semahot* 14.15, p. 210.

16. *Tosefta Shekalim* 1.7, p. 174.

17. *Tosefta Eduyot* 3.3, p. 459; cf. Mishna *ibid.* 8.5. The incident could not have happened before the destruction of the Temple, as is generally assumed, for at that time there were older sages as well as a whole priesthood to defend the purity of the Temple. Even if Joshua had given his opinion on such a subject before the destruction of the Temple he would hardly have dared use the vigorous words attributed to him by Ben Azzai in this connection. Moreover, he explicitly mentions the "dead of the war," which means, of course, the last war with the Romans. But after the destruction of the Temple it was deserted, and the question of the purity of the city could only arise when some effort was made to rebuild it. The Mishna must be rendered, "Concerning bones which were found in the wood chamber, Joshua testified that the sages had taught, 'Each bone must be taken up, and the rest is pure.'"

18. *Yer. Berakot* 7.1, 11a.

19. *B. Shabbat* 12b; *Tosefta Shabbat* 1.13, p. 110.

20. Epistle of Barnabas, XVI.4. Those who assume that the promise to rebuild the Temple was made by Hadrian naturally date this Epistle between 119 and 130. Several writers interpret the words of the Epistle to refer to Hadrian's construction of his pagan sanctuary, an interpretation which cannot possibly be accepted. No one could refer to the establishment of a heathen temple as the fulfillment of a prophecy that "they that destroyed the Temple will themselves rebuild it." See, however, *The Apostolic Fathers*, by Bishop Lightfoot, edited by J. R. Harmer, 1891, p. 240 ff; and see Appendix II, H.

21. Eusebius, *Chronicon,* translated from the Armenian, ed. Karst, Leipzig 1911 (in *Eusebius' Werke*), p. 218; also *Historia Ecclesiae* III.32.

22. *Aboda Zara* 16b.

23. *Yer. Moed Katan* 3.1, 81d.

24. Pliny's Epistles, Nos. 96, 97.

25. *Genesis R.* 64.10, p. 710.

26. Mishna *Eduyot* 8.6.

27. *Sifre* Deut. 106; *Tosefta Sanhedrin* 3.5,6, pp. 418,9; *Temurah* 21b.

28. See Appendix II, I.

29. *Derek Erez Zutta,* chap. 10, *Tosefta Derek Erez, Perek R. Simeon,* in Higger *Massektot Derek Erez,* p. 244. Cf. also *B. Sanhedrin* 97a; *Canticles* R. 2.15; Mishna *Sotah,* end. In *Sanhedrin* the statement is ascribed to Judah; in *Canticles* R. to Simeon ben Lakish; in the Mishna it is cited anonymously. But as Bacher (*Die Aggada der Tannaiten,* I, p. 97) has pointed out, the tradition ascribing it to Gamaliel seems most authoritative and acceptable.

30. *Tosefta Sotah* 13.4, p. 319; *B. Sotah* 48b; *Yer. Sotah* 9.14, 24b; *Canticles R.* chap. 8, to verse 9.

31. Mishna *Sotah,* end.

32. *B. Sanhedrin* 97b.

33. *Mekilta Beshallah, Vayassa,* chap. 4, Horowitz-Rabin, p. 169, Lauterbach II, p. 120.

34. *B. Sanhedrin* 101a.

35. Mishna *Kilaim* 6.5.

36. Dio Cassius 68.24.

37. *Mekilta Beshallah, Vayehi,* chap. 5, Horowitz-Rabin p. 106, Lauterbach I, p. 232. Compare also *Tosefta Berakot* 4.14-15, p. 10, where the account is somewhat confused by an interpolation extending from line 22 to line 26, which attempts to offset the militaristic moral of the main passage.

38. See *Revue des Études Juives* 30.30 ff, 220 ff.

39. For the various reports regarding Julianus and Pappus, see *Sifra Emor, per.* 9.5, 99d; *ibid. Behukotai, per.* 5.2, 111d.; *Genesis R.* 64.10, p. 710; *Yer. Ta'anit* 2.13, 66a; *B. Ta'anit* 18b; *Semahot* 8.15, p. 164.

40. Cf. Joel, *Blicke in die Religionsgeschichte,* I, p. 15; *Yer. Ta'anit* 2.13, 66a; *ibid. Megillah* 1.5, 70c.

41. *B. Baba Batra* 10b, and compare Rashi, *ad loc.*

42. *Sifra Behukotai, loc. cit.*

43. *Tosefta Ta'anit* 2.5, p. 217; *Yer. ibid.* 2.13, 66a; *Yer. Megillah* 1.6, 70d.

44. It is not to be supposed that the revocation of the plan for the building of the Temple caused the abolition of Trajan's Day, as Joel maintains (*loc. cit.*), for the record explicitly states that "the Day of the execution of Julianus and Pappus caused the abolition of Trajan's Day." This can only mean that the festival was abolished because of the Jewish anger at the execution of their heroes .

45. *B. Ta'anit* 29a.

IX. APPROACHING THE PRECIPICE

1. Mishna *Rosh Ha-Shanah* 4.1.

2. *Tosefta Sanhedrin* 2.13, p. 417; *B. ibid.* 11b; *Yer. ibid.* 1, 18d; see also *ibid.* 18c, for the legendary transformation of the historical facts surrounding the permission to fix the calendar in Galilee.

3. Mishna *Yebamot,* end; Mishna *Eduyot* 8.5.

4. *B. Baba Mezia* 59b. That Gamaliel was younger than Eliezer and Joshua follows from the fact, remarked above, chap. V, note 2, that in the record of his journey to Rome with Eliezer and Joshua, when he was not yet Nasi, he is mentioned after them.

5. *Tosefta Ta'anit* 2.5, p. 271; *B. Erubin* 41a.

6. See above p. 53.

7. Mishna *Berakot* 1.9.

8. *Tosefta Hagiga* 2.5, p. 234; *Yer. ibid.* 2.1, 77a; *B. ibid.* 15a; *Genesis R.* 2.3, p. 17.

9. See below, p. 254.

10. *Tosefta Berakot* 3.4, p. 6.

11. *Sifre* Deut. 32.

12. See below, p. 276.

13. See above p. 165; and compare, e.g., Mishna *Menahot* 4.3.

14. Cf., e.g., his ferocious statement in *Mekilta Beshallah, Vayehi,* chap. 1, Horowitz-Rabin p. 89, Lauterbach I, p. 201, cited also in *Yer. Kiddushin,* end.

15. *Tosefta Niddah* 2.2, p. 642; *B. Ketubot* 60b; *B. Niddah* 65b.

16. *Yer. Berakot* 2.1, 4b; *ibid. Moed Katan* 3.7, 83c.

17. Mishna *Sotah* 8.5,7; *Tosefta, ibid.* 7.22, p. 309; *Sifre* Deut. 197.

18. *Deut. R.* chap. 2.

19. *B. Baba Batra* 10a.

20. *Tanhumah Terumah,* beg.

21. *B. Sanhedrin* 65b; *Genesis R.* 11.5, p. 92; *Pesikta Rabbati* 23, 119b.

22. *Tanhumah Tazria* 9, ed. Buber 18a.

23. *B. Nedarim* 50b.

24. *Semahot* 8.13, p. 159; *B. Moed Katan* 21b.

25. *B. Sanhedrin* 68a; *Abot of R. Nathan* I, chap. 25, 41a; *Semahot* 9.2, p. 165.

26. *Yer. Shabbat* 2.6, 5b.

27. *Canticles R.* chap. 1, to verse 3.

28. *B. Gittin* 83a.

29. *Yer. Niddah* 1.3, 49a. It is obvious that the scenes at Eliezer's sick-bed described in *B. Sanhedrin* 68a did not immediately precede his death, for Akiba was present among those who visited Eliezer, but was in Caesarea when the great sage died. Akiba is not mentioned in *Yer. Shabbat* 2.6, 5a, where the deathbed scene is described.

30. *B. Yoma* 85a.

31. *Hagiga* 15b; *Genesis R.* 1.14, p. 12.

32. *B. Moed Katan* 28b.

33. *Baba Batra* 60b; *Tosefta Sotah* 15.11, p. 322. The association of the name of Ishmael with this movement proves that it cannot have been organized immediately after the destruction of the Temple as the sources imply. Nor would Joshua have been the man to argue with the abstainers at that time; it would more likely have been Johanan ben Zakkai.

34. *Genesis R.* 64.10, p. 712.

35. *Tosefta Gittin* 1.3, p. 323; *B. ibid.* 6b; *Yer. ibid.* 1.2, 43c.; for further reference to Ishmael's removal to Galilee, see *B. Baba Batra* 28b.

36. See Mishna *Ketubot* 9.9; *Tosefta Berakot* 2.13, p. 4. *Tosefta Megillah* 2.4, p. 223; *Yer. Rosh Ha-Shanah* 4.8, 59d; *ibid. Megillah* 2.3, 73a. *B. Rosh Ha-Shanah* 32b. and Rashi, *ad. loc; Megillah* 4a.

37. *Revue des Études Juives,* 1932, p. 11; Mann in *Hebrew Union College Annual* IV, 256 ff.

38. *Pesahim* 56a; see also Elbogen *Der. Jüd. Gottesdienst in seiner Geschichtlichen Entwicklung* 3, pp. 63, 140, 587.

39. B. *Aboda Zara* 27b; *Yer. Shabbat* 14.3, 14d; *ibid. Aboda Zara* 2.2, 40d.

40. *Sifra Ahare, per.* 13.14, 86b; B. *Sanhedrin* 74a.

41. *Tosefta Yebamot* 12.9, p. 255.

42. *Yer. Hagiga* 2.1, 77b; B. *ibid.* 15a.

43. *Genesis R.* 82.8, p. 986.

44. This is implied in the statement, *Tosefta Shabbat* 15(16).9, p. 133, that many of them were recircumcised—a truly dangerous operation —in the time of Bar Kokba's successes. As a result of the renegade practices, the ritual of the circumcision was altered, and the operation made such that concealing it would be impossible.

45. B. *Aboda Zara* 18a; *ibid. Berakot* 61a.

46. B. *Sanhedrin* 98a.

47. B. *Hagiga* 15b.

48. *Sifre* Deut. 80. The words, "and they returned to their places," which are found in the ordinary editions of the *Sifre* also after the incident of the four scholars, are an interpolation, as a comparison of the Mss. reveals.

49. *Semahot* 8.11, p. 157. I. H. Weiss has recognized the contemporary allusion in this remark, but he fails to see how it refers to definite parties (See *Dor Dor ve-Dorshav* II, p. 132, note 1).

50. See above, p. 49.

51. *Abot of R. Nathan* I, chap. 24, 39a; *Mekilta Jethro, Amalek* chap. 2, Horowitz-Rabin p. 197, Lauterbach II, p. 182.

52. *Sifre* Deut. 41; *Mekilta of R. Simeon* 19.17, p. 100; B. *Kiddushin* 40b; *Yer. Pesahim* 3.7, 30b; *ibid. Hagiga* 1.7, 76c; *Canticles R.* chap. 2, to verse 14.

53. B. *Sanhedrin* 74a; *Yer. Shebiit* 4.2, 35d; *Tosefta Shabbat* 15(16)17, p. 134.

54. *Pirke Rabbenu Ha-Kadosh,* and thence in Nahmanides' Commentary to *Ketubot* 19a.

55. W. Weber, *Untersuchungen zur Geschichte d. Kaisers Hadrianus,* p. 239.

56. *Ibid.* 241; J. Juster, *Les Juifs dans L'Empire romaine* II, 191, note 2. Dio Cassius 69.12.

57. *Tosefta Hullin* 2.9, p. 502; cf. Mishna *ibid*. 2.4.

58. *B. Erubin* 86a.

59. Mishna *Ma'aser Sheni* 2.9; *Baba Mezia* 3.12; *Eduyot* 1.10; *Kelim* 28.2; *Ukazin* 3.8; perhaps *Niddah* 6.12.

60. Mishna *Shekalim* 4.7.

61. *Tosefta Kelim* III, 2.2. p. 591.

62. *Tosefta Eduyot* 1.10, p. 456; cf. Mishna *ibid*. 2.7.

63. *Tosefta Ohalot* 4.2, p. 600; cf. *ibid. Eduyot* 1.7, p. 455; *Yer. Berakot* 1.2, 3a; *B. Nazir* 52a.

64. *Sifra Tazria, per.* 1.2, 58c; compare, also, his reply to R. Yeshebab, in *Tosefta Ohalot* 16.3, p. 614.

65. Mishna *Shebiit* 8.9, 10.

66. *Sifre* Numbers 148, p. 196; *B. Menahot* 68b.

67. *Sifre* Deut. 1; *Sifra Kedoshim, per.* 4.9, 89b; *Arakin* 16b.

68. *Semahot* 8.8, p. 154.

69. *B. Sanhedrin* 97b.

70. *Yer. Ta'anit* 4.7, 68d; *Lament. R.* 2.2.

71. *Ibid.*

72. *Mekilta Jethro Bahodesh,* chap. 6, Horowitz-Rabin p. 227, Lauterbach II, p. 247.

73. Dio Cassius 69.12; Jerome, *Comm. in Jes.* 2.9; *Idem, Comm. in Matth.* 24.15.

74. Eusebius, *Vita Constantini* III.26; cf., however, W. Weber, *Untersuchungen zur Gesch. d. Kaisers Hadrianus,* p. 243, note 880.

75. Justin, Apology, 1.47; Eusebius, *Historia Ecclesiae* IV.6.

76. Eusebius, *Historia Ecclesiae* IV.5,6.

77. Tertullian, *Adv. Judaeos,* chap. 13.

78. *Sifra Behukotai, perek* 5.2, 111d.

79. *Yer. Ta'anit* 4.8, 68d; *Genesis R.* 65.21, p. 740. The reconstruction of the history of the period which is made in this chapter was made possible only through the help of several distinguished scholars. Professor Alexander Marx was kind enough to discuss the subject with me in great detail and gave me the benefit of several bibliographical references which had escaped me. At his suggestion, I read a brief paper, summarizing the conclusions at which I had arrived, before the Academy of Jewish Research. In the course of the discussion valuable additional suggestions were made to me by

Professor Salo Baron and some others who were present. I am also indebted to Professor Norman Bentwich and Professor Harry Wolfsohn for assistance in the preparation of this part of the book.

X. APOTHEOSIS

1. *Tosefta Derek Erez* in Higger, *Massektot Derek Erez,* p. 311 (See variants); Higger, *Massektot Kallah,* p. 343; Epstein, *Mikadmoniot Hayehudim* p. 115; and Büchler in *Jewish Quarterly Review, N.S.,* IV (1913-4) p. 487.
2. *B. Berakot* 61b.
3. *B. Pesahim* 112a.
4. *Tosefta Sanhedrin* 2.8, p. 417; *B. ibid.* 12a.
5. Mishna *Gittin* 6.7.
6. B. *Yebamot* 108b.
7. Mishna *Yebamot* 12.5; *Yer. ad. loc.,* 12d.
8. *B. Erubin* 21b.
9. *Lament. R.* chap. 3, verse 44.
10. *B. Berakot* 61b; *Yer. ibid.* 9.5, 14b; *Lament. R., loc. cit.*

NOTES TO APPENDIX

1. See above, pp. 158 and 165.
2. Mishna *Baba Batra* 6.4.
3. *Ibid.* 1.6.
4. *Ibid.* 9.9,10.
5. Mishna *Ketubot* 9.2. This interpretation is obviously the only correct one, as can be seen from the discussion in *Yerushalmi, ad loc.*
6. *Baba Mezia* 62a; *Sifra Behar par.* 8.3, 109c.
7. Mishna *Baba Mezia* 2.7.
8. Mishna *Berakot* chap. 6, end.
9. *Yer. Ma'aser Sheni* 1.4, 53a; *ibid. Erubin* 3.1, 20d.
10. Mishna *Nazir* 7.1.
11. *Mekilta Beshallah, Shirah,* chap. 3, Horowitz-Rabin p. 127, Lauterbach II, p. 25.
12. Mishna *Bikkurim* 2.8.
13. *Sifra Shemini, par.* 9.7, 56a; and *Mishna Kelim* 30.2.
14. Mishna *Kilaim* 1.3; 3.3; 3.6; 6.2; 7.5; see also *Shabbat* 9.2. For the

rule prohibiting the preservation of mixtures, see *Tosefta Kilaim* 1.15, p. 74; *Yer. ibid.* 8.1, 31d; *B. Moed Katan* 2b.

15. Mishna *Shebiit* 4.6; *Peah* 4.10; *Sifra Kedoshim per.* 2.5, 87d; cf., however, Mishna *Peah* 3.6; and 3.1.

16. Mishna *Ma'aserot* 3.5. Ishmael admits the principle, but holds that the yard must actually be unprotected.

17. Mishna *Ma'aser Sheni* 4.8.

18. *Yer. Ma'aserot* 3.2, 50c.

19. *Tosefta Sotah* 14.6, p. 320; *B. Shabbat* 56a.

20. Mishna *Shekalim* 4.3.

21. *Sifre* Deut. 107.

22. Mishna *Demai* 6.4. Akiba's bias in favor of the traders appears most clearly in *Midrash Tannaim* 25.15, p. 169; and *Sifre* Deut. 194.

23. See Dalman, *Arbeit u. Sitte in Palaestina* II, p. 6. Akiba's views on the subject are implied in the *baraita* cited in *B. Pesahim* 5a. Judah ben Ilai agrees with him (Mishna *Pesahim* 2.1) and so does Jose, his other plebeian pupil (*Mekilta Bo, Pisha*, chap. 8, 9a, Horowitz-Rabin p. 28, Lauterbach I, p. 64). Judah ben Bathyra opposes Jose in *Mekilta, ibid.;* and Simeon ben Yohai opposes Judah in *B. Pesahim* 28a. Cf. also *Pesahim* 2.1; Mishna *Temurah* 7.8. For the difference in climate between the valley and the hill country, see Dalman, *Arbeit u. Sitte in Palaestina* I.1, p. 221; I.2, p. 282.

24. See statistics in Appendix II, E.

25. See *Harvard Theological Review* XXII, p. 194; and references there given, especially Josephus, Antiquities XIII.13.5; *Tosefta Sukkah* 3.16, p. 197; *B. Sukkah* 48b.

26. *B. Rosh Ha-Shanah* 17b; cf. *Sifre* Deut. 40. In *Yer. Rosh Ha-Shanah* 1.3, it is cited in the name of Simeon ben Yohai, who represented the patrician view in his day, though he was a disciple of Akiba.

27. *Tosefta Sukkah* 3.18, p. 197; *Ibid. Rosh Ha-Shanah* 1.12, p. 210; *Yer. Rosh Ha-Shanah* 1.3, which states expressly that the purpose of the *Baraita* is to justify the water libations; *B. Rosh Ha-Shanah* 16b. The text of *Tosefta Rosh Ha-Shanah* has been influenced by that of *Babli;* the text of *Tosefta Sukkah* is more original.

28. Mishna *Sukkah* 3.4; *Sifra Emor, par.* 16.7, 102d. It may seem strange at a first glance that there should have been so marked a difference between Jerusalem and the country in this regard in ancient times,

but the cost of fruit was between three and six times higher in Jerusalem than elsewhere and presumably this also applied to other vegetable products, including twigs and branches. See Jeremias, *Jerusalem* I, p. 35; II A, p. 36.

29. Mishna *Parah* 8.11.

30. Mishna *Mikvaot* 7.1; for the difference in the average snowfall between Jerusalem and the lowland, see *Dalman, Arbeit u. Sitte in Palaestina,* I.1. p. 233.

31. Mishna *Shabbat* 1.10.

32. *Ibid.* 1.5 ff. The principle enunciated by the Shammaites that "one's property" must rest on the Sabbath because it is part of one's extended personality is altogether in accord with their general theories; but so far as this particular prohibition was concerned, it was a rationalization rather than a real explanation of their position.

33. Mishna *Eduyot* 2.6.

34. *Yer. Shabbat* 14.2, 14b; *Tosefta Eduyot* 1.9, p. 456.

35. Mishna *Baba Batra* 4.1,2,9.

36. *Mekilta Bo, Pisha,* chap. 11, Horowitz-Rabin p. 37, Lauterbach I, p. 84.

37. Mishna *Hallah* 2.3.

38. Mishna *Hallah* 4.4; compare *Yer. ad loc.;* see also Mishna *ibid.* 2.1; 4.5; and *Yer. ibid.* 2.1, 58b.

39. *B. Baba Kamma* 7a; compare the reading of *Mekilta Mishpatim* chap. 14, Horowitz-Rabin p. 296; and *Yer. Gittin* 5.1, 46c. The correctness of the text of *B.* is shown by a comparison with the law which is certainly a derivative from this, fixing the redemption money of a victim of a goring ox. This has already been noticed by Horowitz, *Mekilta,* ed. Horowitz-Rabin, p. 285, line 9, editors' note.

40. *Mekilta Mishpatim* chap. 10, Horowitz-Rabin p. 285, Lauterbach III, p. 85; cf. Mishna *Sanhedrin* 1.4.

41. *B. Baba Kamma* 5a.

42. *Ibid.* 42b.

43. Cf. the Hillelite opinion in Mishna *Hullin* 8.1.

44. Mishna *Bekorot* 2.6; cf. also 2.7,8.

45. *Ibid.* 2.9.

46. *Tosefta Bekorot* 3.15, p. 538; cf. Mishna *Bekorot* 5.1, where Akiba's

view is omitted. The rule applies, of course, only to a firstling which has become unfit for sacrificial purposes.

47. *B. Shabbat* 97a; cf. *Sifre* Numbers 105, p. 103.

48. *Hullin* 49a.

49. *Genesis R.* chap. 46, p. 462; *Leviticus R.* 25.5.

BIBLIOGRAPHY

Bacher, *Agada d. Tannaiten*, I, 271 ff.

Billerbeck, *R. Akiba, Leben und Wirken eines Meisters in Israel* (in Strack's *Nathanel*, 1916-1918).

Bloch, J. S., in *Mimizrach u-Mima'arab*, 1894, p. 47 ff.

Bornstein, D. J., in *Encyclopedia Judaica*. s.v. *Akiba*.

Braunschweiger, *Die Lehrer der Mishnah*, p. 92 ff.

Bruell, Jakob, *Mebo ha-Mishnah*, p. 116 ff.

Derenbourg, Joseph, *Essai sur l'histoire et la géographie de la Palestine*, p. 329 ff., 395 ff., 418 ff.

Dunner, in *Monatsschrift für Geschichte u. Wissenschaft des Judenthums*, 1871, p. 451 ff.

Ewald, *Geschichte d. Volkes Israel*, VII:367 ff.

Frankel, *Darke ha-Mishnah*, p. 111 ff.

Funk, S., *Akiba*.

Gastfreund, I., *Toledot R. Akiba*.

Ginzberg, Louis, in Jewish Encyclopedia, s.v. *Akiba*.

Graetz, *Geschichte d. Juden*, IV:50 ff; see also, Notes 7 and 8.

— *Gnostizismus*, 83 ff.

Halevy, Isaak, *Dorot ha-Rishonim Ie*, 455 ff., 620 ff., 659 ff.

Hamburger, *Real-Encyclopaedie für Bibel u. Talmud*, II:32 ff.

Hirsch, J., *Die Religionsgeschichtliche Bedeutung R. Akibas*.

Hoffmann, David, *Zur Einleitung in die halachischen Midraschim*, p. 5 ff.

Hyman, Aaron, *Toledot Tannaim ve-Amoraim*, p. 988 ff.

Javitz, *Toledot Jisrael*, VI.

Jost, *Geschichte d. Judenthums u. seiner Sekten*, II:59 ff.

Landau, in *Monatsschrift*, 1854, p. 45 ff., 81 ff., 130 ff.

Margolis-Marks, *A History of the Jewish People*, pp. 213 ff.

Moore, G. F., *Judaism*, I:87 ff.; II:106 ff.

Neuburger, in *Monatsschrift*, 1873, p. 385 ff., 433 ff., 529 ff.

Oppenheim, H., in *Bet Talmud* II:237 ff., 269 ff.

Rosenthal, F., *Vier apokryphische Bücher*.

Rubin, *Anshe ha-Shem be-Hokmat ha-Nistar*, in *ha-Eshkol*, V:22.

Schuerer, E., *Geschichte d. jüdischen Volkes im Zeitalter Jesu Christi*, II:442 f.

Stein, L., *R. Akiba u. seine Zeit*.

Strack, *Einleitung in Talmud u. Midrash*, p. 125.

Weiss, I. H., *Dor Dor ve-Dorshav*, II:107 ff.

Wittkind, *Hut ha-Meshulash*.

Zuri, *Rabbi Akiba*.

INDEX

355

LOUIS FINKELSTEIN

Louis Finkelstein was born in Cincinnati, Ohio, on June 14, 1895. He took his doctorate at Columbia in 1918 and became a rabbi in the following year. After many years as professor of theology at the Jewish Theological Seminary, Dr. Finkelstein was appointed chancellor of the institution in 1951. He is the author of many journal articles and a number of books, among them *Tradition in the Making, Beliefs and Practices of Judaism, Pre-Maccabean Documents in the Passover Haggadah, Abot of Rabbi Nathan,* and three volumes on the Pharisees.